Wealth Management

Wealth Management:
A Guide to Determinants of Investor Behaviour

Dr. Himani Grover

KALPAZ

First Published, 2020

Published by

Kalpaz Publications
C-30, Satyawati Nagar,
Delhi – 110052
Ph.: 011-47034999, 9811692060
www.kalpazpublications.com
E-mail: kalpaz@hotmail.com

Printed at: Gyan Press, Delhi

Cataloging in Publication Data—DK
Courtesy: D.K. Agencies (P) Ltd. <docinfo@dkagencies.com>

Grover, Himani, author.
Wealth management: a guide to determinants of investor behaviour / Ms. Himani Grover.
pages cm
Includes bibliographical references and index.
ISBN 9789353243050

1. Finance, Personal. 2. Business enterprises—Finance. 3. Saving and investment. 4. Capitalists and financiers—Psychology. I. Title.

LCC HG179.G76 2020 | DDC 332.024 23

Contents

Acknowledgement

This research was indeed a long, challenging expedition and now when I look back today I realize that I owe my thanks to so many people whom I met along my way and who were always ready to offer their endless support and guidance throughout this journey, without whom this accomplishment of successfully consummating this research would not have been possible.

I owe my sincere gratitude and deepest appreciation to my revered guide, having an attitude and substance of a genius, Dr. Sachin S Vernekar, who has been my mentor and a venerated personality in the field of education. Without his guidance and persistent help this dissertation would not have completed. He is the one who has given me the opportunity to start my career in this line and therefore, I owe him for what I am today.

I earnestly acknowledge the contributions made by all my seniors and other faculty members whose constant guidance has led to successful completion of the work. I am grateful to the executives who spared their valuable time in providing me with useful data and information, required for the research study.

I extend my heartfelt thanks to my parents, my family members especially my beloved husband Mr. Varun Bahl for his understanding and constant support throughout the work. I can't thank him enough for the support he has provided me in writing my thesis. I would also, like to extend special thanks to my friends, my peers Dr. Aarushi Kataria, Shikha Gandhi, Dr. Ashima Bhatnagar, Dr. Bhawna Duggal, Dr. Sonia Malik, Dr. Geetu Tuteja, Dr. Supreet Wahee, Dr. Atul Singh, Dr. Parul Agrawal, Dr. Sanjeevan Rao who have always stood beside me during my tenure of research and have always motivated me to achieve my goals and objectives. Lastly, I would like to thank God for giving me strength and determination for finishing this research. Thank you, God!

Preface

Money holds a significance position in everybody's life. The need of hour is not limited to merely earning money and becoming rich rather it has become crucial to manage the hard earned money meticulously. Management of money involves following a suitable saving and investment plan that utilizes individual's wealth in an organized way. An individual makes investment decisions based on various factors and choose among the various investment plans available. He relies on the available market information, fundamental and technical analysis to make decisions but lacks potential and ability to comprehend this information that suits best to his requirements. Consequently, financial advisors, professionals assist the individual investors in protecting and enhancing their wealth. Thus, it becomes imperative for these professionals to understand their clients well so as to provide customized financial services that meet individual investor's financial goals. This book therefore is based on a research that reviews the effect of some behavioural factors like financial literacy, subjective norms, beliefs and risk appetite on the attitudes of investors toward seeking and using wealth management services.

As a result, the wealth managers can bespoke their strategies and financial plans to provide value to their clients and also achieve greater competitive advantage.

The research was undertaken considering the increasing scope of Wealth Management and because of dearth of literature available on investor's behavior towards Wealth Management Services. It was very challenging rather difficult to collect data from High-Net worth Investors who generaly avail Wealth Management Services but with the help of some friends & family members working in banking sector I was able to overcome this challenge. I am greatful to all of them for their support.

List of Abbreviations

ABE	-	Average Variance Explained
AGFI	-	Adjusted Goodness-of-Fit Index
AHP	-	Analytic Hierarchy Process
AMOS	-	Analysis of Moment Structures
CAGR	-	Compounded Annual Growth Rate
CFA	-	Confirmatory Factor Analysis
CFI	-	Comparative Fit Index
CI	-	Confidence Interval
CRM	-	Customer Relationship Management
EFA	-	Exploratory Factor Analysis
GDP	-	Gross Domestic Product
GFI	-	Goodness-of-Fit Index
HNWI	-	High Net-worth Individuals
KMO	-	Kaiser-Meyer-Olkin
MSV	-	Maximum Shared Variance
NCR	-	National Capital Region
NFI	-	Normed Fit Index
RMSEA	-	Root Mean Square Error of Approximation
SEM	-	Structural Equation Modeling
SMC	-	Squared Multiple Correlations
SRC	-	Standardised Residual Co-variances
TLI	-	Tucker Lewis Index
TRA	-	Theory of Reasoned Action
UHNW	-	Ultra High Net-worth
VIS	-	Variance Inflation Factor

Chapter - 1

Introduction

1.1 Background of the Study

For any person living on this globe, money has its own significance. Merely earning money is no longer enough for a person to become rich; it is equally crucial to manage the money in a careful manner. In other words, creation of wealth must be followed by protecting it. This is possible only if money is managed in a proper and organized way. A secure future for oneself and one's family is possible only when one follows a suitable saving and investment plan that utilizes wealth in an organized way. At present, there are varied investment plans that an individual can choose from. An investor makes investment decisions based on various factors. He makes use of fundamental and technical analysis and also relies upon market information to make informed judgment about his investment. But he might not be able to completely comprehend the information and analysis. This is where financial institutions come into the picture. They help an individual by providing professional services to manage his wealth. Wealth management is not merely providing investment recommendations but includes all aspects of the financial life of an individual or a company. It refers to the facilities provided by financial organizations or individuals to assist investors in protecting and enhancing their wealth. It encompasses various kinds of services including planning of finances, managing the investments, planning the tax returns, handling the cash flow in addition to management of debts. Wealth management can thus be defined, as an activity that aims to maximize, safeguard and handle the financial well-being of a person, family or firm. This field has immense potential and is amongst one of the rapidly growing industry of the financial sector. It deals with every facet of a customer's financial life and provides consultation in a personalized/tailored manner. It includes employment of varied kinds of goods, services and tactics. It is wealth managers that assist people to recognize their financial aims and take steps to attain them. Previously, setting of the goals was considered to be beyond the scope of wealth management; this however has become an intrinsic part of wealth management services in the current times. This sector is becoming more prominent and significant because of the increasing number of rich & super rich people.

Apart from individuals, several private and public sector banks have also begun to offer wealth management services to assist their clients especially the High Net-worth Individuals (HNW) to safeguard and enhance their wealth. HNW individuals are the people who have assets worth more than USD1 million including investable and liquid financial assets but excluding personal assets and real estate (Deposits, 2014). This classification enable banks to provide personalized services to the individuals. In India, wealth management services include providing information and assistance in investing in equity-linked portfolio management services, distinct products tailor-made for a class of people, mutual funds and also insurance. Furthermore, the services have also been extended to provide information and assistance in tax evaluation and planning, investment in real estate, advisory services related to art by varied firms. According to Budge (2007) and Brunel (2002) in India, services of wealth management encompass investment in structured products, equity-linked portfolio services of management, mutual funds, insurance. Firms have initiated to broaden the scope to encompass real estate, tax assessment and planning, estate planning and art advisory within their ambit.

Ceru (2004) defined wealth management as managing surplus funds or wealth to attain a financial goal, for instance, to make sure capital endowed is kept whole or the asset risks are well handled at all occasions. According to him, the main objective of the wealth management is asset accumulation, protection and its distribution. Brunel (2002) enumerated that wealth management is a complicated process and in order to support the process, the system requires incorporating, embedding and interacting with multiple systems for market data, customer information and accounting and transaction data. There are several aspects of wealth management to be discussed in this study. It was stated by Maude (2006) that many businesses perform some forms of wealth management via investment and insurance. A complete plan of wealth management must commonly include ways to sustain, grow and share the benefits. In the opinion of Dun and Bradstreet (2009), "Wealth management is a creative, distinct field and not merely a take on the conventional institutional investment management domain; it can thus be defined to be an all-rounded facility that aims to maximize safe-guard and handle the fiscal aim of a person, a house or even a company." According to Evensky (1997), in wealth management, everything is client-centric; in fact this process commences only when an official association is set up between the wealth manager and the customer. Evensky (1997) further opines that the task of a wealth manager is to successfully develop and personalize the procedure of wealth management to encompass the personal experiences of the customer. Thus, wealth management can be regarded as an association between a customer and an advisor referred to as a wealth manager. According to McCann and Lavayssiere (2008), currently the world is experiencing the best period in context of wealth accumulation. There have never been so many individuals from across varied areas that have grown so rich at the same time. Furthermore, never before have people had so many chances to enhance the wealth they own in such a short time- span. This is the natural result of innovative concepts and utilization of capital in a suitable manner. Beinhocker (2006) opines that wealth across the world has whizzed up to almost a vertical curve and is still ascending even today. Consequently this development and gathering of wealth have improved the creation of services for the so called rich class of people. According to Cognizant Report (2011) India's wealth management sector is poised for right establishment, given the favorable landscape for market as well as expected regulatory boosts for the industry. Moreover, this would offer exciting growth chances that would drive fast expansion of market, combined with a rise in the number of wealth management industry participants. In order to successfully tap into this ability, organizations like financial services have to undertake a customized approach by considering the specific attributes of market in India. Further, this has to be supported by a cost-effective and robust business model that is concentrated on enhanced compliance and transparency, efficient technology solutions and synergistic partnerships. Indian wealth management services encompass investment in structured products, mutual funds and insurance and services related to equity-linked portfolio management.

For High-net-worth individuals (HNWIs), the owner and families of small firms, who desire the help of a credentialed financial specialist, implore the wealth managers to organize estate planning, retail banking, tax professionals, investment management and legal resources. Wealth managers can encompass backgrounds as independent certified financial planners in the USA and UK, chartered financial consultants, chartered strategic wealth professionals in Canada or any professional like MBA (professional money managers) who work to improve the income or profit, growth and tax preferential action of long term investors. One should already have accumulated several quantity of wealth for strategies of wealth management to be very effective. Private wealth management is distributed to High Net-worth Investors. Commonly this includes opinion based on the utility of different business succession, stock option planning, estate planning vehicles and occasional use of hedging for huge amount of stock. A professional service is the combination of investment or financial advice, accounting or tax services and estate planning for a fee (Finacle connect, n.d and Oracle, 2010).

Ceru (2004) pointed out that wealth management is defined as managing surplus funds or wealth to attain a financial goal, for instance, to make sure capital endowed is kept whole or the asset risks are well handled at all occasions. Wealth is nothing but the net assets, after deducting liabilities or debt. The main objective of the wealth management is asset accumulation, protection and its distribution. To start with wealth management, first consider to determine the economic situation and economic goals for a business, before deciding how the money must be handled. For doing this the following processes must be done first: one has to understand the goals and constraints of firms and personal, analyze the economic position using cash flow and net worth analysis and to evaluate the personal risk and business risk profiles (Oracle, 2010). On the other hand, it was pointed out by Brunel (2002) that wealth management is a complicated process and in order to support the process the system requires to incorporate, embed and interact with multiple systems for market data, customer information, and accounting and transaction data.

According to Driga, Nita and Cucu (2009), the emphasis of wealth creation managers is on considerable rise as banks have now shifted their focus on high net worth individuals. In the present scenario, wealth management plays a prominent role in every individual's life especially the investor who invests. It is the fastest growing sectors in the industry of financial services. A complete plan of wealth management must commonly include ways to sustain, grow and share the benefits which would involve the following action plans such as:

- Cash flow planning: This enables the proficient and most favorable use of credit for the firm. The first step is to have bigger understanding about the economic position in order to manage the gain and loss of cash (Budge, 2007). The proper management of cash flow might allow using any surplus funds to the needs based on their availability over the short term, medium or long term and in addition allow meeting the commitment as they become due (Maude, 2006 and Shamsuddoha, 2005).

- Investment planning: Budge (2007) mentioned that the aim of investment planning is to sustain wealth and make sure adequate returns. The investment plan depends on the goals and willingness to take certain risks. This is necessary to notice and perform regular review on the investments performance in order to make sure that these plans are on the track to attain the goals. Further, Driga, Nita and Cucu (2009) added that the investment plan may be changed based on the varying market conditions or investments performance. To design an investment plan, there are several considerations that need to be noticed; they are as follows: the objectives of investment, an asset allocation policy are used in order to meet the objectives of investment and finally the forms of investment products to meet the goals.
- Insurance planning: According to Ceru (2004) this is used for personal protection and business protection. An insurance program should be considered as a part of the plan to prevent against the unexpected economic loss risks. This may include protection for losses due to theft, flood and fire, key-man insurance or marine and other risks to the business and health and life insurance for both the employer and the employees. Personal protection includes losses due to problems like disability, death, critical illness and family. The insurance amount is based on the needs, the situations and the objectives. Insurance protection must be reviewed frequently to make sure that the protection is sufficient based on the present situation (Dwivedi et al., 2008 and Ceru, 2004).
- Tax planning: This is used to minimize redundant cash losses and ensure efficient cash flow management. The main goal of tax planning is to manage the economic affairs to reduce the tax payable. The tax payable amount may affect the decisions on the following categories like investment, savings and borrowings (Ceru, 2004).
- Retirement and safety planning: These are used for the employees to guarantee the maintenance of key staff for firm's continuity. Retirement planning is an important feature of wealth management. As the owner of a business, he will need to make notice on several issues which are as follows: the retirement timing, the amount of money needed to persist daily life, the succession plan as to who and how the firm may run after the retirement are to be ensured. There are several factors to be considered for developing a retirement plan; they are needs of future retirement, the styles or

standards and future expenses of current lifestyle, investment and savings (total funds accumulated), insurance, account inflation and taxation, the circumstances of family such as age, education needs, dependants etc (Isdale, 2006).

- Retirement and succession planning: It was mentioned by Driga, Nita and Cucu (2009) that these are used to ensure that the firm can continue to operate in a smooth manner even if the owner of the business leaves the firm. The succession planning permits the owner of a firm to deal with their firms in a prearranged manner in the action of premature death or permanent disablement. The unexpected loss of the business owner without correct succession planning may affect the business' goodwill and also may cause the problems of liquidity. It is more significant if the members of the family have no idea, interest or expertise in continuing the business. With the help of this planning, the following benefits can be achieved, like minimizing the family risks, disputes and business disturbances, retain the business shareholdings within the family and plan the exit of the owner from the firm (Markets, 2008).
- Estate planning: This is to ensure efficient transfer of wealth to beneficiaries or successors. It is the process of making perfect arrangements for the management and disposition of one's estate at death (Markets, 2008). It can also avoid the arising of administrative and legal complications. The advantages of estate planning are proper management of business, avoidance of legal tussles over the wealth distributions, efficient transfer of capital to family and trusts, wills and foundations are the tools used for this planning (Isdale, 2006 and Maude, 2006).

The wealth management firms offer a wide array of options to an investor to invest. The investment strategy of every investor is distinct. According to Gemes et al., (2014) the global wealth management scenario has considerably improved over a year. The new global regulations, changing investor's behavior, rapid advancement of digitization have changed the way a business is done. It is imperative for the wealth managers to adapt quickly to the changing rules and the changing scenario. The rapid advancement in digitization is influencing the expectations of investors towards wealth management. As more and more individuals are becoming technology savvy and aware, they are looking for alternatives to manage their wealth. Thus, it has become important for wealth mangers to track their behavior and step-up the ladder of success. Investment behavior is referred to as how investors predict, review, judge and analyze the decision making procedures that encompass information gathering (Martin-Oliver & Salas-Fumas, 2011). According to McInish (1982), investment in different assets types is an essential activity which positively influences people. It includes employment of funds with the objective of earning capital appreciation or income. In the present scenario, the financial services sector has been diversified and offer an individual investor, numerous ways to invest. Madhani (2007) described that the investors are more cautious and they are aware of conservation towards risk. Further, investors transform from offshore wealth management to onshore wealth management from exotic products for investment to more time tested conventional products for investment. Investors are accepted to be much more crucial about the products and advice. In addition to that, it was stated by Pang and Warshawasky (2009) that the investors would have greater wealth control and focus on minimizing the share of offering in the product with discretionary mandates. Investor transforms from performance consideration to risk and protects its assets. More investors would search diversification in the relationships between the banks for measuring the risk containment (Madhani, 2007 and Maude, 2006).

1.2 Description of the problem

The theory of behavioral finance has many significant applications. It is important for a finance manager or advisor to understand the intentions and behavior of his client so as to design appropriate customized business model to serve his requirements. Therefore, the financial institutions identify the most influencing factor that determines that behavior which in turn will affect its financial policies and strategies. Investment is a buying of financial product or other value item with an expectation of positive return in the future. Investing has a main effect on future well-being of investor (Dwivedi et al., 2008). According to Gali (1994), wealth management can be described to be an all-inclusive technique to comprehend and offer responses to all chief financial issues that an investor may have to deal with in context of his or her financial life. Wealth management addresses every aspect of customer's financial life in highly consultative and individualized way. It uses a full range of strategies, services and products. Customers of wealth management are demanding tailored and comprehensive services with personalized options in the investment (Madhani, 2007 and Isdale, 2006). The main threat to the growth of wealth management industry is about the lack of proper framework for regulatory approach. Such services are being regulated and main hindrances are being plugged after different scams and frauds (Shamsuddoha, 2005). Moreover, providers of wealth management are struggling to combine a flexible and fluid business model that integrates the products and service offering with information technology and customer-centric platforms (Dwivedi et al., 2008). According to Mindel and Sleight (2010), handling money especially of others is a crucial business. In this, the expert advice of a professional is beneficial. It is the wealth manager who enacts a crucial function in offering suitable wealth management for his customers. The function enacted by a wealth manager is quite different from the functions enacted by an asset or money manager. Akin to the asset or money manager, the wealth manager assists the customer to invest funds but also has his focus in the customer too. The entire focus of a wealth manager is on the customer. His endeavors are aimed at helping customers attain their life goals by suitably handling their financial assets (Dun and Bradstreet, 2009). According to Dun and Bradstreet (2009), the role enacted by a wealth manager is similar to that of the family doctor who takes care of the health of the customer. They believe that the main task of the wealth manager is to examine the financial standing of a customer and then to recommend a variety of banking and investment products that are suitable to handle distinct wealth management issues. Understanding the investor's psychology to provide him customized products and services is associated with a field of study which is known as Behavioral Finance. According to Sewell (2007), 'behavioral finance is the study of influence of psychology on the behavior of financial practitioners and its subsequent effects in the market'. Irrespective of how much an investor is well-aware, or explored profoundly the various investment options, he behaves reasonably before investing because of the fear about future. Various researchers have examined that the investor's financial decision is influenced by internal and external factors (Nagy and Obenberger, 1994; Shefrin & Statman, 2000; Hussein A.H., 2007; Maditinos et al., 2007).

The primary aim of this investigation is to uncover and discover the fundamental factors that impact on the use of wealth management services amongst investors in Delhi (National Capital Region) because to the best of researchers' knowledge there is no available information on the present study. Research on investment behavior has indicated that purpose to employ in an exacting behavior is a role of the individual's attitudes headed for that action and those characters are reliable with performance (Ajzen, 1991; Ajzen & Fishbein, 1980; 2000). Therefore, the attitudinal element was deemed significant in this investigation and variables connected optimistically or pessimistically to the attitudes were taken predictors of the possibility of proper use of wealth management services. The current research is carried out to evaluate the influence of financial literacy, risk appetite, personal beliefs, subjective norms and attitude on investor's investment behavior. Apart from these, this research intends to assess the significant association between attitude, beliefs, and financial literacy risk appetite and investment behavior. Moreover, this research provides strategies in order to be adopted to favor investor's wealth management behavior with special significance to Delhi (National Capital Region).

1.3 Significance of the Study

Studying behavioral finance can help Wealth Management practitioners in building a successful advisory relationship by keeping up a reliable approach to delivering Wealth Management Services, giving what the customer expects, and promising for mutual benefits. This investigation is reasonable for several reasons. Firstly, with the growth of the Indian economy and the rise in the wealth of the people, there is an increasing need of Wealth Management Services. Investors all over the world, intend to achieve their financial goals relying on various sources as a channel to their success in earning adequate returns. One of those important channels is financial advisors. The investors are looking for new measures & approaches to achieve their financial goals despite having lack of investment knowledge. This shows importance of advisory relationship on investment decision-making and therefore, the advisors should understand & seek the factors that impact investor's behavior so as to provide them necessary customized services to maintain this trust be-held by investors in them. Secondly, the analysis of investors' personal beliefs, their knowledge, and their risk-taking ability along with the potential impact of these beliefs, literacy, and risk appetite on individuals' attitudes toward seeking wealth management services marks the foundation of building healthy customer relationship.

The main rationale of this study is to investigate the fundamental factors that persuade the utilization of Wealth Management Services among investors in Delhi/NCR. Various researchers have shown that an individual's intention to perform an action is based on the individual's attitude towards that action and thus that attitude is consistent with the individual's behavior (Ajzen, 1991; Ajzen & Fishbein, 1980; 2000). Therefore, attitude was considered as the corner stone of the study and various elements that relates positively or negatively to attitude was considered predictors that influence an individual's attitude which in turn influence his behavior to perform a specific action.

The study intends to review the effect of (a) personal beliefs about wealth management; (b) knowledge and awareness about wealth management, wealth management services; (c) risk-taking ability; (d) influence of friends, peers, colleagues, family, media (subjective norms) on the attitudes of investors toward seeking and using wealth management services.

1.3.1 Significance of the study to wealth managers

Financial institutions that provide wealth management services are on the increase and these institutions manage assets of large number of wealthy and most profitable clients. Moving forward, in order to retain this large customer base, these institutions will have to find a way to thrive in the midst of the existing market conditions. The present market conditions are not suitable to provide desired returns that are anticipated by wealthy investors. Also, these conditions are difficulty to generate enough profits for the firms itself to survive in the long run. Since, the HNWI forms the largest customer base for the wealth management firms, it is imperative for these firms to provide them value for their money by giving them customized services that leads to higher returns as well as fulfilment of the client's financial goals. Therefore, in order to do that, the managers must know the mind-set of their clients so as to meet their requirements. The institutions that fulfil the requirements of its investor can take advantage of growth opportunities that knocks the industry in the challenging economic environment. The financial firms that are unable to meet the goals of their clients experience lost faith of their investors as well as fear of their sustainability. The investor on the other hand suffers loses and this in turn affects his attitude towards investment and also his future decisions. In this kind of situation it is most likely that the investor will switch advisors resulting in more loses to the existing firm. On the other hand, according to a study conducted by Loucks, Waitman, & Ericsson (2011), some wealthy investors believe that their financial loses were unavoidable irrespective of the fact that their assests were managed by extremely skilled wealth managers. Furthermore, they also examined in their study that the investors switch advisors as they feel that a single advisor may not fuflill their financial needs. Therefore, if the wealth managers provide investment services and strategies that are better tailored to their client's needs, the dynamic perceptions of the investors might be changed. These investors are very sensitive to the advise or services that wealth managers provide. Given these state of affairs, in order to win a customer, determining the key components of their attitude is crucial.

The present study enables these wealth managers to examine the attitude of investors towards wealth management services by assessing the association between the various components of attitude and their impact on attitude and investment behavior. As a result, the managers can tailor their strategies and financial plans to provide value to their clients and also achieve greater competitive advantage. These institutions are able to gain competitive advantage because clients rely high on the firms that are able to meet their needs and fulfil their financial and economic goals.

1.4 Objectives of the Study

This study aims at studying the factors that influence an investor's behavior towards wealth management services and thereby providing a model for wealth managers to design and develop their strategies. The goals of the research from the broader perspective are described below:

1. To examine the different components of the investor's attitude and investor behavior in the context of finance industry.
2. To study the role of these predictors in shaping investor's attitude and thereby resulting in a desired investment behavior.
3. To analyze and investigate the influence of a moderator variable on the interrelationship of predictors and investor's attitude.
4. To study and analyze the function of investor's attitude on the interrelationship of predictors and investment behavior.

1.5 Issues of the Study

The wealth management is a very nascent concept in the history of finance industry. Thus, very little published literature is available on investor's behavior towards Wealth Management Services. Most of the literature on general investor behavior is based on the theory of reasoned action or theory of planned behavior where investors' attitude is considered as an antecedent of investor's intention and thus investment behavior. This study applies the theory of reasoned action as proposed by Ajzen and Fishbein (1980) and focused on examining the various components that influence investor's attitude and which in turn affects investment behavior. The main issues covered in the study are as follows:

1. Identifying the role of financial literacy, risk appetite, personal beliefs, and subjective norms in shaping the attitude of an investor.
2. Exploring the relationship between the predictors of attitude (financial literacy, risk appetite, beliefs and subjective norms) and investor's behavior.

3. Examining the moderating role of risk appetite in influencing the relationship between financial literacy-attitude; beliefs-attitude and subjective norms-attitude.
4. Examining the mediating role of attitude on the relationship between financial literacy, risk appetite, beliefs, subjective norms and investment behavior.
5. Evolving a Wealth Management Behavior model as a guiding framework for wealth managers in designing their financial strategies and financial plans.

1.6 Scope of the Study

The scope of the study is limited to investors investing in wealth management services only i.e. High Net-worth Individuals. It does not include small investors and corporate investors. The study is also limited to Delhi (National Capital Region) only; it does not cover HNWIs living in other parts of India as it is assumed that the HNWIs living in other parts of India will behave in the similar manner. Moreover, the components of attitude taken for the study includes financial literacy, risk appetite, beliefs and subjective norms only, other components which might have significant influence on investors have been excluded from the study. The study is based on the Theory of Reasoned Action in which attitude is said to have a major influence on intention which in turn leads to investment behavior. But the model has been adapted for the present study and intention has not been included in the present scope of the research and thus does not form part of the Wealth Management Behavior model. The study covers financial institutions and banks that provide wealth management services. According to a survey conducted by MarketsandMarkets (2010), the wealth management industry in India is dominated by ICICI Bank, HDFC Bank and Kotak Bank. Also, according to Companies in India (2014) report, ICICI bank along with HDFC bank and other financial institutions are among the top 20 Wealth Management companies in India. So, the present study takes into account the HNWI clients of ICICI bank, HDFC bank, Kotak Mahindra bank, Motilal Oswal Asset management Company and Muthoot Asset Management Compaany. The HNWI clients of rest of the institutions and banks are beyond the scope of this research.

1.7 Overall Methodology of the Study

The overall thesis is based on empirical research on factors influencing investor's wealth management behavior in Delhi/NCR. The study has been divided into two parts i.e. pilot study and questionnaire based survey study.

The pilot study has been carried out by selecting 50 HNWI clients of mentioned banks and institutions and factors that influence their investment behavior were identified. The hypotheses evolved based on literature review, have been statistically tested on the basis of questionnaire based survey conducted through purposive and snowball sampling. The data has been analyzed using multivariate analysis: Structural Equation Modeling using AMOS. On the basis of the results obtained, Wealth Management behavior Model has been developed. The model was further investigated by moderating and mediating effect of variables. The findings and results synchronize with the literature review to a great extent.

1.8 Organization of the Book

The section below gives an overview of the contents that are included in this thesis. The thesis is divided into six chapters. A brief introduction of each chapter is given as follows:

Chapter one gives background of the study and includes the importance of studying investment behavior and its relation to Wealth Management Industry. The problem statement, significance of the study in general and significance to the wealth managers is defined. The objectives of the study and its scope have also been included. The chapter also includes the overall methodology adopted in the study and finally, the structure of the thesis is delineated in brief.

Chapter two reviews the literature related to the Wealth Management and the major determinants of investor's behavior. The literature review outlines the need, challenges and determinants of wealth management industry and also provides an overview of global and Indian Wealth Management Industry. The review leads to the identification of key components of attitude that influence investment behavior. Based on these components relevant hypotheses have been proposed.

Chapter three provides the research design of the study. The variables identified in the literature review have been illustrated diagrammatically in the Wealth Management Behavior model. The framework also depicts the relationship between predictors and outcomes. The model will be tested for its fitness and the proposed hypothesis will be proved through analysis of questionnaire survey. This chapter also describes the design of the questionnaire, its validation, the results of the pilot study, reliability of the instrument and the various statistical techniques to be used in the analysis.

Chapter four outlines the results of the preliminary data analysis which gives an overview of demographic profile of the investors and their preferred wealth management service. The results of the hypotheses testing, validation of the model fitness, relationship between variables has been done in the second part of the analysis. Multiple regressions using SEM has been carried out to prove the hypothesis. Also, moderator and mediator effect have been used to identify the impact of moderator variable on the investor's attitude and mediating effect of attitude on the relationship between antecedents and Investor behavior was examined. On the basis of the results, Wealth Management Behavior Model has been presented.

Chapter five presents the findings of the study. The chapter aims at synchronizing the findings with the literature review. The detailed discussions on the results are briefed in this chapter along with the results of hypothesis testing.

Chapter six is based on learning and conclusions based on the findings and results. The chapter focuses on conclusions drawn from the study, its implications fir wealth managers and investors, recommendations for financial practitioners, limitations of the study and areas of future research has also been discussed. The chapter provides conclusion to the research followed by suggestions or recommendations and best strategies to be adopted for the investor's wealth management and to enhance the wealth management with respect to Delhi/NCR region. This study will provide valuable insights for the investors of wealth management and future researchers.

Bibliography: This chapter has the lists of all works studied, including those mentioned in the text.

Appendices: The appendices include all necessary relevant data supporting the study including the survey about the factors that influence the investor's wealth management behavior with specific reference to Delhi (National Capital Region) region considered in the study and to collect the primary data for the purpose of this study.

1.9 Summary

With the increasing scope of wealth management services in India, the chapter provides an overview of need of studying investor behavior, meaning of wealth management, its products and services and the significance of the study to wealth managers. In the challenging economic environment it is crucial for the wealth managers to tailor their financial plans and strategies according to the mindset and needs of their clients. This is essential for their sustainability in the industry.

The objectives of the study has been designed keeping in view the above situation and thus the study aims at identifying the factors that influence investor's attitude which in turn influence their investment behavior. The scope of the study and the relevant issues has also been discussed in length. The objectives of the study will provide a roadmap to the wealth managers to design their future plans and strategies for HNWI.

Chapter - 2

Literature Review

The review of literature provides information and overview of the prevailing framework and helps to outline the study by exploring the existing literature. The present study reviews the literature available to provide an introduction of the followed groundwork and theoretical structure proposed by the Theory of Reasoned Action (TRA) and presents the relevant components associated with investor behavior.

This chapter explores the meaning and definition of wealth management and also provides some insight on the need for wealth management. A part of the section focuses on the determinants of wealth management. The present study is based on a model developed under the Theory of Reasoned Action: behavioral intention model which identifies two determinants of behavior viz. attitude and subjective norms. Further, the study conceptually establishes relationship between investor's knowledge (financial literacy), beliefs, risk appetite, norms and attitude; and their impact on investor's intention to invest and investment behavior for Wealth Management Services. Further, this chapter discusses about the need for wealth management and challenges associated with the wealth management. Subsequent section discusses about the factors influencing investor's choice of Wealth Management Services and finally concludes with the chapter summary.

2.1 Overview of Wealth Management

The idea of Wealth Management originated in the US in the 1990's. In the beginning, it encompass investment advisory which in turn included financial planning that offered people with services like private banking, portfolio and asset management, taxation advisory etc. Majority of these services are extremely personal and portfolio management being the most common among them. These services includes products like stocks, equity linked and structured savings products, mutual funds and alternative investments.

The Wealth Management Services can be availed by High Net-worth Individuals (HNWIs), small entrepreneurs and other individuals who want their hard earned money to be professionally managed by specialists known as Wealth Managers. After China, India is considered to be the second most appealing market for Wealth Management. According to a research conducted by one of the Asia's leading wealth manager firm, Barclays Capital, a known Investment Banking firm, "China and India persist in being the most appealing Asian markets, both in context of ability to expand businesses and anticipated growth rate of revenues."

Families employ wealth management services not merely to monitor their money, but to employ expert management to advice and invest their wealth, deal with family relationships and also handle the succession planning. The main function of a wealth management firm is to understand the requirements of a client, support them and provide them with all the necessary resources required to manage their wealth. From a customer's viewpoint, wealth management is considered as an investment and financial advisory field which includes a wide spectrum of specialized and aggregated financial services that involves activities like income tax planning, investment portfolio management, risk management, retirement planning and administration (Chan & Chan, 2011). Wealth manager also provide assistance in the implementation of continuity and disposition planning with other such professional guidance to the closely held businesses.

2.1.1 Need for wealth management

It was argued by Basu and Drew (2009) in studying *portfolio size effect* that many wealth management organizations or companies are assessing and seeking avenues to reassemble the lost trust of customers. The firms are looking forward to engage their business customers and also want them for managing the investments of business customers in a very efficient and collaborative manner. Despite of that, wealth managers are also seeking to fortify themselves with comprehensive and complete customer information, at the same time making every possible effort in order to offer the best solution and the prudent advice to their customers (Thunderhead, 2013). With the widespread growth of new products and financial services, financial institutions are increasingly widening their focus even on the small investors and helping them in achieving their financial goals (Lusardi & Mitchell, 2014).

Shun-Yao & Chyan (2011), in their research on *Influence of information on risky investment preferences* observed how the lack of essential financial knowledge to efficiently measure the level of risk involved in a particular investment generates the need of the professional wealth managers to provide them with an advice or manage their wealth on their behalf. Wealth managers provide such investors with a service to directly interact their experienced professionals face to face while taking any major financial decision or investing in any complex investment portfolio. Professional wealth managers possess the knowledge of several investment portfolios available in the market. They exhibit knowledge of how to efficiently balance risk and returns from an investment and also possess special techniques to analyse company's performance and are also proficient in effectively managing a portfolio (Lusardi & Mitchell, 2014). Financial service managers provide a sound advice that is based on in depth understanding of the customer's requirements compared to their actual behavior (Kahneman and Riepe, 1998).

Need of the wealth managers and their financial advice is more critical for the anxious investors. The investors who possess such behavior tend to intuitively and spontaneously take decisions and show less patience even while making huge investments. Consequently, it is important for these investors to opt for personal advisory services offered by wealth managers in order to avoid making big mistakes resulting in big losses because of their behavioural issues (Funfgeid et al, 2008). Also, the investors who follow their gut feeling while making any investments face potential problems in effectively managing their wealth and essentially need professional advice and guidance in regards to their financial matters (O'Donoghue and Rabin, 1998). Investors who feel insecure in making financial decisions and investments are also the primary candidates for the need to wealth management services. Past performance and future returns can be well determined by the financial institutions who hire experienced financial advisors to comprehend the future state of market to take the right decisions (Lusardi & Mitchell, 2014).

Bahbah (2009) in a research on *timeless strategies for building financial security in wealth management*, elucidated that various measures to increase the awareness must be taken to guide the people regarding the importance of wealth management services to manage their wealth. After gaining wealth, it is more important to safeguard it by managing in an effective and diverse manner. By following a proper saving and investment plan; and correct utilization of wealth in a planned way provides a secured future for a family. To achieve this professional financial advisers are appointed to help their clients through professional wealth management. The customer centric solution is one of the best solutions for the needs of wealth management, definitely that would ease to overcome several challenges faced by customers at every level of wealth management business. The wealth management business cycle includes covering acquisition, identification, reporting and servicing (Brennan and Xia, 2002).

2.1.2 Determinants of wealth management

According to Wealth Management advisors, providing advice across different types of products, predicting recent trends in the local and global markets, suggesting rare product bundling and also suggesting investment protection mechanism are key factors for the achievement of wealth management services. The customer's expected quality of service, profit and loss reporting and investment advice from firms are few of the important selection criteria for customers to choose their wealth managers. Technology plays an important role in delivering actionable advice in an efficient manner; it acts as a supporting tool in the client-to-advisor association, and also plays a vital role in retaining the customers. The other factors contributing to the needs of a wealth management strategy includes the business model, diversity of offerings, standard or quality of advisors, customer segregated organizational structure. Wealth Managers need to efficiently train the employees in order to provide better services to their customers.

Moreover, Wachter (2002) in a study on *optimal consumption and portfolio allocation under mean reverting returns* mentioned that the vital differentiators for an accomplished system include higher client servicing capabilities, increased operational efficiencies and strong management oversight. The superior client servicing capabilities consist of family association view, advice based sales, analytics driven advertising, campaign administration, uninterrupted monitoring and reporting performance of wealth. The Strong Management Oversight which includes online monitoring of advisor accomplishment, reducing risk through timely reporting and institutionalizing compliance information across all levels of organizational hierarchy and increased operational efficiencies which includes execution of investment plans, automated planning, online or active collaboration tools. The best solution offered by customer centric solution which benefits wealth management organizations through timely advance, focused marketing, clear portfolio management, improved and advisor productivity, resulting in enduring customer association and enhanced wallet share.

According to Brennan and Xia (2002) in a study on *dynamic asset allocation under inflation* and Watcher (2002) the key objectives for the success in wealth management are increasing focus on client-centricity through specified client segments, understanding of client needs, proactive effort and individualized value propositions and exceeding client expectations. The customer centric solution has proven to be one of the important deciding factors for wealth management organizations, ensuring customer fidelity by providing distinguish services from other competitors and suitably gaining competitive advantage.

Barber and Odean (2001) while examining the *overconfidence in common stock investment* have explained the theoretical concepts and predicted that overconfidence in an investor makes him trade more excessively. A study conducted on analyzing *the investor's behavior* by Maditinos et al. (2007) determines that an individual investor's behavior depend excessively on the social media such as newspaper and the rumors in the market while an intellectual and experienced investor will depend more on the analysis of fundamental facts. Hou, Peng and Xiong (2009) in a study on the *implications of investor attention for price and earning momentum*, concluded that earnings momentum reduces with the attention of investor while the price momentum gets build up and increases with the attention of investor.

Walia and Dr. Kiran (2009) in their research on *analysis of investor's risk perception* have focused on the perspective of an individual investor by understanding the expectation of the investor and his risk appetite. Customers consistently expect to get innovative solutions with higher quality in the provided services. A research conducted by Kabra, Mishra and Dash (2010) on *factors influencing the investment decisions of generations* concluded that age and gender of an individual investor essentially influences his risk appetite. Chandra and Kumar (2011) in a study on *determinants of individual investor behavior* concluded that five major factors that influence investment behavior of an individual investor are investor's foresight, financial knowledge, cautious attitude, skewness in information and the confidence level.

According to Bennet et al. (2011) while examining the *investor's attitude on stock selection decision* found the factors those influence investor's attitude are: goodwill and reputation of the firm, market conditions, industrial regulations and revenue. In a study conducted by Qureshi et al. (2012) on *factors affecting investment decision making of fund managers*, examined the various factors (such as inquisitiveness, risk reluctance, adoption of modern fiscal techniques, industrial regulatory controls) that influences the behavior of an investor and impacts the decisions of the fund manager. Riaz et al. (2012) in a study on *impact of psychological factors on investment decision making* concluded that the availability of information to the investors and how the investor perceive and interpret that information significantly impact and determines the risk tolerance, investor's behavior and decision making in regards to their investments.

Khanifar et al. (2012) in a research on *studying affecting factors on analysts decisions regarding share analysis*, found that financial statements and midterm reports are considered more important than economy market and industry related factors by financial analysts. Kadariya (2012) while studying the *factors affecting investor's decision making* found that both the tangible and intangible information are essential for investors to succeed in capital market. Raheja and Lamba (2013) have mentioned that there are many different investment options available in the market and every individual as per his preference choose to invest in diverse options. Risk tolerance is one of the important factors influencing the investor's decision while choosing for a particular investment option and demographic factors are related to the risk taking capacity of an investor

Obamuyi (2013) in a research on *factors influencing decisions in capital market* concluded that the investment decisions of individual investors are considerably impacted by the educational qualifications, marital status, age and gender of the investor. In a similar study on *factors influencing investment decisions,* Jagongo and Mutswenje (2014) concluded that financial institution's reputation, trustworthiness and creditability status in the market are the most essential factors that significantly impact the investment decisions of an individual investor. Stafford (1994) mentioned in his research that "fundamental elements that clients look for in their service managers are courtesy, cordiality, sincerity and convenience but they also consider reasonable fee, firm's stability, concerned management and organizational strength and security as crucial elements of the service". Khazeh and Decker (1992) while studying the *choice of investors for their banks* determined the essential elements for the selection of wealth manager are service cost or brokerage (price), trustworthiness and creditability (Goodwill) and competitive loan or interest rates (price).

In a research conducted by Vincent F. Yu and Hsiu-I Ting (2011) on *identifying key factors affecting consumer's choice of wealth management services*, the three main elements that form the crucial factor in choosing a financial institution for the wealth management are image, product and services. Sub-elements of image are popularity, reliability, morality, professionalism and recommendation. Sub-elements those come under products category are diversification, fee, returns and risk. Key elements of services are convenience, confidentiality, communications and attitude. Gerrard and Cunningham (1997) elucidated that providing the quick and efficient service and maintaining the confidentiality of the customer's information considerably influences the decisions of the customers.

It was added by Evensky, Horan & Robinson (2011) in *financial advisors guide to managing and investing client assets* that the wealth management strategies compiled for investors focuses on trade-off between profit and risk, wealth creation for retirement planning and safeguarding revenue income. The wealth management, offering diverse range of services like tax planning, financial planning, cash flow & debt management, investment management is based upon requirements of clients. However, wealth managers assist individuals to find their goals and achieve them. Further it was supported by Watcher (2002) that, successful advisors develop a strong and clear association with clients by addressing client's interest with utmost concern. In order to strengthen the advisory relationship, the wealth managers can work with the clients and develop comprehensive plans and strategies for managing their wealth. But nowadays there are different investment options and plans with complicated risks. Hence, greater diversification is required in the initial stages of investment. For instance only some investors hold all their accounts with the same wealth manager. For an investor to make a decision based on the understanding of all the facts and implications, a thorough and consolidated view of his financial report is quite crucial. In order to make profitable decisions, wealth managers need to have access to customer data to examine and analyze it efficiently. Moreover, for wealth managers to take right decisions based on facts, it is essential to have integrated information across all accounts and firms at one single place, rather than spending time and money in assembling all the information from several different sources (Essvale, 2008).

With the increasing workload in life, every individual wants to easily access his or her account information when and where they need it. Thus, the access to the consolidated information through multi-channel communication tools allows the customers to have access to the accurate and most recently updated information by using mobile application, online web access or over a telephonic call. According to Walia and Dr. Kiran (2009), even though returns and risk are two most important determinants of an investor for their investments, they also considerably focus on the media's recommendation, transparency in the disclosures, management fee and maintenance charges, history of the fund and the reputation of the organization. In a research on *strategy and technology for the new wealth management*, Ceru (2004) stated that most of the financial firms are trying to step in and evolve themselves in this "new wealth management" business. An appropriate combination of business strategic model and modern technology would drive the important decisions of financial institutions to implement technology solutions for the continued growth and success of their business in the wealth management sector. Wealth management institutions primarily focus on the customers lying in high net worth (HNW) and ultra-high net worth (UHNW) segments and make use of growing technology to establish their business footprints in the core of this market.

As mentioned by Finkelstein and Poterba (2004) in a study on *adverse selection in insurance markets*, wealth management spans far beyond than just an investment advice and it encloses a blueprint of entire financial activity of an individual. Most of the financial institutions engage in providing this service to help investors to preserve, safeguard and expand their wealth in effective manner. In a research conducted by Basu and Drew (2009), the first step in viable wealth management is identifying attractive customer segments. A firm operating the space of wealth management can achieve success by comparing their own abilities, skill and competence with the needs and requirements of the customers. Moreover, the annual income has a relationship with perception, for benefits of wealth management services. To attract new clients and retain the trust and confidence of the existing customers, a financial institution must be compassionate with the customers and proficient in their skills. Human touch is one of the fundamental and essential elements for the success in the wealth management sector. It is important for the wealth management firms extending their services to the middle-income group of customers with fewer assets to balance the cost to service with the profit anticipated (Evensky et al., 2011).

In a study examining the *challenges to delivering integrated wealth management services to business owners*, Budge (2007) has found that there is a large segment of people from business class sector who are encountering a lot of formidable challenges with managing their assets and wealth in an efficient manner, which is yet be explored by the wealth managers. A research conducted by Isdale (2006) on *strategies for simplifying and increasing the effectiveness of wealth management*, focuses on the initiatives that can be taken by high-income group investors and their wealth managers to make their investment decisions and efforts more effective and efficient. A book by an author Pompian (2012), advises a model to understand the investor's behavior and building an investment portfolio in accordance with the exhibited behavior of that investor. In an article on *issues and concerns with wealth management in India,* Dwivedi et al. (2008) has brought the attention towards the growing Indian wealth management industry and how has it played an important role in bringing relief to the falling Indian economy. Hamilton (1992) discusses the investment model and criterion for choosing wealth managers for efficiently managing their wealth and to yield high returns on their investments.

In a research on *private banking and wealth management services,* Driga et al. (2009) determines the characteristics of the private banking sector and the significant growth it has obtained in the last 10 years as the private banking primarily focuses on the high net worth section of the people. Shamsuddoha (2005) introduces the leading strategy and design approach followed by the wealth managers. Pang and Warshawsky (2009) compares the strategies followed by wealth managers in retirement planning. Amenc, Martellini & Ziemann (2009) focuses on the modern technical approaches and management strategies followed for making substantial gains through asset management in the private banking sector. Brunel (2002) has proposed new techniques and initiatives over the conventional and primitive portfolio management approach for the wealth management sector, which will drive a portfolio manager to take up a much wider role of wealth manager.

In a study on *Investor's perception*, Das (2012) focused on the perceptions of small investors in funds in a study based on Assam. He advocated in his study that success relied on professional competence of FM (fund managers) and their past performance. Mutual fund provides investment opportunities to a group of people who want to deposit their small earning and saving in diversified portfolios including government and private bonds, equities and commodities. It was observed in the study that the viewpoint and attitude of investors depends on the demographic factors such as investor's age, marital status and occupation, which is considered to have significant positive influence on the type of investments an investor, chooses. It was also observed that the female segment of the society and population considered in this research is not fully involved in this wealth management industry. Thus, the fund managers must take necessary actions for tapping the higher income group and female segment for targeting more investments in Mutual Funds Avenue of investments that would steer this sector towards growth and development.

2.1.3 Challenges in wealth management

Recently the wealth management has become one of the most demanding and competitive industry across the globe and is facing many real time challenges including promoting their services, widening their scope of support and building trust among clients. With the increasing use of technology current wealth management clients are interested to use mobile applications to access and manage their accounts. Wealth managers need to build robust and secure IT infrastructure to safeguard their investor's wealth. After the heavy financial setback by wealth management firms, clients have now started hesitating to trust their wealth managers with doubts regarding their integrity (Kumar et al., 2011).

In a study on *consumption and portfolio choice over the life cycle*, Cocco et al., (2005) elucidated that wealth management firms now need to review their primitive business strategies, amend their legacy business model, improve their services and enhance their infrastructure, revise their plans and build up a new business model which is more robust and resilient. Building such a business model and appointing a relationship manager as a single point of contact for clients would strengthen the association and relationship between the clients and wealth managers. Firms must change their business models to meet the global financial investment requirements of their clients. In recent years, the client's faith on advisors have significantly reduced and many clients have started to probe their advisors and have also raised their expectations from their advisors forcing them to fulfill their commitments and focus on a client centric view to deliver amiable experience to their customers. In a similar study, conducted by Chacko and Viceira (2005) on the *dynamic consumption and portfolio choice,* discussed about another challenge faced by wealth management organizations i.e. lack in robust productivity tools. Wealth managers need to upgrade their firm wide technology to build interactive and efficient tools. These tools could be used for collating and providing diverse views of the client, formulating financial strategies, building robust CRM applications and to collaborate with back office systems. It has become imperative for the advisors to use high-end technology tools to run their business with the clients. In general, most organizations are unable to address and handle the increasing client's demands, which include instant access to their accounts information on mobile devices with the required data security in place. Some of the major challenges of wealth management organization are mentioned below:-

- Using redundancy tools

- Lack of integration
- Data security challenges
- Inability to provide robust mobile solutions
- Sub optimal reporting solutions
- Lack of good document management system
- Lack of real time access to market information

The organizations need to focus on technology investments to transmute the business of wealth management in a prosperous way. The world's population is progressing rapidly with increasing urbanization. According to the United Nations (UN), world's population is forecasted to touch around eight billion people by the year 2050. Approximately five billion will be under the age of 59. Currently older generations retain an important share of private banking assets and will continue to do so. However, the disclosure of "Entrepreneur 2.0" survey by United Nations and the growing base of younger clients will create major challenges to the wealth management firms. On an average, wealthy or young clients are higher in numbers than older clients in developing countries. In the emerging markets, proliferating GDP growth will result in immense accumulation of wealth in wealth management markets leading to an expanding fragment of wealthy and young clients across worldwide. The young clients have different expectations and needs than senior clients. Retaining the trustworthiness of clients towards their banks and their relationship manager is an important challenge for the wealth management firms. The long-term and constant relationships bring success for the wealth manager (Cocco et al, 2005 and Campbell and Viceira, 2005).

In a case study on the *Impact of demographics on the selection of the investment avenues*, Sireesha and Laxmi (2013) pointed out that the wealth management firms need to focus on outsourcing their support functions, which can benefit their clients at an affordable cost. Apart from support functions, the important areas of interest are the middle and back offices. Back office functions which include payments, custody, security processing, IT business applications and credit processing activities are the essential roles which can be outsourced. The specific middle-office activities that benefit most from outsourcing are trade execution and client reporting. As described by Walia and Dr. Kiran (2009) in their research on *investors risk perception towards fund services*, it is important for the wealth managers to carefully examine the level of risk that investors is willing to bear and make sure that the designed portfolio adequately satisfies their risk tolerance. According to Gain et al. (2012), in the *study on individual investor behavior* and research conducted by Dhivya and Sekar (2010) on *investor's preference towards financial investment*, the clients look for technologies from wealth managers. So the financial institutions need to use best technologies to satisfy the needs and fulfill the expectations of client by wealth management advisors. However, it is clear that the firms face important challenges in bringing the entire suite of brokerage, banking, trust, investments, retirement products, banking and custody services in an integrated manner. Moreover there is the need to invest in new platforms for handling distinctive asset classes. The main key to success for the wealth managers lies in prudently selecting their partners, understand the fast changing requirements of the local market and then need investigate to integrate various factors, so that the clients see them as seamless and endless provider. The technology called open architecture will involve many challenges for integration of data from multiple money managers; and efficient overlay management will become a key differentiator for firms.

Further, Walia and Dr. Kiran (2009) stated that the clear communication, well organized contact, yearly reviews and timely detailed account statements are needed by advisors to improve or enhance client relationships. The biggest impact of social networking steer people to expect more innovative solutions for their requirements, i.e. clients do not just want to be fed with information; they want and expect it to be analyzed into a conclusive graphs and data so that they can use it to accredit themselves to make decisions. The wealth management advisors need to address the challenges by gathering information from the clients as much as possible and to integrate their distributed function, i.e. to establish a central control over things like compliance, regulated content, integrity controls and brand protection. It is important to know how different organizations interact with their clients to improve and enhance their communications with respect to their competitors.

In order to make the customers accept the services of wealth management, it is essential to recognize what influences the decisions of investors when choosing wealth management services. As a result, some researchers have identified the factors by adopting Analytic Hierarchy Process. The relative significance of alternatives and factors were reviewed by taking feedback from various respondents who are using or intend to use Wealth Management Services (Ananda and Herath, 2008). The results revealed that the foremost concern of investors is the service quality provided by Wealth Managers, followed by their image, the products offered and the risk associated with these products. Hence, to pull the individual investors, special attention and focus is required to invest more time and effort to the new product designs to extract maximum returns with minimum risk (Liu and Hai, 2005).

Vaidya and Kumar (2006) in their research on *Analytic Hierarchy Process*, described the Analytic Hierarchy Process (AHP) as an effective technique for analyzing complex and complicated problem statements and making intricate decisions by selecting among numerous challenging alternatives in a multi objective environment through forecasting and optimal allocation of inadequate resources. It is particularly applied in bringing consensus in-group decisions. Based on mathematical ratios and human psychology, it was originally introduced by Thomas L. Saaty in the period of 1970s and is often called as Saaty method. It was supported by Liu and Hai (2005) and Handfield et al (2002), that AHP is a flexible and efficient technique for making multiple attribute decisions. It segments a multifaceted decision problem into numerous smaller components in the form of a hierarchy. This decision support approach can be used in wide varieties of application catering to various industries like patent valuation, education, supplier selection, purchase decision, operations efficiency improvement, land use planning, waste management, \ etc (Chiu and Chen, 2007). This method enables to make complex decisions by clearly defining the objective, outlining the different criteria and then finally evaluating and comparing various alternatives, eliminating them based on their analysis and choosing the most scored alternative

According to Boyd (1994) in a study on *customer preferences for financial services*, with the fast changing and more complex demands of investors, it has turned out to be very significant for the wealth managers to strenuously focus on the deciding factors of the investors which influence their decisions to choose their wealth managers and advisors. It is a tough challenge for a general customer to differentiate between two wealth managers and compare their services on various different aspects. In the view of Grady and Spencer (1990) in their *analysis of managing commercial banks*, there is an intense competition for both the creditors and lenders types of customers, hence it has become incredibly important for the financial institutions to be more informed and acquainted with the demands and wishes of the customers.

Across Asia, approximately 90 percent of individuals reviewed their financial services providers' to deliver education on running investments and wealth more successfully. The problem identified was that the most significant factor which influenced their choice of banks in both Asian and

Singaporeans list of counterparts was the ability to meet a wide range of client requirements (Bahl, 2012; Dr. Kukreja, 2012).

The study aims to examine the individual investor's behavior in an effort to know their characteristics or personal details, which in turn will help to identify their preferences regarding various sources of investments they make. These study further attempts to highlight the impact of certain demographic aspects such as the age of the investors and their risk tolerance level on the investment decisions.

The factors that influence investor's perception on private and public mutual funds are tax savings, transparency, liquidity, quality of service and flexibility and so on. Thus, it was concluded that fund managers have to improve the Wealth Management Services in order to acquire more clients and attract more investors and to retain the existing clients.

2.1.4 Global Wealth Management Industry

The existing status of Wealth Management and Private Banking industry is changing because servicing client and delivering value is becoming the focal point for marketers. The control of time-honored enterprises is being challenged by the new rivals in addition to the influence of novel norms and client service infrastructures and their way of functioning. According to the 2001 Bi-yearly report of PWC, an investigation conducted discovered that wealth management persists to be a profitable venture with unexploited ability for substantial advancement if enterprises can swiftly respond to fulfilling the varying requirements. Number of millionaire families was about 2.3 million in the year 2003, which had significantly increased by 171 percent from 850,000 in the year 1993 and the yearly world wealth report predicted that the economic wealth of HNWIs in North America will rise at an average yearly rate of almost 11 percent between the year 2003 and 2008 (Shaikh and Kalkundarikar, 2011).

According to the 5th Annual World Wealth Report generated by Merrill Lynch Global Wealth Management and Cap Gemini (2014); the globe's high net worth individuals (HNWIs) saw a rise of populace and wealth in 2010 exceeding 2007 pre-crisis marks in almost all areas. 2010 witnessed international HNWI populace and wealth advancement becoming more established; in fact the HNWIs populace rose to 10.9 million – a rise of 8.3% and HNWI fiscal wealth touched US$42.7 trillion –registering a growth of 9.7% (in contrast to 17.1% and 18.9% respectively in 2009). According to World Wealth report 2012, the world's population of high net worth individuals slid 1.7 % to US $42 trillion after 2011. In 2010, the international populace of Ultra HNWIs rose beyond 10.2% and its worth increased by 11.5%. The international HNWI populace persisted to be clustered mainly in the U.S., Japan and Germany, which in all were responsible for over half (53.0%) of the globe's HNWIs. The single biggest HNW section across the globe is located in the U.S., with its 3.1 million HNWIs being responsible for 28.6% of the international HNWI populace.

Global private wealth management grew by nearly 12% in 2014 to reach a total of $164 trillion. The rise was in line with 2013, when global wealth also grew by just over 12% (Beardsley et al., 2015). Market expansion was driven by the performance of existing assets and creation of new wealth. Overall the ongoing economic recovery and accommodating monetary policies resulted in strong stock and bond performance while rising income and consumption led to strong GDP growth. According to Forbes Billionaires List of 2012, global billionaire count increased to an all-time high of 1,226. US saw additions, due to innovations, strong brands and US market upswing. Amongst BRICs, only Brazil saw an uptake, while India and China saw a downfall. Since larger wealth management assets are in USA which is a largely fee-based market, it indicates revenues held firm there. A BCG report on global wealth also shows client assets/RM improved as firms let go of non-performers and used performance-driven sales. Many of the world's wealth managers enjoyed solid Assets under Management growth in 2012 because of strong GDP performance in emerging economies, rebounding equity markets worldwide, net investor inflows and the fact that the number of HNWI continued to grow two to three times faster than the GDP in most markets (Gemes et al., 2014).

According to Mckinsey Global Wealth Management Survey, 2014, despite the slower economic growth, the number of millionaires is expected to rise by 7.1 % by 2018 to more than 18 million. The total HNW assets are expected to rise by 49% to USD 76 trillion. The Asian markets excluding Japan, is expected to create USD 9 trillion of wealth. The major developing countries to show an uptrend in HNW includes China, India and Saudi Arabia. Emerging markets are inclined towards UNHW clients and enjoy higher assets growth.

According to Allianz Global Wealth report, 2014, the total financial wealth of the private individuals was raised to little below 10% year on year in 2013, the maximum degree of growth observed globally since 2003. Investment in equities and other securities were the primary cause of steering the economic growth of the year: amount of capital invested in equities and fixed-income securities increased by 16.5% that year, which is even higher as compared to the growth in the years contemporary to the crash of the financial market and global crunch, to higher than EUR 45 trillion globally. However most of the investors made profits by opting for liquidity and making most of their investment in bank deposits. Savings deposits and term deposits were raised by 5.5% in the year 2013 (in comparison to 6.7% in year 2012) to gross amount of nearly EUR 34 trillion globally towards the end of the year 2013. The third most preffered asset class in the security investment portfolio, specifically private domestic and everyday claims towards the insurance sector and pension institutions, observed substancial consolidated growth of 7.2% at global level during the year 2013. Contrary to this securities asset class, infact, this progress was steered not only by valuation gains, but also by significant capital invcstment. As a matter of fact, the capital investment into this securities asset class was more than as compared to any other investment option.

On the other hand, the same report outlines that wealth distribution in most of the developed nations observed to be deteriorated. Particularly, the relative amount of asset and capital increased in the posession of the richest 10 % of the individuals. Which inturn resulted in the considerable increase in the inequality in most of countries in Europe particulary in Italy, Ireland, Switzerland and France. It has been observed that the decline in the growth of securities as a result of a crisis, majorly have the harder impacts on the low and middle class investors categories (Brandmeir et al., 2014).

Looking forward, the global wealth is projected to grow at a CAGR of 5.4% in next 5 years and will reach an estimated figure of $198.2 trillion USD by the end of 2018.

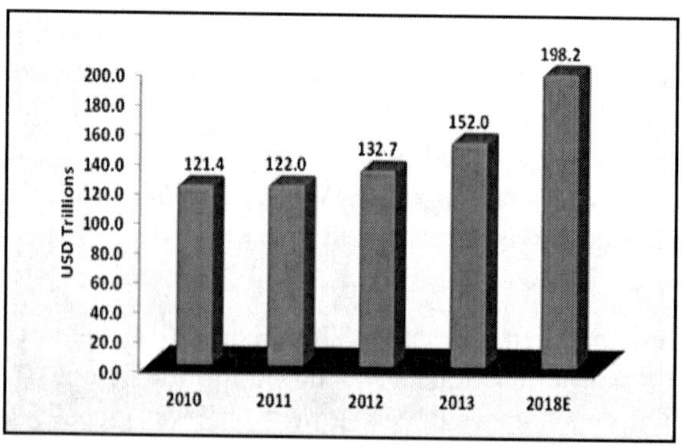

Source: Karvy Private Wealth's Fifth India-Wealth-Report-2014. Available at : http://cafemutual.com/UploadPdf/635545862001818750_India-Wealth-Report-2014.pdf

Figure 2.1: Global Individual Wealth

2.1.5 Wealth Management in India

The development of India makes it an alluring market for wealth management firms as India's GDP has been steady around the 9% mark along with a robust future position. It is anticipated that this development would be persistent and India is anticipated to rank number 3 in terms of international economies by 2030. Thus, probable entrants in the wealth management domain find India to be an alluring market because of the growing economy with a considerably huge growth rate and the expectation that it will be ranked number three in terms of global economies by 2030; this encourages them to develop an early base and enhance their market revenues (Cognizant Report, 2011)

In contrast to their global equivalents, the wealthy populace of India is comparatively younger and thus, they have a varied perspective towards wealth management. The variation in the demography provides a chance to develop new plans to deal with the requirements of the younger populace and influence new technologies including the social media and mobile-based applications which enable investors to bring investment opportunities at their fingertips and these advancements have turned out to be key differentiators in this industry.

Wealth management service industry in India is widely fragmented which is not astonishing because this sector is still in its early years of growth and is still not mature. Till now, majority of the organized firms have emphasized chiefly on the individuals living in metro cities, resulting in around one-fifth of the Indian high net-worth individuals (HNI) populace remaining unexploited. India is regarded as one of the rapidly developing wealth management markets.

In contrast to its large populace, the Indian HNW market is quite small; with 153,000 HNWIs India ranked 16th in the world by the HNI Population (Asia-Pacific Wealth Report, 2014). However its development is rapid across the globe, providing the wealth managers a large scope to expand. The robust financial performance of the Indian economy is the cause for the development of the HNW populace as it has enhanced the ratio of HNW entrepreneurs and trade owners. According to a research report by Data monitor (2011), the characteristic of Indian high-net worth individual is most probably a male, whose age is above 65 years and who has earned his wealth mainly via entrepreneurship. In context to his portfolio, he is partial towards real estate, preferring to apportion the biggest share of his wealth to real estate investment funds, as he considers real estate to be a sound investment.

The growing volatility in Indian markets makes a shift in the focus of clients to low risk products with the expectation of higher returns at competitive prices. This poses a challenge for wealth managers to redesign their business models in order to sustain and maintain their market share in the evolving market.

According to the Karvy Private Wealth (2014), total wealth in India grew 27.5% to INR257.4 trillion (US$4.1 trillion) in 2014, with physical assets of INR122.7 trillion (up 52.3%) and other assets growing 37.7% to INR134.7 trillion. Furthermore, Karvy forecasts that Indian wealth will double over the next five years. The total Indian Individual wealth in Financial Assets stands at INR134.71 Lakh Crore in FY14 and Indian Individual wealth in Physical Assets (Real Estate, gold, Silver, Platinum) stands at INR122.70 lakh crore. Hence, the total Indian Individual Wealth in FY14 is estimated at INR257.41 Lakh Crore, an increase of 27.47% over FY13.

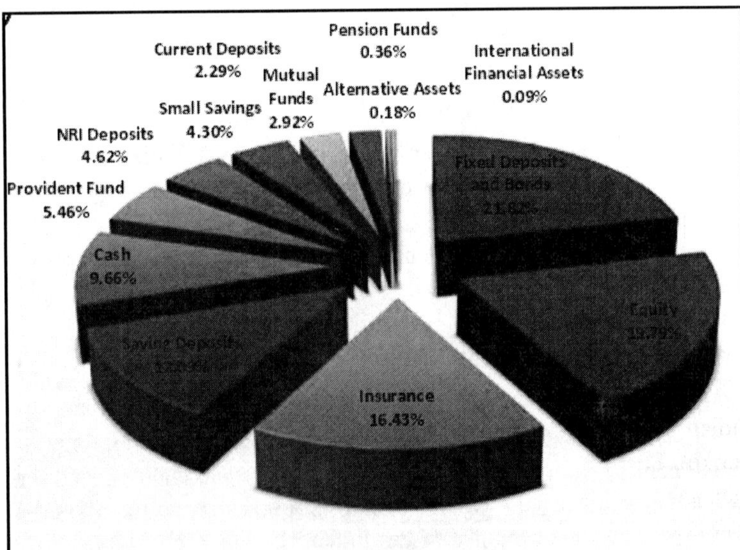

Source: Karvy Private Wealth's Fifth India-Wealth-Report-2014. Available at : http:// cafemutual.com/UploadPdf /63 5545862001818750_India-Wealth-Report-2014.pdf

Figure 2.2: Distribution of Individual Wealth in Financial Assets

The figure 2.2 above shows the distribution of individual wealth in Financial Assets. Fixed Deposits and Bonds occupy the top position with an aggregate investment of 21.82% followed by Direct Equity with an investment of 19.79%, Insurance (16.43%) and Saving Deposits (12.09%).

The figure 2.3 above shows the distribution of individual wealth in Physical Assets. Investment in Gold occupies the top position with an aggregate investment of 50.96% followed by Real Estate with an investment of 41.07%. Diamond, Silver and Platinum holds a very small amount of investment of 6.33%, 1.59% & 0.05% respectively. Owing to India's financial growth, increase in investment and rising income level, the wealth management market has seen a healthy growth. Households prefer investing their savings in physical assets rather than financial assets.

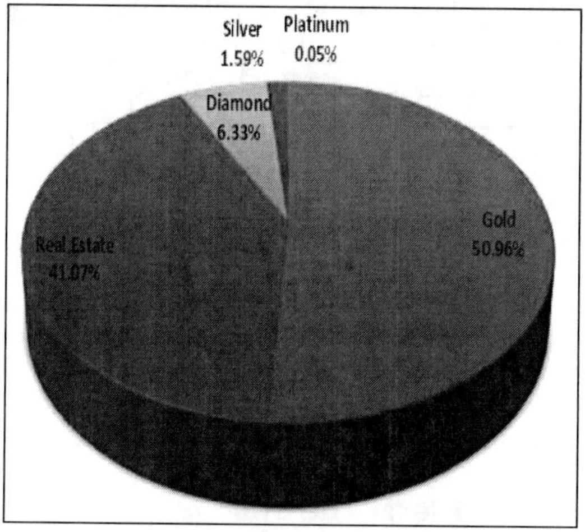

Source: Karvy Private Wealth's Fifth India-Wealth-Report-2014. Available at : http://cafemutual.com/UploadPdf/63554 5862001818750_India-Wealth-Report-2014.pdf

Figure 2.3: Distribution of Individual Wealth in Physical Assets

Looking forward, there are a lot of opportunities available for Indian banks and financial institutions to boost the wealth management market. The wealth managers must start creating the awareness of wealth management in smaller cities where people are not yet aware of these services or they cannot access these services because of lack of resources. These small cities might have potential wealthy people which the wealth managers should not ignore. Also, the growing wealth of Indian entrepreneurs and private company employees is an opportunity that may take Indian Wealth market to a new level because these people need professional advice to manage their money as they create wealth and build up companies.

As a result of the economic and financial growth of India and the significant increase in the individual's wealth, wealth management industry has seen a boom in its demand. India is one of the rapidly expanding wealth management industries with the total HNWI population growing at over 20 % CAGR (Allianz, 2014).

It is expected that the total worth of the liquid wealth held by rich people in the developing countries like Brazil, China, and India will become three times from $1.5tn to $4.6tn between 2006 and 2015 (World Wealth Report, 2014).

Top 8 Asian Cities by HNWI Population

City	Ranking	2012	2022	Change (%)
Tokyo	3	5,440	6,763	24
Beijing	6	2,285	5,262	130
Mumbai	7	2,105	4,988	137
Hong Kong	8	3,205	4,780	49
Delhi	11	1,945	4,278	120
Osaka	13	2.970	3,813	28
Shanghai	14	1,415	3,704	162
Singapore	23	1,345	1,930	43

Source: Survey by Knight Frank; http://www.2point6billion.com/news/2013/03/18/asias-high-net-worth-individuals-concentrated-in-china-india-12062.html

Figure 2.4: HNWI Population In Asian Countries

2.2 Theories on Individual's Behavior

This section provides an abstract of the theoretical framework adopted during the course of this research, reviews the literature available to provide an introduction of the followed groundwork and existing theoretical model, architecture and design described and explained in the Theory of Reasoned Action (TRA) which presents most relevant components associated with investor behavior.

2.2.1 Theory of Reasoned Action

The present study forms its basis on the components presented under the Theory of Reasoned Action (TRA), which was originally described and elaborated in 1967 as an extension to the expectancy-value structural framework and has been applied to comprehend an individual's behavior and predict it. This theory presents a proposition that every individual thinks wisely and logically uses the available information to reach his/her decisions (Ajzen and Fishbein, 1980). It has been stated that an investor does consider the consequences and benefits of their actions before making any decisions about their conduct or behavior related to any investment they make. Hence it resulted into a conceptual theory known as "*a theory of reasoned action*".

The Theory of Reasoned Action (TRA) basically refers to a framework build from behavioral intention and fundamentally describes the relationship between attitude and behavior of an individual.

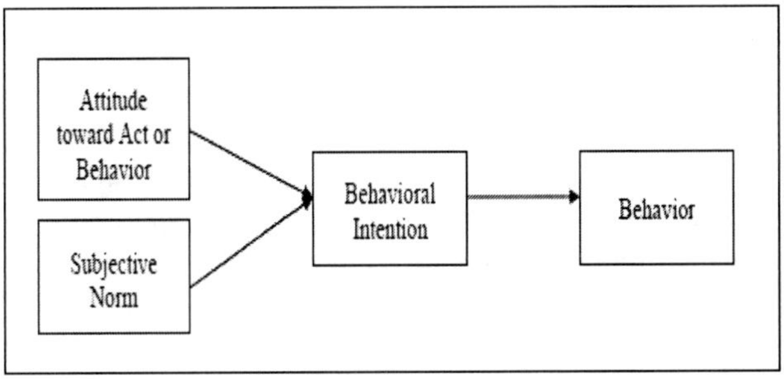

Figure 2.5: Theory of Reasoned Action

According to this theory, an individual's intention is derived from a function of two essential attributes. The nature of the first attribute is personal to the individual and the second attribute reflects the influence of the society on that individual. This evidently concludes that an attitude and social pressure forms a person's intention (Azjen and Fishbein, 1980). Attitude, a personal factor, determines whether a certain behavior should be exhibited or not. The second determinant referred to as subjective norm, determines the influence of social pressures on an investor's behavior (Azjen & Fisbein, 1980). This theory provides us with one of the most influential techniques to effectively predict human behavior and the related behavioral characteristics. Research on this theory was primarily only focused on the voluntary behaviors because the other kinds of behaviors could be result of external elements influencing the behavior. Habitual actions and impulsive behaviors are also excluded during the development of this theory. This theory has proven to be relatively effective in understanding the human behavior and its related dispositions (Sheppard and Hartwick, 1988). This theory presents useful conceptual model, which offers a technique to conveniently determine the intermediate variables and elements in developing a relationship between attitude and behavior. This Theory proposes that individual's behavior is influenced by his behavioral intentions to exhibit or perform a specific behavior. Intentions of an individual refer to his decisions to act in a particular way. Intentions can be determined by a mathematical function of two fundamental elements. First element is the attitude towards performing an act or behavior, which is an evaluative reaction that results from perceived implications often associated with behavior. The second element is the influence of significant others generally referred as subjective norms, which is derived from the beliefs about the expectations of close referents and the individual's motivation to follow their expectations. Thus, *Theory of Reasoned Action* can be mathematically represented as below

$$I = bA + cU + e_t$$

In the above equation *I* refer to the *individual's intentions*. *A* refers to the *individual's attitude* towards the act or behavior. U refers to the *beliefs* about the expectations of referents and significant other to exhibit a specific behavior, which represents subjective norm. 'b' and 'c' are the specific constants associated with attitude and subjective norm respectively. Whereas e_t represents random error element. As described by Fishbein individual's intentions are influenced by the behavioral beliefs (F), which refers to the anticipated implications of acting in a specific way. The subjective norms are driven by normative beliefs (N) which refers to the expectation of the significant others about what is expected behavior comprised of. Hence this theory can be compiled by mentioning that the intentions to engage in a specific behavior influence the individual's behavior. Secondly the individual's intentions are encapsulated by attitude towards the behavior and the subjective norm. Subjective norms are driven by normative beliefs and the desire to be in consensus with the significant others and the attitude is driven by behavioral beliefs and the evaluation of the anticipated outcomes.

Limitations in Theory of Reasoned Action

Even though theory of reasoned action is most widely preferred in research, several criticisms have been raised against this theory because of some of its limitations. Many researchers have presented an argument that apart from attitude and subjective norm there are other determinants of one's intention, to which this theory does not cater. Most common of them are cognitive reactions towards individual's attitude (Ajzen and Driver, 1992), habit of an individual (Triandis, 1980), self-identity (Granberg and Holmberg, 1990) and moral obligations for an individual (Schartz and Tessler, 1972).It does not accurately determine behavioral constraints due to lack of resources and opportunities such as time, skill and money. This theory also had some limitations in predicting behavioral intentions in a situation when the individual does not have free control on his behavior.

In order to overcome these limitations, another theory referred as Theory of Planned Behavior was developed by adding another variable referring to perceived behavioral control.

2.2.2 Theory of Panned Behavior

Theory of planned behavior was developed by Ajzen in 1985. This theory is considered as one of the most widely used theories in human psychology in observing and predicting human behavior. Theory of planned behavior has evolved as one of the important theories with a broad spectrum of influence and is used in research on human behavior (Lai & Hung, 2010). This theory proposes that the perceived behavioral control of an individual is the important influencing factor of his behavioral intentions while making any decision (Chiou, 1998). The model of perceived behavioral control is consistent with concept of perceived self-ability within a general model to study relationship between attitude, subjective norm and behavioral intention developed by Bandura (1982) with the acumen of how wisely an individual would take action to handle a particular situation. This theory also measures the most challenging behaviors that require the special skills, knowledge, opportunities, resources and cooperation from others (Ajzen, 1991). The extent to which one's intentions to act and behave in a particular way is carried out, is driven by the amount of control and availability of resources one has over his behavior. Since this study is primarily based only on Theory of reasoned action, theory is planned behavior is out of scope of this research objectives and has been mentioned above just for the reference.

2.3 Determinants of Investor's Behavior

The following literature reviews some of the factors' that influence investor's behavior and relate each other in the relevant investor behavior research.

2.3.1 Financial Literacy

Financial literacy means how literate a person is in terms of financial and investment techniques. In other words, it means how well an individual understands and possesses knowledge of financial and banking industry. If such knowledge is not present, an investor tends to make poor investment decisions, which sometimes prove to be fatal for his financial health. Education is said to have a relation with the knowledge and financial maturity of an individual (Lin, 2007).

Lodhi (2014) in a study on *factors influencing individual investor's behavior* defined financial literacy as a set of skills and knowledge, which helps a person to take informed and prudent financial decision with their knowledge of financial market. Lusardi & Mitchell (2014) referred financial literacy as the ability of the investor to analyze financial information and take informed decisions for their financial investments and to effectively manage their wealth and debt. Baker et al., (2014) stated that financial literacy is a human capital form that entails skills and knowledge regarding personal finances encompassing financial theory, mathematical ability, knowledge of financial instruments and potential to apply knowledge efficiently. In a research conducted by Becchetti, Caiazza and Coviello (2013) on *financial education and investment attitudes*, financial literacy has been referred as the development and growth of the investor and financial service consumers in enhancing their knowledge of financial products and concepts with seeking advice from professionals and gathering more financial information; and enhancing their skills and getting more confident in making financial decisions by understanding the financial risks and making right use of opportunities. As reported by Olsen (2008) gaining financial knowledge is broadly classified into two fundamental categories, first step is associated with the financial literacy in which an individual understands the basic financial concepts and obtain knowledge on how the different financial products work and the functioning of the financial system and the second step is associated with the financial empowerment that tells them how to make use of their knowledge in step one to enhance their decision making skills. Cole and Shastry (2009) mentioned that in terms of finance, understanding of the compound interest and the ability to carry out calculation to derive the present value are the important predictors of the effective financial planning.

According to Al-Tamimi and Kalli (2009) in their study on *financial literacy and investment decisions*, need of financial literacy has gained a lot of attention due to the extensive development of the new financial products, and the increasing complexity of the finance system surrounded by stringent regulations and the continuous advancements in the economic and political system. With the increase in the earnings people now have more money to save and invest. Financial Literacy is becoming increasingly important for the people to optimally utilize the credits, which has relatively become easy with the increasing completion in the banking industry. Victor and Jonathan (2007) while studying the *disclosure regulation and credit market outcomes*, observed that the individuals who lack in understanding of the calculation of interest rate associated with the series of payments are more likely to get into indebtedness by borrowing high amount and leading to poor financial condition.

It was identified that investors with high financial literacy does not develop their portfolio based on their knowledge rather they count upon the professionals to do this task for them (Muller and Weber, 2010 and Doran et al, 2010). According to Hira and Loibl (2005) financial literacy in the past few years has attained a lot of consideration in many different applications and broader scope in different industries especially the government companies, consumer industry, banking institutions, marketing and advertising industry.

In a research conducted by Braunstein and Welch (2002) on *financial literacy and overview of practice, research and policy*, it was examined that business analysts and strategy designers and other involved business communities are giving attention to the inadequate financial knowledge with the consumers in industry; and lack of intelligent and powerful tools to help them take efficient economic decisions to generate profit and good returns; and also to effectively manage their own business accounts and financial issues. Such lack of adequate financial knowledge can impact an individual's various daily activities such as sale and purchase to the effectively managing their earnings, planning for their financial budget for their better tomorrow.

Friestad and Wright (1994) in their study on the *persuasion financial knowledge model* determined that financial literacy could be broadly categorized into two major elements; subjective knowledge and objective knowledge. Objective knowledge refers to the exact and precise information available and the subjective knowledge refers to the belief regarding the state of information available. Cavazosa (2013) opined that financial literacy is increasingly gaining the focus and is becoming an integral dimension of the research out of the various determinants of the human investment behavior, exclusively while observing the global economic crisis. In the middle of changing financial world, investors are required to make prudent financial decisions and in such a situation, lack of financial knowledge may result into various negative impacts on individual's financial health. From the investors perspective it could result in getting into over-indebtedness situation. This may lead to severe consequences on the financial health and situation of the investor (Keese and Schmitz, 2010). Financial Literacy also impacts the ability of an individual to make savings for future and long-term objectives and goals such as saving for higher education, planning to buy a house and also doing sound planning for his retirement. It also allows an individual to efficiently manage their assets and liabilities, understand the importance and significance of insurance, how to evaluate various risks involved in an investment and the returns generated from it. Chen and Volpe (1998) in *an analysis of personal financial literacy*, observed that individuals with higher financial literacy tend to make more appropriate judgment and often make more prudent investment decisions for their saving and more wisely utilize the credit available to them. It if difficult for a person with less financial knowledge to take the right precautions and measures to protect himself from the risk of financial crises and they are more impacted by the fluctuations in the financial market. In a wider context, a person with lack of skills or inadequate financial knowledge to manage his finances has to sometimes compromise with increasing competition and their operations. Well-informed Investors with good financial knowledge result in bringing efficiency in the market and more competition. In a related study Edmiston and Gillett-Fisher (2006), concluded that the decision made by high financial literate individuals more closely reflect the perspective and opinion of the professional financial experts.

In a study conducted by Sherraden and Boshara (2008) on *how to increase the effectiveness of financial education and saving programs*, it was observed that it is not necessary for an individual to first attain financial knowledge and then make huge gains by making wise investments, but it might also be the case that when an individual starts making lot of investment then he becomes more and more knowledge about the financial system and products. Consumers with higher literacy expect the product to be suitable to their demands and meet their financial investment objectives and the providers of those products and services have to meet tough competition to create them with all the desired features and characteristics appropriate to the demands of the consumers.

With the increasing concern of the financial literacy, several educational programs on saving, basic accounting, maintaining the credits and debts are being conducted on a wider scale to train the youth and develop financial skills in them, which can help them to focus on their objectives to achieve their goals. Mixed results have been obtained from the analysis and research on benefits of conducting various training sessions on financial literacy. Only few programs those were conducted with a particular and definite objective were successful in developing and strengthening some specific areas related to financial management of a consumer which includes saving, managing the debt, insurance and; engaging in and adopting the welfare plans sponsored by the employer. But it is not necessary for an individual to exhibit an enhanced and efficient behavior by merely attending to those financial literacy programs. It depends on the pattern and composition of the training along with the personal characteristics of the individual such as reluctance to changes, which significantly influences the results of such trainings in bringing a positive impact contributing to their bright future. Training coordinator and instructor have a bigger challenge to design the entire training module with the information and content of the training to selecting the audience and right candidates for it and to decide how and when to conduct the training. All these variables combined together account for the effectiveness and positive results of such financial literacy programs. In a research conducted on financial literacy Al-Tamimi and Kalli (2009), have tried to determine the impact of demographic factors on financial literacy, particularly occupation, employment status, monthly earning, gender, age and education. They mentioned that the level of financial knowledge significantly differ by the gender of an individual. Men were found to have higher level of financial knowledge as compared to women.

According to Park, Mothersbough & Fieck (1994) in a study on *assessment of consumer knowledge* and Brucks (1985) in a research on *the effects of product class knowledge on information search behavior*, the level of the knowledge of an investor accounts for the information he possesses and influences his behavior of making decisions. As per Park, Mothersbough & Fieck (1994), there are two determinants of the knowledge that is objective knowledge, which determines or refers to the accuracy of the information and the second determinant is the subjective knowledge, which is individual's perspective of what and how adequate is his knowledge. In a related study on *dimensions of consumer expertise*, Alba and Wesley (1987) have mentioned in their research that even though the objective and subjective knowledge are correlated but they are fundamentally different in two important forms. Firstly, an individual with his subjective knowledge can sometime under or overestimate his knowledge, as he cannot accurately realize about how much and how less he knows. Subjective knowledge can be determined as a measure of level of confidence an individual has in his knowledge and hence it signifies the level of self-confidence. Subjective knowledge increases the ability and the confidence in an investor to take his decisions and exhibit a behavior. Glaser and Walther (2013) in a research on *financial literacy as a dual process theory and investment behavior*, studied the importance of financial literacy in making more intelligent investment decisions and found that the investment behavior of individuals with higher level of financial literacy is primarily influenced by two instincts i.e. cognition and intuition. Danes,

Casas and Boyce (1999) observed the improvement in the financial behavior of an individual with the increase in financial knowledge and consequently reported significant changes in their saving and investment patterns.

Studies performed by Garrett, Bernheim & Maki (2001) on *education and saving and the long term effects of financial education*, examined from their research that the effects of financial knowledge commonly support the concept that financial knowledge improves the financial behavior of an investor. Hira and Loibl (2005) observed that financial management behavior is positively influenced and driven by the financial knowledge. Elliehausen, Lundquist and Staten (2007) in their research on *the impact of credit counseling on subsequent borrower behavior*, examined that individuals with higher financial knowledge have exhibited more responsible financial behavior. In a study based on four important aspects of financial management; investing, saving, credit management and cash-flow management, Hilgert, Hogarth & Beverly (2003) derived a positive connection between the financial literacy and the investment behavior of the investor. Perry and Morris (2005) in a study on *the role of self-perception, knowledge, and income in explaining consumer financial behavior*, examined the link between the financial literacy of an investor and his investment behavior and found that an investor with higher financial understanding tends to exhibit more responsible behavior towards making investment. Clark (2012) observed more responsible attitude, effective investment behavior and less risky decision-making in individuals with higher financial knowledge. Choi et al. (2004) found that the substantial impacts of the financial knowledge are probably overstated by measuring the dimensions of intended behavior of the investor.

In a research conducted by Lusardi and Mitchell (2011) it has been determined that financial knowledge and investment planning are tightly correlated and higher financial literacy leads to successful retirement planning. Gustman and Steinmeier (2004) also concluded that the individual's knowledge of benefits of pension and their understanding of the social security are related to their efficient retirement planning. A similar research conducted by Bernheim, Skinner and Weinberg (2001) found that retirement planning behavior of an individual is positively related to the financial knowledge. Financial literacy is also positively related to optimal financial, investment and retirement decisions (Clark, 2012). Education was found to have a significant influence on wealth management decisions (Lin, 2007). Education plays an imperative role in helping every individual in making his or her financial decisions. Investors might need additional assistance in planning for their retirement and deciding for long-term investment. A study conducted by Cole & Shastry (2009) on *the effect of education, cognitive ability and financial literacy on financial market participation*, it was observed that with the higher financial knowledge an individual is more likely to prudently plan for their retirement.

Wang & Jing (2009) while studying the *buying behavior, social support and credit card indebtedness*, conducted a research to examine the risk taking behavior of an investor based on the subjective and objective knowledge that the investors possess. He mentioned in his research that investors repeatedly take risks while making their investment decisions. They may earn huge returns in their investments by taking risk, for some investors, as they lack in some fundamental financial concepts, they may sometimes make poor decisions putting their capital at risk. Literature based on financial literacy predicts two important theories. First theory as explained by Edmiston and Gillett-Fisher (2006) in a study on *financial education at the workplace* derives more insight to the relationship between the financial literacy and taking risk while making investment decisions. Second theory that was formulated by Lyons et al. (2006) states that financial experience and financial education has positive effect on the financial behavior and knowledge of an individual. A study conducted by Siegal and Hoban (1982) examining the *relative risk aversion revisited*, indicates that financial knowledge and personality of an individual has positive influence on the risk taking behavior and investment decision-making. Several studies have been conducted to investigate the relationship between individual's personal characteristics and the degree of risk he can bear. Barnewall (1987) in a research on *Psychological Characteristics of the Individual Investor* determined the investor's behavior from the aspect of taking risk in their investment decisions and found that they are active or passive. Passive investors are those who have inherited wealth or have gained it by putting someone else's money at risk. Such investors require more safety of their investments and have less risk tolerance. While the active investors are the one those have gained wealth by their own by putting their own money at risk. Such investors tend to have greater risk tolerance as compared to first former category. Filbeck, Hatfield and Horvath (2005) have determined how risk tolerance of an individual relates to the individual's personal traits. They concluded that the level of risk tolerance in the individual are directly associated with the perception, thinking, intuition and individual's preferences. Individuals who have higher inclination to their feeling have less risk tolerance and those who are more inclined to listen their minds have high risk-tolerance.

Grable and Lytton (1998) in a study on *investor risk tolerance and testing the efficacy of demographics as differentiating and classifying factors* determined that gender of an investor has influence in making decisions that involves risk. Riley and Chow (1992) examined that the age of an investor has positive influence on the risk tolerance. Lyons (2004) while studying the *profile of financially at-risk college students* concluded from his research that investors who lack the financial knowledge and experience tend to be at more risk of being unable to repay their debts. Lodhi (2014) determined that the length of the investment duration is also important criteria of making the investment choice. Long-term investments are less risky as compared to short-term investments. It is concluded that financial knowledge of an individual's increases their capacity of taking risk, as with higher financial knowledge an investor can wisely and efficiently analyze the financial reports and information available in hand.

In a similar study Lusardi and Mitchell (2014) has tried to determine the basic financial concepts of the individuals by assessing them on their elementary knowledge on inflation and Interest rate calculation. The findings of the study concluded that the knowledge of the individual investor about the diversification of risk is a vital factor of making decisions of investments. Lyons & Neelakantan (2008) & Lyons et al., (2007) found that Investor needs to be educated to understand the market risks, how to hedge them and how to invest in precarious investments so that there is enough growth in their savings. Lodhi (2014) identified that investment knowledge and other investment related information help investors in minimizing asymmetry of facts and permits him to invest in risky assets. It has been proved that financial literacy is positively correlated with the risk taking i.e. financial knowledge of an investor increases his risking taking capabilities. This is based on the observation that a more financial literate person has the understanding to efficiently analyze the financial statements and annual reports of a company to give him an idea about the future performance of the company and the profit that can be made by investing in that company.

Maditinos et al. (2007) in a study on *investors' behavior in the athens stock exchange*, examined from his research that the level of financial literacy has a significant relation with the investment decision making of an individual. Investors with higher knowledge of financial matters generally adopt a different approach while making their investment decisions as compared to investors with investors with less financial literacy. Investors with high financial knowledge tend to make greater use of financial information published in reports and newspaper, while the people with lesser financial knowledge tend to rely more on the noise and sentiments prevailing in the market and the advice from their friends, colleagues, family and other social sources. In a similar study, Al-Tamimi and Kalli (2009) have determined that financial literacy has a relation and significant impact on the investment decisions of an individual. They have also derived a relation between the occupations of an individual with the financial knowledge he possesses. An individual working in the sector of banking, accounting and finance will eventually have greater level of financial knowledge. It was observed by Lusardi and Mitchell (2014) that financial literacy is associated with the individual's ability of efficiently saving money and making sound investment decisions. If a person with low financial knowledge will make a mistake he will have to pay a significant price for his mistake.

Mirshekary and Saudagarah (2005) while studying the *perceptions and characteristics of financial information users in developing countries* examined how the investors use the annual reports, financial statements and other sources of information of different organizations to make their investment decisions. Some researchers also noticed that knowledge of finance does not influence on the quality of investment decisions (Perry, 2008; Braunstein and Welch, 2002; Gathergood, 2012; Bodnaruk and Simonov, 2012).

Rooij et al., (2011) in a study on *financial literacy and stock market participation* referred that participants of stock market have a higher financial literacy level than average population. Bayer et al., (1996) determined that with the gain in financial knowledge an investor tend to make wiser investments. Schooley and Deborah (1999) in a research on *investor's asset allocations versus life-cycle funds* mentioned that investors with higher financial knowledge are found to have more equity stocks in their portfolio account as compared to other financial products. Cole and Shastry (2009) observed the influence of the financial literacy on the cognitive ability of an individual which consequently increases the participation of the individual in the investment and financial activities. Rooij et al. (2011) concluded that the individuals who are well- versed with financial knowledge are expected to participate more in the equity shares.

2.3.2 Beliefs

Li and Li (2014) while studying the *evidence from belief dispersion and stock trading volume* found out that there exist a positive and firm link between dispersion of trust about the prevailing economic situation between investors and trading volume of share market. It was also noticed that dispersion of modifications in belief is also positively correlated with the volume of trading activities in equity market. This outcome is consistent with study of Kelley and Tetlock (2013) and Campbell (2007). In a research conducted by Weinstein (1980) on *unrealistic optimism about future life events,* belief has been referred as a human cognitive factor, which persuades an individual who has belief over any element or matter to take an action on account of his belief. In addition to that belief also plays an important role in building an attitude towards or against the positive or negative objective respectively. In case the belief of an individual induces a positive attitude, he is more committed to perform an action. Another piece of evidence was founded by Ben (2012), who says that individual investor's decisions are primarily motivated by their beliefs rather than their preferences. Also, it was found that some Investors believe that majority of the population also shares the relatively same opinion as themselves and those who have a different point of view or disagrees with them are partial and biased (Egan et al., 2014).

Beliefs and preferences are central determinants of individual investor's trading and risk-taking behavior (Hoffmann, Post and Pennings, 2013). Belief and trust are the important determinants of the exhibited investment behavior of an individual (Guiso, Sapienza and Zingales, 2008).Wang and Jing (2009) observed in their research that individual belief and their gut feeling is one of the important determinants of individual's investment behavior. In a similar study conducted by Roger, Griffin and Ross (1994) on *exploring the planning fallacy*, it was observed that the individuals with stronger and firm beliefs also tend to exhibit greater confidence in their actions. Through a research conducted on the investors in the equity market, it was found that individual who had more belief in some particular securities or instruments to yield high returns and believed that those instruments would help them to achieve their financial goals, have displayed higher confidence investing in those instruments and also continued to invest in them despite of any market situations or any other influencing factors against those instruments.

According to a study on *Understanding Information Technology Usage* conducted by Taylor and Todd (1995) in a situation when there is a possibility of finding differences in opinion between different referent groups, subjective norm of an individual can be divided into his normative *belief* and his motivation to adhere to one referent group over other, which determines his choice of engaging into specific behavior or not. It was found that determinants of degree or extent of normative belief and motivation to follow someone's opinion influence the financial decisions made by an individual. In another related research carried out by Srivastava (2012) on *rational investment decisions of irrational household investors*, it was determined that the investment attitude of an individual equity investors is largely influenced by his strong belief that long-term investments mostly generate higher returns and possesses lower risk than short term investments. It was due to this belief that many new investments were made in 2007, despite of the major economic crises and financial breakdown observed in the same year. Al-Tamimi and Kalli (2009) in their findings mentioned that Investment decisions are highly influenced by the beliefs and least influenced by the rumors. In a research conducted by Cole and Shastry (2009) it was observed that the lack of trust in individuals significantly reduces their participation in the investment activities. In a study by Glaser and Walther (2013) it was observed that the investment behavior of an individual is dependent upon their personal belief and trust towards different financial theories.

In a study on *why do forecasters disagree and lessons from the term structure of cross-sectional dispersion,* Patton and Timmermann (2010) reported in their research that the variation in the investor's belief helps in identifying the influence of publically available information and analyzing them to understand its effects on the actions of an investor. It was concluded that individual's personal belief is the driving element of the conducted investment behavior in financial market. In a research conducted by Morris and Shin (2002) on *social value of public information*, reported that Belief is an important determining element of the average public opinion about the prevailing financial situation in an economy. Karpoff (1986) and Varian (1985) observed in their research that the primitive, traditional and fundamental beliefs of individual influences their interpretation of the information which in turn effects their perspectives and any changes in their belief subsequently leads to a significant change in their trading patterns. Hoffmann, Post & Pennings (2013) in a study on *how investors' Perceptions Drive Actual Trading and Risk-taking Behavior* determined that most of the individual investors in India preferred to invest in mutual fund based on equity portfolio rather than directly investing in equity. This action was based on their belief that the fund managers would better manage the equity portfolio and it's good to trust and rely on experts than taking their own decisions.

In a similar study on *Religiosity, Ethical Ideology and Intentions to Report a Peer's Wrongdoing* Tim, Ken and Gene (1996) found the religious belief to be positively influencing the individual's attitude. Results were consistent with the research conducted by Dolan et al., (2012) who reviewed the determinants that play an important role in changing the financial behavior of an individual. It was observed that the financial behavior is changed with the change in the mind and thinking of a person; subsequently it was found that the personal beliefs and perception of an individual significantly influences his thinking and can change his mind which in turn can drive a change in his financial behavior. Lodhi (2014) characterized belief and preferences as the psychological factors, which influences the individual's investment behavior and decision making. In one of the related study Azam, Quaddus and Lubna (2013) observed that an individual who *believes* that exhibiting a specific behavior will lead to positive results and good returns will have considerably favorable attitude towards performing the said behavior. Such a positive *belief* determines the attitude, which in turn determines the intention of a person. In addition to this it was also concluded that normative *beliefs* also determines the degree of influence of subjective norms on an individual's life.

Brimble, Vyvyan and Ng (2013) conducted a study on *belief and investing preferences* to examine the influence of investor's values and religious belief on their attitude and investment preferences. The results were negative and no significant relationship was found between the religious beliefs and their investment behavior. Agle and Buren (1999) observed that conventional and religious beliefs had a very minute connection with individual's attitude. Therefore it is extremely important to explore more on this front to understand the influence of personal belief on the investor's attitude and examine the behavior of an investor considering belief as the ground element.

2.3.3 Risk appetite

There are many different definitions and diverse literature on risk in finance, but most arguments contain the concepts of unexpected results and uncertainty. According to Walia and Dr. Kiran (2009) risk tolerance represents the minimum and maximum limits for an investor's ability to bear risk. Hui, Zheng and Wang (2013) and Gai and Vause (2006) have collectively referred Risk Appetite as the investor's preference and willingness of an investor to bear risk, which is further dependent upon the level to which an individual dislikes the uncertainty and the degree of such uncertainty. Tversky and Kahneman (1974) in a *study on Judgment under uncertainty; heuristics and biases* reveal that predicting and forecasting under uncertainty do not usually follow probability rules.

Elmiger and Kim (2003) in a study on *how to grade the risk in your investment and how to measure risk* defined risk as the compromise or tradeoff between the large returns and the huge risk as an after effect or outcome of making insecure and unstable investments. In a similar prospect theory by Tversky and Kahneman (1992) claimed that people tend to be reluctant to take risk in the "profitable zone" and are ready to bear risk in the "losing zone". Lopes (1987) referred risk to a state or circumstances in which the after effects of a decision made by an individual depends on the results of future events with anticipated consequences. From a strategic management view risk is defined as a factor of individual's subjective awareness and knowledge of results as an outcome of a particular action or decision. According to Walia and Dr. Kiran (2009), investors consider their level of monthly earning to decide the limits of risk that they can bear for a specific investment. Risk is a measure of uncertainty of any undesired or unfortunate events to happen. In a similar research conducted by Hui, Zheng and Wang (2013) on *investor sentiment and risk appetite of real estate security market* determined that the level of risk appetite of an individual depends on the hesitation of individual to bear any uncertainty in investment returns and the positive or negative fluctuations in the finance market. Williams & Heins (1964) while conducting a study on *risk management and insurance* advised that the possibility of predicted outcome differs from the unpredictability of the actual results.

From the perspective of a rational investor Walia and Dr. Kiran (2009) mentioned that maximizing returns and minimizing risk are the two fundamental criteria gaining the focus of the wealth managers while creating their service strategies. As described in a study conducted by Sharpe (1966), it was illustrated that the slope of the regression line and explains the volatility of a particular instrument corresponding to the market standard, has been accepted as the most suitable yardstick for the risk measurement. Walia and Dr. Kiran (2009) examined that the uncertainty in the returns of an investment is primarily due to the lack of knowledge and skills to analyze the financial information because of the increasing complexity in the finance industry. With this uncertainty in place, the associated risk with a particular investment is an important factor for the decision makers to derive their investment decisions. In a similar study conducted by Kaplan and Garrick (1981) risk has been determined as an uncertainty factor, which could probably result into considerable loss. Schwartz and Tesssler (1972) observed that anticipated returns on the investments are positively correlated with the systematic market risk; higher returns are generated from high-risk investments. Walia and Dr. Kiran (2009) examined that an important and crucial challenge for the investors is their lack of insight and understanding to efficiently measure the risk factor associated with the investment. Therefore, deviating from the standpoint of standard finance, behavioral finance also examines subjective factors, where observed risks include both emotional and perceptional aspects. Two main attitudes toward risk are risk aversion and risk seeking, both could manifest in one individual under different circumstances (Olsen 2007, Olsen 2008). It was proved that one of the important factors influencing investor's attitude is their tolerance for risk (Bennet et al., 2011).

Alanko (2009) in a study on *what drives investors' risk appetite* determined that risk attitude and risk allocation are correlated and goes hand in hand. During the period of the study, he observed that a situation of recession in an economy creates risk aversion among the investors in the market. Walia and Dr. Kiran (2009) in their research concluded that the risk aversion behavior of an individual determines his decision to completely refrain from risk or only take minor risk i.e. whenever a person is given a choice between 100 % guaranteed moderate returns and high risk and high return, majority of the people choose for the moderate returns which are guaranteed. In a similar research, Alanko (2009) observed that risk attitude of individual person determines the allocation of the investment and decision making attitude.

Srivastava (2007) in an *analysis of behaviour of investors in India* observed that past experience of successful investing in funds maximizes risk tolerance of investor and vice versa for unsuccessful past experience. Walia and Dr. Kiran (2009) opined that before designing any innovation solution for the investors, wealth managers carefully consider the trade-off between the risk and returns; and comprehensively evaluate different investment schemes on various risk elements to satisfy the need of all investors to obtain maximum returns. Tarashev et al., (2003) observed that dynamics of financial market would modify systematically with effective risk aversion level of investors. Walia and Dr. Kiran (2009) examined that wealth managers with their technical skill and professional management are consistently trying to make the markets more transparent and efficient in order to easily determine and effectively manage the risk factor.

Talati and Sanghvi (2011) in *an analytical study on investors' awareness and perception towards the hedge funds* mentioned that Gujarati investors would like to invest in fixed deposits of banks which are nationalized and government securities where they get security of their investment with nominal returns. Investors prefer to take risk in land, equity markets, gold and other such commodities. Walia and Dr. Kiran (2009) determined that uncertainty of the returns and changing perspective of an individual investor towards risk are influencing his decision to invest in the high-risk instruments. Anand and Murugaiah (2004) in a study on *marketing of financial services: strategic issues* observed that the satisfaction of an investor is built upon the dependence and trust confide on the wealth managers in order to gain benefits. Despite of having skills and expertise, most of the wealth managers are not able to retain their trust for investors by ensuring them risk free returns and could not compensate for the extra risk borne by the investors. Walia and Dr. Kiran (2009) found that out of the various factors which influence the decision of an investor, associated risk and expected returns are the important determinants which indicate the direction of an investor towards a particular investment option.

Khitoliya (2014) while studying the *investors awareness and perceived risk attitude* found that investors mostly discuss with relatives and friends about different schemes available in mutual fund prior taking investment decision, which is not fair in decisions of investment. Kumar and Persaud (2002) proposed a method to determine the factor of risk aversion by analyzing the distribution of abnormal returns from an investment. As determined by Walia and Dr. Kiran (2009) investors are normally more conscious while making any decisions for their investments and rationally demands higher returns at low risk, but it is nearly impossible to obtain exceptionally higher returns in an efficient market. Related research has been conducted by Donkers et al. (2001), Diaz-Serrano and O'Neill, (2004), to measure the risk preferences of the individual investors. Ali and Waheed (2013), in their research observed that personality traits encompassing extraversion, openness to experience, conscientiousness, agreeableness and neuroticism would have a significant correlation with investor's attitude regarding risk assumption.

According to Alanko (2009) investor's attitude and decision making related to risky investments plays a vital role in understanding investor's behavior and perception towards risk and this study can provide wealth managers with a deep insight and useful information to improve and focus on investor's demands and customer satisfaction. Hallahan et al., (2004) observed the individual investor's risk appetite and risk tolerance. Dohmen et al. (2005) has conducted extensive and comprehensive research to understand the individual's behavior and their willingness to bear risk. Guiso and Paiella, (2005) also conducted research on individual investors to observe and determine their risk preferences. As observed by Walia and Dr. Kiran (2009) in order to fulfill the demands and requirements of the investors, wealth managers are designing more innovative, productive and cost-effective tools based upon the risk appetite of the individual investors.

Potential research and study has been conducted by several researchers to figure out the various determinants of the risk in the financial industry. Alanko (2009) determined that the risk aversion behavior increases with the age of investors concluding that risk appetite is negatively and non-linearly related to the age. A related study has been carried out by Barsky et al. (1997) on *preference parameters and individual heterogeneity* determines the impact of age on the investment risk appetite of an individual. Nosic and Weber (2007) while studying the *determinants of risk taking behavior* presented an argument age, gender, education and other demographic variables are only the intermediaries of the determinants of risk. Lytton and Grable (1998), Hanna and Wang (1997) and Joo and Grable (1997) have presented some contradictory result concluding that age has a linear relation or no influence on the risk appetite of the investor's behavior. In a related study, McInish (1982) and Wallach and Kogan (1961) found that investor's risk appetite gradually reduce upon their retirement with the rational to carefully spend their saving and pension to maintain their present living standards. Taking high risk in their investments could jeopardize their entire life savings. Haarala (2008) concluded that an investor with the increasing age tends to be more risk averse. Gai and Vause (2006) have proposed a method to determine investor's risk appetite and existing market sentiments at the time of investment. Risk Appetite and risk aversion are often conversely used terms to mutually indicate the market sentiments.

In a study by Hui, Zheng and Wang (2013) on *investor sentiment and risk appetite of real estate security market* proposed a new framework to determine the risk appetite of an individual investing in real estate and equity market; and observed that degree of risk appetite differs from individual to individual and from time to time. Froot and O'Connell (2003) examined that investor's confidence is positively related to the risk tolerance and the market sentiments is the important determinant of the investor's confidence. In a related study on *investor sentiment in India,* Sehgal, Sood and Rajput (2009) determined that the sentiments of the investor play a key role in influencing the economic and market variations. Prevailing sentiments in the financial markets predominantly drives the economy and influences the stock prices in the market, which in turn have the significant influence on the investor's behavior and attitude. Finding of their research were consistent with the results of study conducted by Baker and Jeffrey (2006), Fisher and Meir (2000) and Eichengreen and Mody (1998).

Nosic and Weber (2007) deduced that regardless of the method used measure the risk, risk attitude is always predicts the risk taking behavior of an investor. Alanko (2009) conceptually established a relationship between the individual's risk tolerance of and his attitude and behavior towards risky investments. Hui, Zheng and Wang (2013) examined that risk aversion is a combination of multiple economic and psychological theories, which indicates the investor's attitude in the situation of uncertainty. Risk aversion is the essential element of the investor's behavior towards risky investments.

2.3.3.1 Risk appetite as moderator

The research undertaken by various behavioral finance experts proves that the investment behavior is not only affected by physical considerations but also by mental traits (Kannadhasan, 2006). Psychological and behavioral factors to a great extent determine the investor's behavior. Theorists believe that the behavior of investors is governed by their attitude and risk bearing capacity (Eisenhardt, 1989; Wiseman & Gomez-Mejia, 1998; De Long, Shleifer, Summers, & Waldmann, 1990; Weber, Blais, & Betz, 2002; Mohanta & Debasish, 2011). Risk appetite or risk bearing capacity is considered an important aspect in analyzing the investors' attitude (Illing & Aaron, 2005). It is proved to be a key factor driving investor behavior (Kannadhasan, 2006). Shift in risk appetite causes shift in investors' attitude and thus behavior. Being central to the concept of investors' attitude and behavior, it is believed to have a significant impact on other factors influencing attitude (Fung, Tam, & Yu, 2009). It is because of this reason; risk appetite is taken as a moderating variable in this study in order to examine its role in influencing the relationship between financial literacy, beliefs, subjective norms and attitude. Moreover, no studies so far have been undertaken to prove risk appetite as a moderator in explaining the relationship between predictors and investor's attitude.

2.3.4 Subjective norms

Subjective norms are related to the influence of society such as friends, relatives, peers and other influential members on the behavioral intention of the decision-maker. In case of investment decision-making two major influences are the influence of close friends or relatives and the influence of the advisors who recommend various policies to the decision-maker. Ajzen and Fishbein (1980) defined *Subjective Norm* as the individual's perception regarding the influence of significant others in conducting a specific behavior or to decide whether a particular behavior be exhibited or not. According to the Theory of Reasoned Action, an individual investor will most likely have an intention to perform a certain behavior if a person who is important to him thinks that he should perform such behavior. However it has been observed that even though many individuals do not exhibit a specific behavior, it is more likely that they do not have an intention. This concludes the fact that even though an individual is not in favor and has no inclination towards a performing a particular or specific behavior, he may still conduct such behavior under the social influence and pressure (Venkatesh and Davis, 2000).

Subjective Norms refers to the belief of an individual whether his significant others have the same opinion as himself about whether or not to engage in particular behavior. It was mentioned that subjective norms depends upon the normative expectations of close friends, family and relatives (Cavazosa, 2013).

Azam, Quaddus and Lubna (2013) in a study on *behavioral modeling of the individual's acceptance* referred *subjective norms* as the individual's perspective towards the social pressure exerted on him to perform or not to perform the said behavior. Subsequently it was observed that subjective norms are hypothesized to be a function of normative beliefs. An individual who believe that his friends, family and colleagues expects him to perform a behavior, he will tend to exhibit it under the social pressure of their expectation. In the study conducted on *growth intentions and actual growth*, Kolvereid and Erlend (1996) has characterized *subjective norms* into two groups of psychological determinants. The first group consists of elements identifying the investor's belief about the opinion of their family, friends and colleagues to participate or not to participate in any investment or big financial decision in a business. The second group of elements identifies the degree to which the opinion of family, friends and colleagues influence the financial decisions of an individual. The positive score in findings of the research substantiated that the support of the significant other does significantly matters for an individual to take decisions confidently. Applying the theory of planned behavior as well; subjective norm has a considerable influence on investor's investment decision (Sharma and Gupta, 2011; Croy, Paul and Craig, 2009).

Social influence theory suggests that the perspective of peers and other close referents are essential factors in the investment decision-making. Study conducted by Sheppard, Hartwick and Warshaw (1988) on *theory of reasoned action* observed a positive relationship between subjective norms and intentions of an individual to engage into specific behavior. According to Taylor and Todd (1995) in a situation when there is a possibility of finding differences in opinion between different referent groups, *subjective norm* of an individual can be divided into his normative belief and his motivation to adhere to one referent group over other. In a research conducted by Hussein, Hassan and Al-Anood (2009) on *financial literacy and investment decisions,* it was concluded that the investors with less knowledge about the financial system rely extensively on the suggestions and opinion of close relatives, colleagues, friends, peers and family and take their advice before making any investment related decisions. According to Hong, Kubik & Stein (2010) in their research on *social interaction and stock market participation,* they pointed out that a market seems more attractive to an investor, when he sees his peers participating.

Sheppard, Hartwick and Warshaw (1988) studied *the theory of reasoned action* and mentioned in their research that friends play an indispensible role in one's life. Friends of an individual have a significant influence in making almost all the crucial decisions in life, which include studies, marriage, professional career, buying a property or making any huge investments. In a similar research on *attitude, subjective norm and perceived behavioral control*, Cavazosa (2013) observed that in most of the cases it is the friends who introduce one to the investment for the first time in life. In another study conducted by Shin et al., (2010) on *financial socialization and the role of parents work and education*, it was examined that while taking any big decision, friends are considered to be the major source to get motivation and inspiration. Primarily in case of taking any investment decisions, it was observed that whenever an individual has any doubt of any heavy risk associated with the investment, friends are the first one to be contacted for advice and their perspective in regards to that investment and then compare their beliefs with their friends perspective and only goes ahead if both of their opinion matches and they both reach the consensus. These results were consistent with the findings of research carried out by Wang and Jing (2009), which was based on the influence of friends on one's investment decisions. It was founded from the conclusions that some individual's make investments just because their friends are also making investment. They have no intention or goal to get huge returns on their investments, but the actual motive is just to be associated with their friends and they make investments just for the sake of friendship. Gali (1994) conducted a study on *consumption externalities, portfolio choice, and asset prices* and observed that it was quite common for an individual to copy and follow their friend's investment decision who they think have higher financial knowledge and invest in the same portfolio or instrument in which their friend has invested. This behavior of copying investment decision of friends was particularly observed more during the initial and new investments. Bursztyn, Ederer and Ferman (2012) while studying on *understanding peer effects in financial decisions* found that peers have economically and statistically considerable influence on the investment decisions. It was observed that the investment choices of people often look similar to the choices of their peers and friends. This peer influence was found across various studies of economics and social psychology. Peers play an important role in motivating a person in taking financial decisions. When a person makes any investment, his peers also tend to follow the same investment pattern, which results from the two major concepts of social learning and social utility.

In a study conducted by DeBono and Omoto (1993) on *individual differences in predicting behavioural intentions from attitude and subjective norm*, subjective norms are referred to the impression of normal social pressures to exhibit a behavior. Influence of employees and neighbors depict the financial behavior of an investor in his investment pattern (Cole and Shastry, 2009). Evidently, the varied conclusions related to the influence of subjective norm on intention indicate a concrete relation among them. Hence it is logical to conclude that an individual investor, who possess and exhibits an inclination towards favorable subjective norms, tends to have greater intention to invest than those who do not possess the same preference. Septyanto and Adhikara (2014), Listyarti and Suryani (2014), Gain et al., (2012) found out that subjective norms positively influence investment intentions. They also observed that financial information particularly accounting information and intentions of investors has a positive significant effect on investment decisions.

Chiou (1998) conducted an extensive study on *the effects of attitude, subjective norm, and perceived behavioral control on consumer's purchase intentions* to identify and determine the effect of subjective norm and attitude on the consumer's behavior and intentions. The study resulted into conclusion that the elements like subjective norm and attitude do have positive influence on the perceived behavior of an individual. The theory of reasoned action suggests that the behavior is influenced by intention and consequently intention is influenced by subjective norm and attitude. It refers subjective norm as a function of motivation and belief associated with any referred object. On the other hand, some studies prove insignificant links between these two constructs i.e., subjective norms and investment behavior (Lewis, Agarwal et al. 2003).

2.3.5 Attitude

Attitude is said to be associated with future investor behavior. It is observed to be a driving element of the individual's exhibited behavior. In simple words, attitude predicts behavior. As described in the theory of reasoned action, attitude is considered as a significant factor influencing the behavior of an individual. Attitude is described as a psychological and cognitive tendency that is exhibited by assessing any particular element with some degree of favorableness or unfavorableness (Eagly and Chaiken, 1993). *Attitude* of an individual towards a specific behavior refers to his judgment about whether performing the said behavior would result into positive or negative returns. Thus attitude is hypothesized to be a function of one's belief about the outcomes of exhibiting a particular behavior. Attitude towards an act is also a function of individual's anticipated consequences associated with conducting any particular behavior and is derived from the implications of that behavior (Azam, Quaddus and Lubna, 2013).

Attitude is primarily formed by three components i.e. cognitive, affective and behavioral elements. One of the oldest studies carried by Schuman and Johnson (1976) revealed the evidence to substantiate the positive relationship between the attitude and behavior. Almost a decade later Snyder and Ickes (1985) in a study on *personality and social behavior* mentioned in their finding that there is moderate relationship between attitude and individual's behavior and found some positive patterns which link these two human attributes. In a research conducted by Murgea (2008) on *investor's psychology cycle on the romanian capital market* and Sehgal and Singh (2012) on *psychology of investors based on value and life style survey* it was found that psychological factors have considerable influence on the attitude and behavior. An individual in good mood is intended to be more optimistic while making investment decision and contrarily becomes more pessimistic when not in good mood.

It is the attitude of an individual which helps him to decide whether a particular behavior be conducted or not, considering both the positive and negative aspects of it (Fishbein and Ajzen 1980). Also, behavioral intention has been described as the preferences and inclination of an individual with respect to a psychological phenomenon. In case the attitude of an individual is more inclined towards a distinct behavior, the probability is more that the individual will intend to conduct that particular behavior. However, if an individual has an aversion towards a specific behavior, it is unlikely for that individual to have the intention to possess such behavior (Ajzen and Fishbein 1980). Attitude of an investor towards risk taking involved in an investment plays an important role not only affects his investment behavior but also influences the economic growth and development (Kisaka and Mwewa, 2014). A lot of research has been conducted in this field to claim that an attitude has a significant impact on the intention and behavior of an individual (Michael, 2011; Ramayah and Suki, 2006; Teo and Pok, 2003; Shih and Fang, 2004; Mathieson, 1991). As a result, in the context of individual investment, it is reasonable to assume that if an individual investor is more favorable of the investment, they are more motivated to take the action than those who are less favorable. According to Kaiser, Oerke and Bogner (2007) while studying *behavior-based environmental attitude* and Dickson (2000) in a research on *attitude, knowledge, belief and personal values relating to intentions*, observed that it is easier to attain the prediction about the behavior of an investor by determining his attitude while making a decision for buying a particular product. In their research, attitude is considered as the persuading factor which influences the intention of an investor to choose for the wealth management services. On the other hand, despite having a positive attitude towards investment most of the investors still do not have any intention to invest in volatile market (Kothari and Mindargi, 2012).

Funfgeld and Wang (2008) in a study on *attitude and behavior in everyday finance* revealed an important dimension of an attitude of an investor i.e. the degree of anxiety. The investors who possess more anxiety in their attitude tend to intuitively and spontaneously take decisions and show less patience even while making huge investments. An anxious investor is always unsure with the feeling of insecurity and doubt in mind. In a study conducted by Mandell and Klien (2009), it was observed that the attitude of an individual is sometimes also influenced by the past life history and difficult times spent in life. These results were consistent with the finding of research conducted by Bentler and Speckart (1979) who proposed that the behavioral history of a person has been observed to influence the individual's current attitude and behavior. Borden et al., (2008) observed in their research that for some of the individuals their investment behavior and attitude is considerably influenced by their ethnicity and cultural background. Ismail et al., (2013) reported from their research that the financial attitude of an individual relates to the borrowing behavior i.e. more stronger is the financial attitude means less preference of an investor to borrow money.

Bennet et al (2012) in a research on *the impact of investor's sentiment on the equity market* found out that market specific factors had a positive effect on investor's attitude and opinion in India. Singh and Jha (2009) and

Das (2012) identified that investor's preference is primarily based on liquidity, potential and safety. Felicia (2014) verified that there was change in investor's attitude prior and after the financial crisis regarding investments. According to Kisaka and Mwewa (2014) general agreement formed by scholars after extensive study on identifying relationship between attitude and behavior is that there exist both direct and indirect determinants of the exhibited behavior. Personal traits and demographic elements are the indirect determinants while the intention is the biggest direct determinant of individual's behavior. Intentions of an individual are formed by three basic components; First, Attitude towards exhibiting a behavior; Second, the Subjective Norms and finally the perceived behavior.

2.3.5.1 Attitude as Mediator

Besides looking into the relationship between attitude and investment behavior, the study also examines the role of attitude as a mediator. This is done to assess whether there is any observable relationship between financial literacy, risk appetite, beliefs, subjective norms and investment behavior or the relationship is the cause of mediation created by attitude. Mediation is a form interrelationship between variables that describes causation. It is normally used to provide a more precise explanation to the causal relationship between a predictor and outcome (Hair et al., 2010). A mediator corresponds to a dominant variable through which an independent variable influences a dependent variable (Baron & Kenny, 1986). The previous studies emphasize that the investor's attitude is one of the predictors of investment behavior and is determined by various components. In other words, since the predictor variables influence investor's attitude, which in turn influences investment behavior, it can be concluded that attitude has a mediating effect and might explain the relationship between predictors and investment behavior. Very few studies have been undertaken to prove attitude as a mediator in explaining the relationship between predictors and behavioural intention and actual behavior. A study conducted by Çabuk, Tanrikulu, & Gelibolu, (2014) showed that attitude plays a major role in terms of direct impact on intention to buy and indirect effect as a mediator on how predictor variables affect intention to buy. To the best of researchers' knowledge there's no study conducted that examines the impact of attitude as mediator on intentional behavior and actual behavior.

2.3.6 Investment behavior

Investment behaviors as defined by Slovic (1972) is a process by which investors display their conduct of judgment, prediction, analysis and review of strategy planning and decision-making, which includes investment psychology, information accumulation, defining and understanding, research and analysis. According to Azjen & Fishbein (1980), a specific future behavior of an individual can be predicted by his behavioral intentions. In a study on *values, attitudes, and interpersonal behavior,* Triandis (1980) referred intention as self-directions to exhibit a specific behavior and is presumed to consequently influence the behavior. Armitage and Conner (2001) in their research on *efficacy of the theory of planned behavior* observed the inherent relationship between the individual's intentions and behavior. In a related study Brubaker and Fowler (1990) reported a positive link between them and found that any changes in the intentions of an individual subsequently results in behavioral transformation. In an extensive research on self-instructed attitude and financial behavior Byrne (2005) factorized individual's attitude and financial behavior into five fundamental characteristics, which together forms intentions and leads to conduct of particular behavior. These characteristics are anxiety, spending tendency, need for saving, decision patterns, and interest in financial affairs. Based upon these characteristics, individual attitudes were studied to obtain more insight in understanding their behavioral patterns.

Wang (2001) observed that due to overconfidence in the behavior of investors, they usually overestimate the role of their own information and therefore excessively trust their capacity. Excessive optimism in the behavior usually comes from overconfidence and captures the perception that future incidents would be better and more positive than present situation. Walia and Dr. Kiran (2009) determined that the investor's optimistic behavior and awareness about the volatility in market also influences the investor's decision to invest in high-risk investment options. In a similar study on *the positive role of overconfidence and optimism in investment policy*, Gervais et al., (2002) concluded that over-optimistic investors may believe that bad investment would not harm their portfolio and therefore expect too much from the market and from investing opportunities. Excessive optimism also has positive impacts on investing attitude and encourages people to invest, since too much risk aversion would decrease trading volume. Johnson et al., (2002) determined that excessive optimism has negative effects when it leads to highly risky investment. Moreover there exists a link between overconfidence and excessive optimism.

Locke and Mann (2005) in their study on *do professional traders exhibit loss aversion* have mentioned in their research that there are some preferred investment behaviors that assures the considerable gain and success in making investment decisions. Such investment behaviors are characterized by the following consistent investment strategy, maintaining patience during financial crises, rational thinking and disciplined trading. Investment strategies are primarily based on reversal strategies, momentum in the market and past performance of different financial products. Camerer, Loewenstein & Rabin (2004) while studying the *behavioral economics: past, present, and future* mentioned in their research that human psychology and theories of economics are being studied to broadly explore and understand the individual's behavior related to financial matters. Barberis & Thaler (2003) in *a survey of behavioral finance* focused on the factors and circumstances, which results into significant deviation from the expected rational behavior of an individual.

However, it has been observed by Azjen & Fishbein (1980) that the measures of intention are not always good indicators. Intentions keep on changing with time and the intentions measured before observing the behavior can contradict with the intentions measured while observing the behavior. This concludes that larger the time gap, less precise is the prediction of individual's behavior from his intentions, which tends to broaden the difference in the relationship of behavior and intention. As per their research, occurrence of unexpected events and unforeseen situations may result into changes in intentions of an individual investor. According to Walia and Dr. Kiran (2009) wealth managers are making use of new technology and data mining capabilities to design modern approaches for investment decision-making and strategic planning to forecast the future trends and analyze the investment behavior of an individual in the wealth management industry.

Speed & Smith (1992) in a study on *retail financial services segmentation* and Harrison (1994) in a research on *segmenting the market for retail financial services* tried the market segmentation approach to learn and analyze the behavior of an investor. Market Segmentation intends to determine financial behavior patterns by grouping the investors into different segments based upon their financial requirements. Azjen & Fishbein (1980) have determined various reasons, which can deviate intentions of an investor such as sudden accident, loss of job, natural disasters, abrupt sickness, unanticipated pregnancy, any severe injury or disability, any causality in family or close relatives or sudden fall of the stock market or economic breakdown. Walia and Dr. Kiran, (2009) concluded that the behavior of an investor with respect to his willingness to bear risk is associated and impacted with the market sentiments and risk tolerance. Several researches have been conducted to determine the different elements of investment behavior that influences the trading behavior of an investor.

Linnainmaa (2011); Grinblatt, Keloharju and Linnainmaa (2012) presented that IQ of an individual is an important element of the individual's investment behavior. Christells et al., (2010) reported that cognitive character of an individual is the important characteristic of his behavior. Kumar, Page and Spalt (2011) focused on how the religious beliefs influence the behavior of a person. Biais et al., (2005) studied the relation between the self-control and individual's behavior. Muehlfeld, Weitzel and Witteloostuijn (2013) examined the effect of motivation on the investment behavior of an individual.

Lam (2008) in his study instituted that attitude, past behavior and subjective norms have significant positive impact on investor's intention to make investments. Results derived from his research are similar with the outcomes of Das (2008) and Srivastava (2007). Byrne (2005) and Corter and Chen (2006) observed that past experience of successful investing in funds maximizes risk tolerance of investor and vice versa for unsuccessful past experience. Behavior exhibited in past investment affects future behavior of investment. According to Walia and Dr. Kiran (2009), it is important for the wealth managers to be aware and carefully consider the rationality present in the investment behavior.

2.4 Summary

This chapter gives an overview of wealth management, its needs, its determinants and challenges. The scenario of global wealth management industry and Indian wealth management industry is also presented. This chapter has described the groundwork and the existing research model and theoretical structure build on two important frameworks explaining the investment behavior along with the conclusions of the existing literature, which exhibited significant information for the design of this research framework. The model identified various variables under study: financial literacy, risk appetite, beliefs, subjective norms, and attitude and investment behavior. The literature related to the relationship between these variables has been reviewed and related hypothesis have been proposed. Based on the relationships discussed in the study, attitude of an investor is formed on the basis of his financial literacy, risk appetite, beliefs and subjective norms and finally, the relationship between attitude and investment behavior is formed. Also, the research undertaken by various behavioral finance experts proves that the investment behavior is not only affected by physical considerations but also by mental traits (Kannadhasan, 2006). Psychological and behavioral factors to a great extent determine the investor's behavior. Theorists believe that the behavior of investors is governed by their attitude and risk bearing capacity. Thus, risk appetite is taken as a moderating variable in this study in order to examine its role in influencing the relationship between financial literacy, beliefs, subjective norms and attitude. Besides looking into the relationship between attitude and investment behavior, the study also examines the role of attitude as a mediator. In other words, since the predictor variables influence investor's attitude, which in turn influences investment behavior, it can be concluded that attitude has a mediating effect and might explain the relationship between predictors and investment behavior.

Hypotheses has been presented and classified into three different types. First one is classified as direct path hypotheses, second is classified as Moderating hypotheses and third one is Mediating Hypothesis. These hypothesis are used to validate the research model proposed during this study. Structural Equation Modelling used along AMOS version 4.0 has been applied to verify the proposed hypotheses in accordance with the theoretical model. Analytical tools and methods employed to accomplish the goals of this research have been thoroughly explained in detail in Chapter 3. The analyses of the data and observations justifying and substantiating the finding of the research have been described in Chapter 4 and Chapter 5.

Chapter - 3

Research Methodology

3.1 Introduction

Research Methodology is a systematic process used to collect information and data, perform a careful investigation and statistically analyze it for the purpose of making business and economic decisions. The methodology could comprise of publication research, data collection methods, how to conduct interviews and surveys and other research approaches. Research may include information from present and historical studies.

The research methodology is integral and the most crucial component of thesis writing as it focuses on different types of research techniques and demonstrates the different methods, methodologies and important dimensions followed in the research study and help us to make a choice between them depending upon our research problem and preferred approach. It is imperative to include a basis of the concepts and theories that underlie these methods. There are many different ways to approach the research that fulfills the requirements of a dissertation. The methods and techniques are chosen in order to fulfill the research objectives successfully.

This study has been carried out to evaluate the effect of financial literacy of an investor, risk appetite of an investor, his personal beliefs, subjective norms a on the attitude and behavior of individual investors towards using wealth management services. This chapter outlines the different research approaches followed in the different phases of research study. The main sections of the chapter includes the design of the study, development of instrument which describes the procedure used in designing the instrument, pilot study, data collection and the data analysis which explains the statistical tools used to analyze the data.

3.2 Objectives of Research

The prime goal of the research is to find solution and key to answers a business or economical problem and to fulfill an indefatigable quest of inquisitiveness. Although every research is conducted and carried out with specific objective, below are few of the general objectives for research.

1. To obtain an understanding of a concept or to acquire new insights into it. Research with such an objective is categorized as formulative or exploratory research.
2. To precisely illustrate the specific characteristic attributes of a person, circumstances or a class of individuals. This research carried out with such an objective follows the descriptive research approach.
3. To observe how frequently an event takes place and the dependent variables associated with that event. It can be obtained by following diagnostic research technique.
4. To examine the hypothesis of cause and effect relationship between the dependent and independent fluctuating factors respectively.

The study has been carried out as a part of research degree (Doctor of Philosophy (Ph.D) with the aspiration of building a better career in the field of education. The research tries to discover new facts involved in wealth management services; the study verifies and tests the initial hypothesis and the influential facts associated with the wealth management services; the study tries to examine the cause and effect relationship between the dependent and independent variables being measured; the research tries to analyse the public response regarding their choices made while opting for wealth management services; the research intends to establish new concepts and theories through determining the factors impacting the services offered for wealth management; the study develops new insights to wealth management industry and presents some suggestions about the focus areas for the growth and success of this industry.

To summarize, the study aims to fulfil the following research objectives:

1. To examine the components of investor's attitude and investor behavior in the context of finance industry.
2. To assess the relationship between financial literacy, risk appetite, beliefs, subjective norms, investor's attitude and investment behavior.
3. To examine the moderating effect of a risk appetite on the relationship between financial literacy-attitude; beliefs-attitude; subjective norms-attitude.

4. To examine the mediating role of investor's attitude on the relationship between financial literacy- investment behavior; beliefs-investment behavior; risk appetite-investment behavior; subjective norms-investment behavior.

3.3 Conceptual Framework for the Study

The conceptual model of the study is based on the Theory of Reasoned Action given by Ajzen & Fishbein as discussed in section 2.2.1. Because of the comprehensiveness of the model, which requires several studies to affirm its validity, an adapted version (see Figure 3.1 below) - which is considered the conceptual model for the present study - was designed. The Research Model, which can be called as Wealth Management Behavior Model, examines investor's behavior towards wealth management services. As per this framework, four factors forming a person's attitude were selected and considered to be the predictor variables of attitude. These variables were assessed based on the existing literature. The new model examines the direct influence of attitude on investor's behavior. The other variable having direct influence on the investor's behavior i.e. behavioral intention is not taken in the scope of this study.

The model below specifically looks at how financial literacy, risk appetite, investor's beliefs and subjective norms influences attitude and then how attitude influence investor's behavior to make their investment in wealth management services.

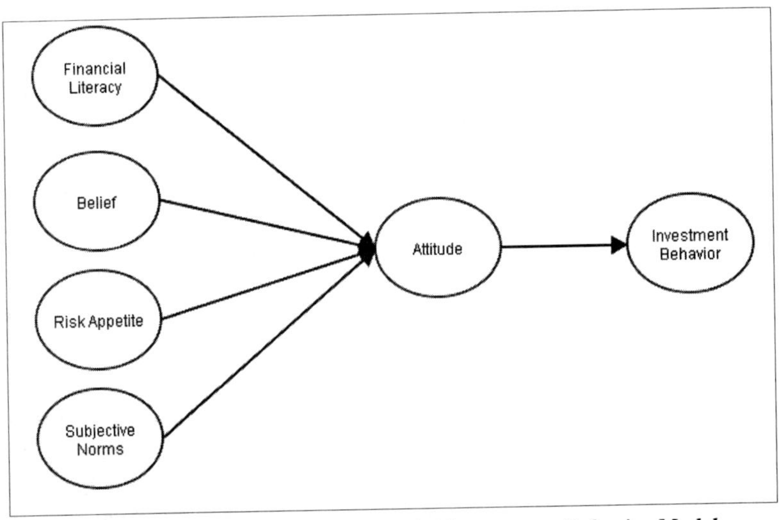

Figure 3.1: Research Model - Wealth Management Behavior Model

3.4 Hypothesis Formulation

Hypotheses are the statements that explain the relationship between variables of the study. Various hypotheses formulated for this study are specified below:

3.4.1 Hypothesis based on inter-relationship between variables

1. H1a: Financial literacy has significant influence on investor's attitude.
2. H1b: Risk Appetite has significant influence on investor's attitude.
3. H1c: Beliefs have significant influence on investor's attitude.
4. H1d: Subjective Norms have significant influence on investor's attitude.
5. H1e: Investor's attitude has significant influence on Investment behavior.

3.4.2 Hypothesis based on Moderation

6. H2a: Risk Appetite moderates the relationship between financial literacy and attitude towards investment.
7. H2b: Risk Appetite moderates the relationship between beliefs and attitude towards investment.
8. H2c: Risk Appetite moderates the relationship between subjective norms and attitude towards investment.

3.4.3 Hypotheses based on Mediation

9. H3a: Attitude mediates the effect of financial literacy on investment behavior.
10. H3b: Attitude mediates the effect of beliefs on investment behavior.
11. H3c: Attitude mediates the effect of risk appetite on investment behavior.
12. H3d: Attitude mediates the effect of subjective norms on investment behavior.

3.5 Research Methods

Research method is the guiding path of the research, which is aimed at designing and laying the foundation of the study in a manner that results in solving of the formulated issue (Sekaran, 2006). Research methods can be classified into different types such as descriptive or analytical, applied, or fundamental (basic research), quantitative or qualitative, conceptual (often referred as theoretical and literature based) or empirical, inductive or deductive. Each of these methods is used in solving problems, learning the significance and importance of fundamentals of interest and gathering significant information in research field. Research can be carried out by following one of the above or a combination of above approaches depending upon the type of research and field of study. These research methods cater to different phases of research processes; conceptual, design and analyze phase. Below is a brief description of different research approaches.

3.5.1 Descriptive Research

The research method adopted for the study was *Descriptive.* Greenfield (1996) depicts that descriptive examination answers the inquiries of who, what, where, when and how. It does not answer the inquiries of why. Descriptive exploration manages everything that can be measured or numbered. Descriptive exploration is mainly carried out when the researcher needs to have quantitative thoughts of the variables under examination. This study additionally tries to build cause and effect relationship among variables. It describes the association between underlying factors that influence Investor's attitudes and their actual behavior, toward seeking and using Wealth Management Services. To the best of the researcher's knowledge, this study is the first attempt to quantitatively assess investor's attitude towards seeking and using Wealth Management Services in Delhi/NCR. Thus, the utilization of a descriptive and causal research design was deemed appropriate. Descriptive-Causal studies have been widely used to assess individual's attitude towards actual investment behavior (Gill & Biger, 2009; Srivastava, 2007; Bennet et al., 2012; Gain et al., 2012.

3.5.2 Applied Research

This study falls in the category of applied research as it caters to wealth management industry and tries to identify and analyze the factors impacting its popularity and growth. *Applied Research* intends to find an answer or aid to a particular issue being faced by a society, a business organization or a specific industry. It is aimed at deriving insight to a social or business problem and establishing conclusions. (Malhotra and Birks, 2007). In general this research approach is intended to identify social, economic or political trends those are likely to influence a particular institution or industry. Evaluation research and market research illustrates two different types of applied research.

3.5.3 Quantitative Research

This study follows the quantitative approach as it involves the collection of substantial datasets, which are subject to significant and comprehensive quantitative analysis in a meticulous and precise manner. *Quantitative research* is a process of measuring variables and verifying existing theories and hypothesis (Cooper & Schindler, 2014). Data is has been used to generate new hypothesis based on the results of the data collected about different variables. The process is initiated with the formulation of a questionnaire with the objective to gather statistical data from the responses of the population. Questionnaire seemed to be a logical and easy way collecting and consolidating information and data from people. Questionnaire may consist of open and close-ended questions. It may also include multiple-choice questions for the respondents to choose the most relevant response to a question. It is quite difficult to design and formulate a Questionnaire. *Quantitative* research is a method where the researcher decides what to study; asks specific, narrow questions; collects quantifiable data from participants; analyzes these numbers using statistics; and conducts the inquiry in an unbiased, objective manner (Malhotra and Birks, 2007). Further, the study aims at establishing the relationship between variables in the problem. The questionnaire survey method is found to be suitable to collect information from the sampling unit. The questionnaire was developed and pre-tested before giving to the respondents. On the basis of the conceptual model developed through literature review, hypotheses were generated and tested statistically using multivariate analysis. The multivariate statistical tool, Structural Equation Modeling is used to identify the relationship between different antecedents of investment behavior. The survey method was deemed appropriate for this kind of problem as it is easy to administer and the data obtained is considered reliable because the responses are limited to the alternatives mentioned (Malhotra, 2010).

3.5.4 Empirical research

This study is based on Empirical research approach. This research is based on data, deriving information and finding that can be confirmed by experiment and observation. It is often termed as experimental research. In this approach a working hypothesis with an assumption to the apparent presumed results is first attained and then work has to be carried out to collect enough facts and figures in the form of data to substantiate the hypothesis perceived in beginning. Finally the researcher formulates the experiment design to bring the desired information. Empirical research is appropriate when different research variables are interrelated and we need to affirm it with evidence in the form of data.

3.5.5 Deductive Research

This study is based on deductive research approach. Deductive research is primarily linked to datasets, surveys and quantitative experiments. This technique follows the "top-down" approach. It begins with building a broad theory around the research topic and then narrows it down into more specific hypotheses, which can be tested. It is further compressed and curtailed by gathering observations to support the hypotheses.

3.6 Research Processes

Research process is divided into different phases involving identifying, locating, assessing, analyzing and then developing and expressing our ideas to reach to the conclusion (Crotty, 1998). Below are the broadly classified phases in the entire research process.

3.6.1. Identify the research topic

The first step in the research process is to define the research problem and identify initial hypotheses. In this phase, research area/subject was identified as "Factors influencing the investor's wealth Management Behavior in Delhi/NCR". The research subject has been discussed in detail with the supervisor and a draft prepared on research proposal has been submitted to the academic committee.

3.6.2. Review the literature

During this phase preliminary search has been conducted which included gathering background information and identifying important concepts related to research area. The objective of preliminary search is to obtain fundamental information regarding the problem under study.

The review of literature additionally helps the researcher to figure out the groundwork that has already been carried out by different researchers in the past, how those researches were lead and carried out, and the finding those resulted from those studies. Review has been conducted through books on wealth management, Internet search engines, published journals and banks websites.

3.6.3. Clearly define terms and concepts

There are various different terms and concepts those are used to describe the primary objective and intent of the researcher to carry out the research and utilized at different phases during the entire research process. These terms and concepts are meticulously elucidated as they get applied in the course of research. They can have various different definitions and can be described and interpreted in many forms depending on the context in which they are applied. Therefore it is necessary to define these terms n concepts more narrowly relating closely to their application and our research objectives. By doing so it becomes easier for the researcher to manager the scope of the research and to easily gather the appropriate data needed to conduct the research.

3.6.4. Define the population and select a sample

It is necessary to define the scope of the research by precisely defining the target population and selecting the appropriate sample. In this process the researcher particularly focuses on specific subset of population for questioning, observation and measurement purpose to collect the statistical data from the selected population. Population can be defined by a specific group of people in a community belonging from particular age group, males or females, people belonging from and residing in a particular geographical region or a group of people belonging to particular ethnic background. Population can also be defined by a specific group of miscellaneous events or objects. Population is the complete collection belonging to such a particular group. The target population of research is mostly too huge and broadly geographically scattered to directly study. Therefore, the selected group of population is further narrowed down into a smaller group called sample by defining only a specific section of that entire population group to be considered and studied for our research. People belonging to sample are referred as subjects of participants. Sampling process has been classified into different phases such as determining the population of interest, defining the sample frame, specifying the sampling method and sample size and finally followed by sampling and gathering the necessary data.

3.6.4.1 Participants of the study

The population means the total units from which the sample is to be taken. It may be limited or unending. A limited populace is the one in which the amount of things is definite, while an unbounded populace is the one the things can't be resolved (Crotty, 1998). For this study, investors who are categorized as High Net-worth and have availed one or the other wealth management services living in Delhi-NCR Region were considered as populace from where the sample was taken. The figure 3.2 below shows the HNWI population of Delhi in 2012. Based on this data, the population of the study was taken as 1,945 people who are HNWI.

Top 8 Asian Cities by HNWI Population				
City	**Ranking**	**2012**	**2022**	**Change (%)**
Tokyo	3	5,440	6,763	24
Beijing	6	2,285	5,262	130
Mumbai	7	2,105	4,988	137
Hong Kong	8	3,205	4,780	49
Delhi	11	1,945	4,278	120
Osaka	13	2.970	3,813	28
Shanghai	14	1,415	3,704	162
Singapore	23	1,345	1,930	43

Source: Survey by Knight Frank; http://www.2point6billion.com/news/2013/03/18/asias-high-net-worth-individuals-concentrated-in-china-india-12062.html

Figure 3.2: HNWI Population in Asian Countries

3.6.4.2 Sample frame

This indicates the sources from which the samples were to be taken. For this study, HNWI investors living in Delhi/NCR, India were the respondents. Majorly the ones falling in the age group of 21 and above years were looked into. They were from different educational backgrounds and occupation. From the gender prospective the researcher might look into a mix of males and females. The study covers financial institutions and banks that provide wealth management services. According to a survey conducted by MarketsandMarkets (2008), the wealth management industry in India is dominated by ICICI Bank, HDFC Bank and Kotak Bank. Also, according to Companies in India (2014) report, ICICI bank along with HDFC bank and other financial institutions are among the top 20 Wealth Management companies in India. So, the present study takes into account the HNWI clients of ICICI bank, HDFC bank, Kotak Mahindra bank, Motilal Oswal Asset management Company and Muthoot Asset Management Company.

3.6.4.3 Sampling technique

Sampling design is the method that is chosen by the researcher to select upon the sampling target from the sampling frame (Cooper & Schindler, 2014). There are two types of sampling techniques that can be used: Probability Sampling and Non-probability Sampling Technique. Probability Sampling is one in which every element has an equal chance of being selected whereas in non-probability sampling, the researcher uses his own judgment in selecting the samples and every element does not have an equal chance of getting selected (Malhotra, 2010). For this study, Non-probability Purposive/Judgmental and Snowball Random Sampling were used. Judgmental or purposive examining strategy was utilized considering that the respondents chosen will have adequate basic knowledge of investment since they happen to be using various investment avenues. As the information regarding the population or the universe was not fully available, the questionnaire study was also carried out using snowball random sampling technique.

3.6.4.4 Sample estimate

A specimen of 700 wealth management clients' was chosen. This sample size was taken by considering the formula given by Nargundkar (2008):

$$n = \left(\frac{Zs}{e}\right)^2$$

Where,

Z = Z score from the standard normal distribution for the Confidence Level. We have assumed 95% confidence level in our estimate and therefore, the z value corresponding to 95% confidence level is 1.96.

S = Population Standard Deviation

S = Range / 6

If we are taking Likert scale of 5, then range = 5-1,

Therefore, S = (5-1) / 6 i.e. 4 /6 = 0.67

E = tolerable error, for the study the tolerable error taken is ±0.05 which means that my estimate will lie within ±0.5 of the actual value with 95% confidence level.

In this case, therefore, the sample size is

N = [(1.96 x 0.67)/ 0.05]2 = 689 (approx.)

Also, as suggested by Hair et al. (2010), recommended size of sample should be between 150 to 400 for Structural Equation Model (SEM).

The table 3.1 below presents there search methods and the sampling techniques used for pilot study and questionnaire study.

Table 3.1: Description of Research Methods and Sampling techniques Used

Study phase	*Objectives of the Study*	*Research method Used*	*Sampling Technique used*
Pilot Study	To ensure validation of the questionnaire	Questionnaire Survey method	Purposive Sampling
Questionnaire Study	To bring out the relationship between different variables under study	Questionnaire Survey	Purposive Sampling & Snowball Sampling

3.6.5. Develop the instrumentation plan (Research Design Phase)

This stage marks the beginning of the *design phase*. The instrumentation plan serves as a blueprint and road map for the complete study, determining who will be involved in the research study; how, when and where the data will be gathered. This phase of the study also includes defining and formulating the questionnaire based on the prototype report and gather substantial information to confirm or deny hypothesis. During this phase, variables have been identified, clearly defined and labeled. Below are the different steps involved in the preparation of the questionnaire.

3.6.5.1 Design of questionnaire

The questionnaire is "basically a collection of questions that fit the research topic and its objectives, and the answers to which will provide the data necessary to test the hypotheses formulated for the study" (Kothari, 2004). Fundamentally the Questionnaires consists questions in well-framed statements, which help the researcher to gather the opinion of the people and their answers in the form of their agreements and disagreements to the questions, precisely analyze and evaluate those opinions, experiences and behaviors received from the respondents (Nachmias and Nachmias, 1981). There were various steps involved in the development of the questionnaire for this research. This process commenced from identifying and clearly defining the research topic, identifying the issue, goals and objectives, determining the variables and specifying the indicators, identifying the relationship between variables and research topic, phrasing the questions, finalizing the layout and deciding the sequence. Phrasing the questions requires significant knowledge of the subject matter (Yin, 2002). Hence, the questionnaire designed for this research is based on the conceptual model presented in second chapter, applying the identified research variables during the literature survey and enriched through the pilot study. Questionnaire makes use of structured questions in the close ended format wherein the respondents need not describe their responses by writing comments in their replies, but just need to select one out of the pre-coded list of answers available for each question in the questionnaire, which most closely reflects their view/experience. The questions have been framed using clearly defined statements and specific to this research topic in such a manner that the respondents can easily understand it. Each question has been developed in a way that the question conveys only one 'thought' at a time. The statements utilized in framing a question are detailed and conform quite closely to the perception of the respondents. Significant consideration has been paid to the order the questions in the most effective sequence. The order of the questions significantly influences the respondents in developing their interest and their provided responses. Questionnaire must begin with the questions that raises the interest in the survey and should begin with easier questions, gradually moving to more specific questions looking for the respondents' viewpoint on a particular aspect associated with the research. Questions follow some sort of psychological order and the related questions on a specific aspect have been grouped together.

Questionnaire is intended to determine and measure the variables and indicators to test the hypothesis of interest through gathering data on facts, activities and respondent's attitude and behavior. Variable refers to characteristic that represents multiple properties and these properties can differ in quality and quantity. Based on these properties, variables are classified as dependent, independent, control, continuous and discrete. This research is conducted to study the qualitative effect of these variables. In order to measure such variables, qualitative analysis has been applied on the comparative basis to determine the magnitude of these variables.

Likert scale has been used for measurement of variables in the questionnaire to measure respondent's preferences or level of agreement with a specific or group of statements. The respondent's opinion has been recorded on a scale ranging from 1 to 5, 5 being strongly agree and 1 being strongly disagree. With the assumption that equal intervals on the scale indicate equal measures of the property/variable, the scale may be assumed to be approximately close to the 'interval scale' (Kothari, 2004). The interval data generated by the interval scale helps to apply statistical methods like mean and standard deviation. Interval responses are obtained by using Likert scale. Product moment correlation technique along with t-test and F-test can also be applied and tested while measuring responses on interval scale (Kothari, 2004).

During interactions with the investors in banks (during snowball inquiry, pilot study, questionnaire validation and pre-testing stages), it emerged that

Wealth Management as a term was still new to the finance sector and most of the people still believe that this term is associated with High Net-worth Individuals only. Hence, considering the objectives of the research, the set of questions in various dimensions have been designed in independent study areas. Questions have been framed to measure the variables in the particular study area and also their influence on investment behavior.

The questionnaire also contains some control questions, which may indicate the reliability of the respondents. Few questions similar to those asked in earlier parts/sections are asked again in different context(s) to introduce cross-check(s) on the respondents' reliability. Concise description about the objective of the research along with directions and guidelines on how to fill the questionnaire are enclosed with the questionnaire.

3.6.5.2 Questionnaire format

Information has likewise been gathered from some banks offering wealth management services i.e. survey and to a few experts poll was disseminated either by means of email or generally. Larger part of reaction accepted through email. A self- administered survey designed carefully to ensure clarity and specifically to let respondents complete by their own without anyone's intervention was obtained from the wealth management services clients residing in Delhi/NCR region. Preventive and precautionary measures were taken to mitigate replication in the response samples. The questionnaire shared with the clients intend to measure the following variables: financial literacy, investor's beliefs related to investment, investor's risk appetite, subjective norms influencing investor's behavior and investor's attitude towards Wealth Management Services. Indicators to determine these variables were obtained from reviewing the existing literature.

The Questionnaire contains two sections; first section is based on measuring the demographic variables and second section has 63 statements revolving around their experiences and preferences for wealth management services. The questionnaire used for this research is split into six independent study parts for different dimensions namely financial literacy, risk appetite, beliefs, subjective norms, attitude and investment behavior.

3.6.5.2.1 Financial Literacy

The financial literacy indicators used in the questionnaire aimed to assist wealth managers in designing their strategies according to the financial knowledge of the investors. The knowledge items sought to measure if consumers are aware of various institutions providing wealth management services; whether they know which investment decision is best for them or not etc.

3.6.5.2.2 Investor's Belief

The belief indicators used in the questionnaire are defined and included for the purpose to assist wealth managers in designing their strategies according to the beliefs of the investors. These items measure the beliefs of people towards their investment; towards the company they are investing; towards a particular stock; towards the economy; towards their own choice of investment etc.

3.6.5.2.3 Risk Appetite

Various statements were included to measure the risk appetite of an investor through the obtained responses. The knowledge of risk appetite helps the wealth managers to design the portfolio in such a manner so as to balance the risk-return tradeoff. These items measure the mind-sets of the investors in various situations like in times of losses; in times of fluctuations in the economy. It also assesses the thinking of investors towards investment in some companies and stocks.

3.6.5.2.4 Subjective Norms

Subjective Norms refers to the perception of an individual towards the opinion given by people close to him. The items measure how investors react towards the information/opinion given by their friends, relatives' family, peers, advisors on investment issues. The items also assess the reaction of investors towards the advertisements, publications regarding various financial products. The investors' decisions were also assessed on the basis of their intuition and past experiences.

3.6.5.2.5 Attitude

Attitude refers to the feelings about a specific object. This measure will assist wealth managers to make improvements in their products so as to develop a positive attitude among investors The items measure the factor on the basis of investor's attitude towards financial products; their perception about the company; the duration of their investment; their behavior in times of uncertainty; their assessment about the future performance of the stock; their perception about the services of the wealth manager; their objective of investment etc.

3.6.5.2.6 Investment Behavior

Investment Behavior refers to the behavior of investor towards the type of investments they make or their investment pattern. Studying investment behavior aids wealth manager in designing strategies for clients to fulfill investor's long-term goals. The items measured the behavior of investors by assessing their frequency of availing wealth management services; their attitude towards wealth management service providers; their opinion about the future of wealth management etc.

3.6.5.3 Questionnaire Testing

After completing the questionnaire validation, it has been pre-tested by means of a pilot survey conducted on a small sample of respondents (50 respondents). Respondents selected in pre-testing the questionnaire belong to same target population from which the actual survey was taken as suggested by (Thakur, 1993). This pre testing has been conducted with a purpose to confirm the respondents understanding of the terms and concepts used in the questionnaire, to take the respondents opinion on the complexity of the question statements, to confirm that they interpret the question in the same way, as it is required and to note down the respondents suggestions to incorporate them for the final preparation.

3.6.5.4 Validity of the Questionnaire

Validity of a questionnaire specifies the degree to which it satisfies the purpose and objective of the researcher and the degree to which it solves the prime motive to measure the necessary variables to be evaluated (Kothari, 2004). In case the research design is unable to clearly fulfill the primary purpose of research, it is referred to as research error and insufficient validity. High degree of validity reflects the accurate approximation to the real value.

3.6.5.4.1 Face validity

Face validity refers to an estimate of the non-quantifiable extent or degree to which the test or questionnaire apparently conforms and accomplishes the purpose of the test to the participants. Face validity is an indicator of operationalization and is a measure of subjectivity and obviousness of the test. It refers to the transparency of the test and how unambiguously a test appears to the respondents. It indicates how apparently a test measures the variables or their effect what it is required to measure. Tests that clearly present the purpose, relevance and significance to its participants are considered to have high face validity. It measures how effectively or genuinely a test can be used to make the important subjective judgments in the entire study. Since the face validity is not quantified and substantiated be means of any statistical tools, we must not solely rely on this face validity and make use of other quantifiable techniques to measure the validity of the our tests in order to derive any conclusions. To establish face validity of the questionnaire, senior experienced academicians and researchers were requested to provide their opinion about the research variables and suggestions on improvement and also to indicate whether the operational definitions of the variables correspond to the concepts. Finally, the necessary changes were made to revise the questionnaire as per the suggestions and recommendations of the experts.

3.6.5.4.2 Criterion related validity

Criterion-related validity also referred as concrete validity or instrumental validity. I order to measure the Criterion-related validity we determine the effectiveness of our operationalization in accordance to a given criterion. This criterion is an already established and predefined standard procedure of measurement. The accuracy of measuring Criterion-related validity of a test is determined by calibrating and comparing it against a measure of known validity or predefined standard. In criterion-related validity we normally determine the effectiveness of our test and its operational performance based on our theoretical model applied in research. It determines the degree to which a measure is relevant to derive a conclusion. The validation was performed with the guidance and assistance of senior experienced academicians and researchers. Finally changing the questionnaire to incorporate their suggestions.

3.6.5.4.3 Content validity

Content validation is guided by the question: "Is the content of this measure representative of the content or the universe of content of the property being measured?" (Kerlinger, 1973). Content validation is a subjective measure and refers to the degree to which the variables used in the measurement process are relevant and represents the construct that we intend to measure in our study. It determines whether a measure represents all the characteristics and features of the construct applied in the research and whether that measure covers the entire relevant content domain of the construct. We need to first determine what comprises of the entire domain and how is it relevant to that content. Content validity has a bit of subjectivity element in its measurement, which needs some degree of acceptance about what a particular characteristic represents. Determining content validity is an essential beginning step in designing and defining a new measurement process. Content validation has been measured by obtaining the opinion of the senior experienced academicians/researchers by sharing with them the questionnaire along with the objectives of the research and providing the operational definitions of the variables. Their views are noted on which questions measure which variables and which objectives of the study are being achieved through the questions and which aspects of the objectives of the research are not being addressed through the existing questionnaire. Questionnaire was reviewed again and necessary changes to the format and content were made according to the collaborated suggestions.

3.6.5.4.4 Construct validity

Construct validation is closely associated to empirical scientific inquiry. The objective of construct validity is not to validate the test, but its goal is to validate the theoretical model or construct behind the test (Kerlinger, 1973). Construct validity is the degree to which a measure confirms to predict a correlation with the proposed theoretical model. It is used to determine the validity of the measurement procedure such as a questionnaire, which is employed in accessing and measuring a particular construct. A construct is referred to a group of behaviors and human traits such as belief, intention and behavior etc. that are interrelated in a relevant way and are used to create a model or a framework designed for the research objective. Construct validity is also referred as an extent to which inferences made on the basis of observations and measurements carried on the data from the surveys are relevant, adequate and appropriate to measure the theoretical constructs required for the research. Almost all the items for various constructs for organizational antecedents have been taken from scales developed by various authors. However, some of the variables have been adapted for the research objective. Hence, the construct validity is being checked for the study variables.

In order to prove the construct validity of our measurement procedures we need to present empirical evidence to substantiate that the data conforms to the presented theoretical model. Required evidence can be produced by content analysis, factor analysis, ANOVA etc. Confirmatory factor analysis is the most commonly used method to examine construct validity.

Factor analysis is a statistical method for determining the number and nature of the underlying variables among larger number of measures (Kerlinger, 1973). It facilitates understanding of the formation of a correlation matrix. In particular, it helps in observing the correlations between a large number of interrelated quantitative variables by grouping then under into new factors. The variables those get assigned to same factor are more highly correlated than those that get assigned to different factors.

The factorial validity aims at determining whether the data collected for a specific set of measures reflect the latent constructs. Principal component factor analysis considers only the common variance related with a given set of variables (Kerlinger, 1973). Usually, the initial factor extraction doesn't give interpretable factors. Rotation makes larger loading even larger and smaller loadings even smaller. Therefore, process of rotation provides factors that can be named and interpreted. Varimax rotation has been used as it clearly distinguishes between different factors (Kerlinger, 1973). Entire domain of the construct has been thoroughly examined for the evaluation of the construct validity.

3.6.6 Data collection

The collection of data is a critical task in gathering and consolidating the information required to address the research objective. The choice of method employed for the data collection depends on the data collection techniques and type of variables being measured. Data can be gathered from people in the form of survey, through a questionnaire, by direct observations and recording the event, interviews and focus groups.

Data collection is the process of collecting data from the target population in order to test the hypothesis generated for the study. There are two methods by which information can be accumulated. They are primary sources and secondary sources. Primary sources are the sources used by the researcher to gather firsthand information from the target population, whereas, secondary sources include information which have been collected previously for some other investigations by some other investigators (Malhotra, 2010).

The primary data for the study was gathered by means of structured statements that contain information related to the constructs of the study. Each construct is measured using a 5-point Likert Scale. The study aimed at collecting data from 700 respondents but the actual data, excluding the missing information and incomplete questionnaire came out to be 674 giving an overall response rate of 96% approximately. The data was collected via banks and other financial institutions, in Delhi/National Capital Region of India, who provide Wealth Management Services.

3.6.7 Analyze and interpret the data

3.6.7.1 Pilot study

Pilot study or the pre-testing refers to the preliminary analysis conducted to check the feasibility of the research approach and pre-testing of the questionnaire or research instrument before starting the research on a full scale. Pilot study gives valuable insight and increases the chances of success in the subsequent research process by raising alarm and signs of warning of any major failures and identifying any deficiencies in the research design at the initial stage and by letting any changes or corrections to be made at the right time and phase. The purpose of the conducting this pre-testing was to make sure that the questions prepared and included in the questionnaire for the data collection are easy to understand by the participants, and to wipe out any chances of misunderstanding, ambiguity and prejudice. Pre-testing has been conducted by sharing the questionnaire to 50 volunteers belonging to similar group of target population to collate their views, opinion and suggestions on the different aspects of the questionnaire. Each volunteer was later interviewed to note down their perspective on the basis of the questionnaire, in order to identify the difficult questions and any confusions faced by them in the questionnaire. Volunteers were requested to provide their feedback on any challenges faced in filling up the questionnaire and the improvements that can be made to the questionnaire to make it easier to understand and clear to respondents. Their suggestions were noted on the language used in the questionnaire, questionnaire format, clarity of questions, sequencing or order of questions etc. The difficult and ambiguous questions were reframed and reviewed again with the respondents for the sanity check. Finally, the questionnaire was restructured to confirm that the different elements such as content, form, order of questions, space formatting, arrangement and physical outlook of the questionnaire are desirable for obtaining the appropriate response from people taking the survey thought this revised questionnaire. This revised version of the questionnaire has been attached in Appendix-II Part A.

3.6.7.2 Reliability analysis

Reliability of a test is the degree to which a set of variables or items that form the scale of measurement will provide consistent results every time if the survey is repeated multiple times and the questions are replaced with similar questions (Malhotra and Birks, 2007) and is determined by evaluating the magnitude of systematic variation in the measurement scale.

Reliability analysis has been conducted by determining the internal consistency reliability by measuring the Cronbach Alpha coefficient of a scale, which is the most commonly, used test reliability technique for internal consistency (Pallant, 2007). Cronbach Alpha co-efficient (á) may lie between negative infinity to 1 but normally ranges from 0 to 1. Value of Cronbach Alpha co-efficient closer to 1 means high internal consistency and value 0.7 as the acceptable limit (Hair et al. 2010). A value of á less than 0.7 signifies unsatisfactory results (Malhotra and Birks, 2007). The following table 3.9 summarizes the Cronbach's coefficient alpha from the pretesting of six constructs with 63 cases.

Table 3.9: Summary of Reliability Analysis

Constructs	*Items*	*Cronbach Alpha Coefficient*	*Reliability Results*	*Inter-item Correlation*
Attitude	15	0.828	Good	0.366- 0.907
Risk Appetite	13	0.955	Good	0.284- 0.876
Subjective Norms	10	0.861	Good	0.202 - 0.956
Beliefs	11	0.967	Good	0.499- 0.864
Investment Behavior	06	0.887	Good	0.454- 0.982
Financial Literacy	08	0.862	Good	0.454 - 0.998

Inter-item correlation is another measure to estimate internal consistency that determines the correlation or the covariances among the variables or items in the scale (Hair et al. 2010). From the pre-testing, all inter-item correlation values exceed 0.3 (see Table 3.9), (except few exceptions in subjective norms and risk appetite). This shows the reliability of the test and measurement tool.

The Cronbach alpha values of all the constructs are greater than 0.7, which is observed to be good and satisfactory. This shows high internal consistency amongst each variable.

3.6.7.3 Data Analysis & Hypotheses testing

The data has been analyzed using The Statistical Package for the Social Sciences (SPSS v 21.0) and by Structural Equation Modeling using AMOS (4.0). Descriptive statistics including frequency distributions, measures of central tendency, and measures of variability are used to illustrate the primary attributes of the respondents. These primary characteristics include demographic attributes such as gender, age, education level, occupation, income etc. Moreover, apart from preliminary analysis, a multivariate approach was conducted to deduce association between financial literacy, risk appetite, beliefs, subjective norms, and attitude and investment behavior of the respondents. Data collection by using questionnaire for the survey was anticipated to generate adequate information to fulfill the objectives of this study.

3.6.7.3.1 Statistical tools used

The statistical tools used for the study was Structural Equation Modeling (SEM). It has been used to establish relationship among multiple research variables inter-dependent on each other (Malhotra and Birks, 2007).

The main objective of the research is to develop a behavioral model that describes the behavior of individual investors towards Wealth Management Services. So, in order to fulfill this goal, Structural Equation Modeling was recognized as an appropriate tool. Structural Equation Modeling is a statistical method to perform multivariate analysis that comprise of factor analysis and multiple regression and enables the researcher to determine the interrelationship between variables (Hair et al. 2010). SEM involves the evaluation of two models: a measurement model and a path model (Byrne, 2010).

A measurement model represents the relationship between the measured variables and their constructs whereas the path model or the path diagram represents the multiple dependence relationship between the variables (Hair et al. 2010). The hypothesis generated will be tested statistically by using SEM to confirm how far the model is consistent to the data. The findings will be based on goodness of fit indices (GOF). The goodness of fit indices are the measures that describes the consistency of the model with the set of observations (Maydeu-Olivares & Garcý´a-Forero, 2010). In other words, the indices highlight the differences between observed and expected values under the model (Hair et al. 2010). The researcher's theory is said to be perfect, if the observed and expected values are same.

For the study in particular, a model has been generated to predict the factors influencing investor's attitude towards Wealth Management Services and their Investment Behavior. The relationship between the variables (financial literacy, beliefs, risk appetite, subjective norms, and attitude and investment behavior) is regressed on various combinations including demographic variables. Moreover, the mediating effect of attitude on the relationship between financial literacy-investment behavior, risk appetite-investment behavior, beliefs-investment behavior and subjective norms-investment behavior is also assessed. The hypotheses related to these relationships have been tested using SEM AMOS.

Therefore, SPSS version 21.0 and AMOS version 4.0 has been used to conduct analysis and develop the behavioral model for the research.

3.6.7.3.2 Data screening

In order to proceed further for analyzing the data, it is necessary to ensure that the data fulfills the assumptions of multivariate analysis and is ready, clean and usable for further analysis. The following issues were addressed to ensure the usefulness of the data.

3.6.7.3.2.1 Missing data

Missing data is a condition where values available for a given research variable are not valid or appropriate for analysis (Hair et al., 2010). The missing data may create several problems for the researcher in analysis. Hair et al., (2010) identified that the general impact of missing data is reduction of sample size, therefore, any statistical result, which is based on certain number of data points to compute estimates, will not run. Moreover, the missing data also leads to biasness issues. A statistical result based on non-random missing data will lead to inaccurate results. The following four-step procedure is deemed appropriate in determining missing data and taking the right measures to fix it. (Hair et al., 2010):

1. Identifying the type of missing data
2. Determine the extent of missing data
3. Analyze the randomness of the missing data processes
4. Select the Imputation method

The missing data analysis has been conducted through SPSS and it is observed that the percentage of those variables which fall under missing data category is around 7% which is less than 10% of the acceptable limit and can be ignored (Hair et al., 2010). Moreover, no specific non-random patters in missing values were found. The next step involves imputing the values of missing data. According to Hair et al., (2010), if the missing data is under 10%, any of the appropriate imputation method can be adopted. Imputation refers to the technique of estimating the missing values or the research variables based on the available data from the rest of the variables for which we have the valid values and inferring the responses the respondent would have given if they had answered the question (Malhotra, 2010). Since the extent of missing data was too low, Mean Replacement Method has been used to impute values. Mean substitution replaces the missing values for a variable with the mean value of that variable calculated from all valid responses (Hair et al., 2010). Finally, the data set was ready to be further analyzed.

3.6.7.3.2.2 Multivariate Outliers

The next prerequisite to be fulfilled before analyzing the data is detecting outliers. Outliers characterize the abnormal behavior of the data i.e. the data points that are digressing far away from the normal data variability (Byrne, 2010). Outliers are the observations that are considerably different from the other observations on one or more characteristics (Hair et al., 2010). In other words, they are unique cases with unusually high or low values or a rare combination of values for some variables that make the observation different from rest of all. It refers to the data points those seemed to be significantly different from the majority of the data points in the distribution of data. These outliers can significantly skew data from a normal distribution and determines how appropriately a sample represents the population. These can considerable effect the accuracy of the statistical analysis techniques and significantly influence the results produced from them (Byrne, 2010).

There are five main reasons of the occurrence of the outliers.

(a) Data entry errors or out of range data.

(b) Inappropriately identifying the missing values in the data populations.

(c) Data set not belonging to the intended sample, i.e. sample could be biased.

(d) There is a measurement error or data is biased.

(e) Sample distribution of data for a particular variable does not follow the normal distribution

Outliers may be beneficial or problematic depending upon the context in which they provide the information. Beneficial outliers may indicate a peculiar characteristic of a population which would otherwise would not have been exposed in the normal course of the analysis, whereas, problematic outliers indicate characteristics which does not represents population and may mislead the statistical results as they are against the objectives of the analysis (Hair et al., 2010).

The outliers were detected using AMOS. In order to detect multivariate outlier, *Mahalanobis d-squared* D^2 is calculated. *Mahalanobis distance* refers to the distance of each observation or data point from the mean center of all observations providing a single value for each observation

(Hair et al., 2010). The mean center is determined as the intersection of the mean of the variables being considered. Multivariate outliers are detected by accurately determining the important parameters of Mahalanobis distance and comparing them with corresponding critical value of Chi-Square (÷ 2) distribution. (Rousseeuw and Van Zomeren, 1990). The critical value of Chi-Square (÷ 2) is determined from a table with corresponding degree of freedom (*df=number of variables or predictors*) with p value (probability) <0.001. If the *Mahalanobis distance* of an observation exceeds the critical Chi-Square (÷ 2) value, the observation (data point) is considered as an outlier. The Mahalanobis distance along with two probability values p1 and p2 are displayed. The p1 column depicts the probability of any observation exceeding the squared Mahalanobis distance of that variable. The p2 column depicts the probability that the largest squared distance of any observation might exceed the Mahalanobis distance calculated. Although we expect small figures to be present in the first column (p1) (Arbuckle, 1995), small figures in the second column (p2) indicate towards the observations that are reasonably distant from the middle under the hypothesis of normality. To detect Multivariate outliers using SPSS AMOS, observations with p1 value below 0.05 are considered influential outliers i.e. the correlation between the variables for these responses are abnormal and significantly different as compared to the rest of the sample (Gaskin, 2012)

Table 3.10: Observed AMOS Output - Detection of Outliers

Observation number	*Mahalanobis d-squared*	*p1*	*p2*	*Observation number*	*Mahalanobis d-squared*	*p1*	*p2*
52	202.215	0	0.028	636	63.326	0.405	0.496
57	202.119	0	0.036	360	62.973	0.349	0.5
41	201.703	0	0.039	95	61.737	0.33	0.502
14	200.003	0	0.042	641	61.404	0.292	0.509
10	199.6	0.002	0.045	627	61.258	0.297	0.521
78	198.822	0.002	0.052	578	60.919	0.298	5.532
42	198.703	0.003	0.058	643	54.168	0.344	0.553
40	197.703	0.003	0.062	1	53.852	0.385	0.556
530	197.413	0.004	0.067	511	53.203	0.393	0.558
67	197.219	0.005	0.069	517	52.576	0.41	0.56
16	189.171	0.01	0.072	532	52.355	0.322	0.562
98	187.953	0.03	0.075	519	47.914	0.342	0.564
85	183.033	0.04	0.078	62	47.01	0.282	0.569
44	178.906	0.08	0.098	637	46.934	0.271	0.571
65	175.28	0.12	0.103	644	46.746	0.311	0.572
369	174.733	0.16	0.106	491	46.702	0.395	0.58
55	174.619	0.19	0.123	529	44.886	0.395	0.581

(Contd...)

416	165.434	0.215	0.127	518	44.443	0.378	0.587
574	164.02	0.22	0.139	9	43.676	0.378	0.601
432	157.968	0.245	0.143	670	41.535	0.265	0.609
80	153.713	0.248	0.165	13	39.766	0.232	0.61
56	142.46	0.253	0.167	614	38.835	0.198	0.621
82	137.265	0.256	0.184	374	38.114	0.176	0.644
77	134.051	0.257	0.189	378	37.63	0.295	0.657
596	133.418	0.259	0.2	161	37.381	0.3	0.659
58	129.818	0.263	2.204	597	35.108	0.278	0.676
8	122.486	0.266	0.221	59	33.861	0.282	0.678
514	121.645	0.279	0.222	674	33.568	0.296	0.681
84	114.975	0.298	0.23	671	32.641	0.293	683
90	106.879	0.31	0.267	342	31.952	0.301	0.69
555	102.525	0.314	0.276	638	31.33	0.305	0.693
581	99.195	0.356	0.299	659	28.781	0.363	0.694
647	98.928	0.358	0.321	568	28.649	0.383	0.698
64	95.76	0.36	0.342	598	28.546	0.342	0.702
579	84.402	0.362	0.367	463	27.079	0.356	0.708
159	82.66	0.101	0.378	542	26.734	0.394	0.71
504	81.203	0.222	0.402	593	26.633	0.384	0.721
632	77.564	0.361	0.41	510	25.666	0.32	0.725
164	76.33	0.21	0.421	594	25.428	0.338	0.728
576	72.06	0.323	0.43	566	21.56	0.344	0.732
663	71.843	0.323	0.451	86	20.858	0.366	0.736
68	71.321	0.316	0.454	307	20.202	0..317	0.739
70	70.371	0.339	0.465	610	19.425	0.292	0.742
626	69.286	0.347	0.469	640	18.677	0.328	0.745
657	69.1	0.338	0.471	96	18.15	0.347	0.75
459	68.736	0.345	0.473	667	18.115	0.311	0.752
642	68.025	0.383	0.476	310	17.852	0.395	0.759
666	67.829	0.43	0.482	524	17.698	0.395	0.762
163	67.377	0.32	0.485	367	17.607	0.378	0.765
585	65.437	0.421	0.49	6	17.19	0.381	0.768

The results for the outliers are shown in the table 3.10 above. For the study, though 13 observations show the characteristics of outliers but since they are not extreme, it was not considered necessary to delete them as per (Byrne, 2010).

3.6.7.3.2.2 Multivariate Normality

The necessary steps to analyze the missing data and outlier detection has been undertaken to clean the data and make it appropriate for carrying on the multivariate analysis. The next step involves complying with the assumption of multivariate analysis i.e. assessing multivariate normality. Normality refers to the distribution of the data for a particular variable (Gaskin, 2012). The most critical and important assumption while conducting SEM analyses in general, and in adopting of AMOS in particular (Arbuckle,

1995), is that the data observations are multivariate normal. First, normality of each item would be assessed using: Standard deviation, Skewness and kurtosis.

If the gathered data distribution varies from normal distribution, the multivariate normality should be determined by two characteristics; kurtosis and skewness (Hair et al., 2010). Normality of the data has been measured by deriving the values of kurtosis and skewness from the available data (Byrne, 2010). Kaplan(2008) observed that â2 values those exceeds 7 indicate towards the early departure from normality. Prerequisite to the assessment of multivariate normality is the need to check for univariate normality as the latter is a necessary, although not sufficient, condition for multivariate normality.

The value of skewness refers to the symmetry of the distribution. While the other essential characteristic kurtosis gives an indication towards the "peakedness" of the distribution (Pallant, 2007), or the flatness of the distribution in comparison to the normal distribution. A negative value of kurtosis signifies a flatter distribution whereas a positive value signifies a peaked distribution. A positive value of skew indicates a left shift of the distribution where as a negative value of skew indicates a right shift of the distribution. Normally, a skewness of degree 1 signifies moderate or limited skewness (Kaplan, 2008). Moreover, the degree of multivariate Kurtosis denotes the amount of deviation from multivariate normality. Values of kurtosis below 1 are considered trivial and insignificant; a value in the range of 1 to 10 implies moderate non-normality whereas values above 10 imply significant non-normality (Kaplan, 2008).

The table 3.11 below shows the results of multivariate normality extracted by using AMOS.

Table 3.11: Assessment of Normality

Variable	*min*	*max*	*skew*	*c.r.*	*kurtosis*	*c.r.*
FL8	1.000	5.000	-1.048	-11.107	.897	4.753
FL3	1.000	5.000	-1.058	-11.214	.917	4.859
FL5	1.000	5.000	-.812	-8.605	-.325	-1.724
FL6	1.000	5.000	-.815	-8.636	-.319	-1.688
FL2	1.000	5.000	-.797	-8.446	.012	.061
FL1	1.000	5.000	-.854	-9.055	.124	.656
IB2	1.000	5.000	-.729	-7.727	-.277	-1.469
IB5	1.000	5.000	-.841	-8.909	.320	1.698
IB4	1.000	5.000	-.833	-8.826	.322	1.705
IB6	1.000	5.000	-.736	-7.802	.139	.739

(Contd...)

IB1	1.000	5.000	-.634	-6.723	-.227	-1.205
IB3	1.000	5.000	-.631	-6.691	-.271	-1.438
B2	1.000	5.000	-2.369	-25.105	7.799	41.332
B8	1.000	5.000	-1.928	-20.438	4.822	25.555
B7	1.000	5.000	-2.091	-22.167	4.730	25.068
B10	1.000	5.000	-2.001	-21.210	4.698	24.896
B9	1.000	5.000	-2.379	-25.217	6.485	34.366
B12	1.000	5.000	-1.982	-21.007	4.706	24.939
B3	1.000	5.000	-2.253	-23.879	6.833	36.212
B6	1.000	5.000	-2.475	-26.229	6.966	36.913
B4	1.000	5.000	-2.524	-26.751	7.281	38.584
B11	1.000	5.000	-2.092	-22.169	5.333	28.259
B1	1.000	5.000	-2.486	-26.350	6.870	36.405
SN3	1.000	5.000	-.971	-10.292	.500	2.649
SN4	1.000	5.000	-1.011	-10.716	.669	3.548
SN10	1.000	5.000	-.994	-10.531	.653	3.463
SN1	1.000	5.000	-1.080	-11.442	1.058	5.605
SN7	1.000	5.000	-.944	-10.001	.411	2.176
SN8	1.000	5.000	-1.053	-11.157	.719	3.811
SN5	1.000	5.000	-1.059	-11.222	.776	4.115
SN6	1.000	5.000	-1.102	-11.679	.964	5.109
SN2	1.000	5.000	-1.273	-13.489	1.728	9.158
SN9	1.000	5.000	-1.247	-13.217	1.589	8.419
R13	1.000	5.000	-.731	-7.750	-.189	-1.004
R1	1.000	5.000	-.763	-8.082	-.106	-.561
R4	1.000	5.000	-.760	-8.055	.228	1.208
R8	1.000	5.000	-.595	-6.303	-.273	-1.446
R7	1.000	5.000	-.590	-6.249	-.172	-.914
R9	1.000	5.000	-.805	-8.529	-.104	-.550
R11	1.000	5.000	-.805	-8.531	.122	.648
R2	1.000	5.000	-.829	-8.784	.187	.989
R3	1.000	5.000	-.816	-8.648	-.072	-.383
R5	1.000	5.000	-.481	-5.096	-.855	-4.528
R10	1.000	5.000	-.589	-6.244	-.478	-2.533
R6	1.000	5.000	-.581	-6.162	-.463	-2.453
A1	1.000	5.000	-1.870	-19.823	3.771	19.986
A3	1.000	5.000	-1.811	-19.194	3.795	20.113
A4	1.000	5.000	-1.763	-18.681	3.808	20.182
A2	1.000	5.000	-1.812	-19.201	3.908	20.711
A7	1.000	5.000	-1.705	-18.066	3.167	16.781
A8	1.000	5.000	-1.728	-18.318	3.099	16.424
A12	1.000	5.000	-1.634	-17.320	2.989	15.838
A10	1.000	5.000	-1.919	-20.337	3.862	20.465
A14	1.000	5.000	-1.614	-17.103	2.796	14.816
A13	1.000	5.000	-1.655	-17.540	3.119	16.530
A6	1.000	5.000	-1.692	-17.933	3.431	18.183
A11	1.000	5.000	-1.609	-17.052	3.131	16.593
A9	1.000	5.000	-1.746	-18.508	3.642	19.298
A15	1.000	5.000	-1.693	-17.940	3.279	17.379
A5	1.000	5.000	-1.813	-19.219	4.275	22.657
Multivariate					83.658	4.853

From the above assessment, positive values lie between .012 to 7.799 and negative values lie between –.072 to –10.855. Using the rule that, a value in the range of 1 to 10 implies moderate non-normality, the study, therefore shows moderate non-normality.

According to Kaplan (2008), a distribution that is univariate normal can still be multivariate non-normal. The index of multivariate normality appears at the bottom of the table showing the value of kurtosis and its critical ratio. Byrne (2010) observed that the values greater than 5.00 indicates non-normal distribution of data. From the collected observations, the z-statistic of 4.853 implies that the data samples are normality distributed.

3.6.7.3.2.3 Multi-collinearity

Multi-collinearity is an expression of relationship of an independent variable with a set of independent variables (Hair et al., 2010). Multi-collinearity reduces the independent variable's power to predict the variance in dependent variable to the extent of its association with the other independent variables. The most perfect situation for any study would be to include independent variables which are highly correlated with the dependent variable but have little correlation between themselves (Hair et al, 2010). In order to assess multi-collinearity two measures are most commonly used; Tolerance and Variance Inflation Factor (VIF). The tolerance is defined as the amount of variability of the selected independent variable not explained by the other independent variables. The more the value of tolerance, the small is multi-collinearity. On the other hand, the VIFs determine the extent to which the variance of an estimated regression coefficient increases if predictors are correlated (Martz, 2013) When significant Multicollinearity issues exist, the variance inflation factor will be very large for the variables involved (Investopedia, 2015)

In relevance to the study, multi-collinearity check was conducted for variables namely; financial literacy, risk appetite, beliefs and subjective norms. The rule of thumb is that VIF > 4.0 when multi-collinearity is a problem. Some authors use the more lenient cut-off of VIF >= 5 when multi-collinearity is a problem (Garson, 2012). The table below shows that all VIF values were below 3 and therefore, there was no multi-collinearity. The detailed results are attached in the Appendix B.

Table 3.12: Multi-Collinearity Results (VIFs)

Dependent Variable	*Independent Variables*	*Variance Inflation Factor (VIF)*
Financial Literacy	Beliefs Subjective Norms Risk Appetite	1.102 1.068 1.087
Beliefs	Subjective Norms Risk Appetite Financial Literacy	1.057 1.292 1.309
Subjective Norms	Risk Appetite Financial Literacy Beliefs	1.301 1.351 1.126
Risk Appetite	Financial Literacy Beliefs Subjective Norms	1.136 1.137 1.074

Once the assumptions for Multivariate analysis are checked, the data can further be analyzed using SPSS and AMOS.

3.7 Limitations of the Study

Although the conducted research fills the gap in the literature regarding identifying the factors influencing investor's Wealth Management Behavior, it still has some limitations.

- A survey conducted on a much larger and diverse population could have been more useful and advantageous for the research. All the participants of the survey are the clients of various banks and financial institutions in Delhi/NCR. To conduct a more comprehensive research, clients from different parts of the country would also have also been considered for the survey. Moreover the participants perspective belonging to different demographics could also been studied with different ages, income groups, levels of educational.
- The study examined only four factors as predictors of attitude which are considered as the major influencers but there might be some other factors also which affects investor's attitude and thus investor's behavior which and are not considered as part of this study.
- The macro environmental factors such as political, economic, social, technological that might affect individual's behavior have not been included in the empirical study.
- The factors influencing investor's behavior are undertaken from the point of view of investors. Financial Practitioners viewpoint has not been considered in determining these factors.

- The research model which is based on theory of reasoned action given by Ajzen and Fishbein (1980), was adapted for this study and thus behavioral intention which is considered to be the major influencer of individual's behavior, was not made part of it.
- The theory on which the research model is based itself suffers from certain limitations and was revised by introducing another variable known as perceived behavioral control. This study does not cater to perceived behavior of the respondents.
- The respondents chosen for the study are the clients of selected banks and financial institutions. The various other banks and financial institutions were not considered in the scope of the study.
- Impact of demographic variables on investor's attitude was not considered, though various previous researches have shown that demographic variables like age, gender, and occupation have a major influence on individual's attitude and behavior.

3.8 Summary

This chapter discussed the various methods and methodology used for conducting the research including the purpose of selecting these methods, development of questionnaire, its administration, validity of the instrument, reliability of the instrument, data screening and data analysis process. The data collection included the population, sample size, sample size determination and sources of data collection. The sampling methods and its process were discussed in reference to the study. The questionnaire was tested by conducting a pilot-study which ensured the validity and reliability of the instrument. In addition, the statistical techniques followed for data analysis were also examined in detail. Data was screened for any missing values and outliers followed by testing of various assumptions underlying Multivariate analysis like Multivariate Normality, Multicollinearity. Finally, issues related to ethics in business research were addressed. The result of the data analysis is discussed in Chapter IV.

Chapter - 4

Analysis and Interpretation

This chapter explains the analysis conducted on the consolidated data from the questionnaire. The objective of this study is to understand and analyze the investor's knowledge, beliefs, risk appetite, norms and attitude on investment behavior towards Wealth Management Services. The first part of the data analysis is to analyze the data gathered in the form of responses and get rid of any questions that were not suitable and appropriate to be included in the analysis. Observations from the participants who failed to respond to at least 90% of the questionnaire items were discarded from the obtained responses before conducting any statistical analysis on them. Subsequently, descriptive analysis was conducted comprising of means and frequencies calculations those are employed to determine the characteristics of the obtained samples. Structural Equation Modeling has been used to achieve the goals of the research as described in the hypotheses. Statistics associated with proposed wealth management behavior model have been analyzed within the context of the study and the Theory of Reasoned Action.

4.1 Preliminary Data Analysis

The preliminary data analysis is done to exhibit the results of: (1) Reliability of the research variables by testing Cronbach's Alpha coefficient; (2) Demographic profile of the respondents; (3) Respondent's preferred Wealth Management Service. Further analysis will be conducted by adopting descriptive statistical methods. This analysis will fulfill the following objectives: (1) to study the demographic profile of the HNWI investors in Delhi/NCR region; (2) To study the investors' most preferred products and services provided by Wealth Management Companies.

4.1.1 Reliability Analysis

A reliability analysis was done to check the internal consistency of the variables. Cronbach Alpha coefficient, commonly used indicator, was assessed for all the variables. The alpha coefficient for all the variables was sufficiently high and acceptable (above 0.9) as seen in the table 4.1 below. It was better than the one obtained under pilot survey. The reliability tests indicate that the items would produce consistent results if data collection were repeated (Malhotra and Birks, 2007).

Inter-item correlation is also sometimes used to check the internal consistency of the measures. Values of inter-item correlation exceeding 0.30 or more are considered better (Robinson, Shaver, & Wrightsman, 1991). The correlation was large in all the cases (r = 0.5 to 1.0) but medium (r = 0.30 to 0.49) in case of risk appetite and financial literacy. The correlation is said to be small when r = 0.10 to 0.29 (Cohen, 1988). The results of the study support the minimum values required to prove the internal consistency test.

Table 4.1: Statictics of Cronbach's Alpha and Inter-Item Correlation

Constructs	*Items*	*Cronbach Alpha Coefficient*	*Reliability Results*	*Inter-item Correlation*
Attitude	15	0.976	Good	0.565- 0.893
Risk Appetite	13	0.946	Good	0.439-0.989
Subjective Norms	10	0.969	Good	0.680-0.991
Beliefs	11	0.946	Good	0.516- 0.750
Investment Behavior	06	0.910	Good	0.521- 0.957
Financial Literacy	06	0.905	Good	0.454- 0.998

4.1.2 Demographic Profile of the Respondents

The descriptive statistics related to demographic data was conducted; the characteristics of investors were based on age, annual income, educational qualification, occupation and gender. The results are shown in the table 4.2 below.

Investor's Demographic Characteristics		
Characteristic	*Cases*	*% Percentage*
Age		
20-30	85	12.6
31-40	190	28.2
41-50	286	42.5
51-60	66	9.8
61 and above	47	6.9
Total	**674**	**100**
Annual Income		

(Contd...)

20,00,000-30,00,000	142	21
30,00,001-40,00,000	206	30.7
40,00,001-50,00,000	189	28
50,00,001 and above	137	20.3
Total	**674**	**100**
Education		
Postgraduate	182	27
Graduate	325	48.2
Higher Secondary	100	14.8
Elementary	67	9.9
Total	**674**	**100**
Occupation		
Private Company Employee	274	40.6
Self-Employed	176	26.1
Government Employee	86	12.7
Others	138	20.6
Total	**674**	**100**
Gender		
Male	518	76.8
Female	156	23.2
Total	**674**	**100**

The significant proportions of respondents in the above survey (about 76.8%) are male. This percentage represents the investing habits of men and women. It is interesting to note that men are more inclined towards investing and trading than women. According Jasen (2015), men are found to be more confident about investing whereas, women are found to be more goal-focused and less interested in trading. Moreover, this will further contribute towards investigating the influence of gender on Wealth Management Behavior.

A large number of investors are from the age group 41-50 years (42.5%), 31-40 years (28.2%), 20-30 years (12%). It is noted here that more people have started investing at the young age because of their concern towards dynamic economic conditions in place along with the availability of various sources of investment education (Leong, 2015). These young investors believe that saving alone in a bank is not sufficient to be at par with the increasing standard of living and therefore, they need to secure their future by investing in various other potential avenues. Contrarily, the number of older respondents in the age group 51-60 years (9.8%) and 61 and above (6.9%) are already leading a stable lifestyle and are less inclined towards exploring new investment options and have comparatively less risk-appetite. The respondents are grouped into younger and older subjects so as to know whether there are any differences in their investment behavior.

The study classifies investors into different education levels; undergraduate, graduate and postgraduate. It has been observed that, majority of the investors are either graduate (48%) or post-graduate (27%) and the increase in education level of an individual significantly influences his investment behavior. Education brings more awareness and higher acumen of the economic factors which steers them to adopt sophisticated and complex investment options. Moreover, an educated individual will be able to trade-off between cost-benefit while analyzing various investment options.

The study also tries to build an association between occupation and investment behavior. The occupation of investors in the study is classified into private company employee, self-employed, government employee and others (professionals like lawyers, doctors, architectures etc.). The majority of investors in this study were either a private company employee (40.6%) or self-employed (26.1%).

Wealth Management services are offered to people whose account deposits are above a certain defined limit by the banks or financial institutions and which varies from one bank to another. However, the amount of deposits depends on the income level of an individual. Therefore, the study classifies the respondents on the basis of their income. It is apparent from the above table that majority of the investors being offered Wealth Management Services lie in the income group 30,00,001-40,00,000 (30.7%) and 20,00,000-30,00,000 (21%).

4.1.3 Investment Preferences of Respondents

The turbulent economic environment has enabled investors to diversify their risk by not putting all their eggs in one basket rather explore more avenues to park their funds. The respondents were asked to rank the various wealth management services in order of their preference (1-most preferred, 9-least preferred). The table 4.3 below shows the mean ranks and other relevant descriptive for different investment options under Wealth Management.

Table 4.3: Investor's preferred Wealth Management Services/Products

Investment Option	*N*	*Mean*	*Standard Deviation*	*Mean Ranks*
Private Equity/Depository Services	674	1.724	2.562	1
Insurance	674	5.952	2.437	6
Mutual Funds	674	4.955	4.732	5
Fixed Income Products	674	7.194	2.786	7
Real Estate	674	4.382	2.223	4
Loan/Credit Services	674	2.581	2.435	2
Portfolio Management Services	674	2.723	2.642	3
Estate Planning	674	9.034	2.314	9
Advisory Services	674	7.932	2.142	8

The results show that private equity followed by loan/credit services are the most preferred investment services among the HNWI investors. Portfolio Management Services is the third preferred choice followed by investment in real estate. Mutual Funds occupy the fifth position because some investors find mutual funds a non-reliable avenue for investment (Dr. Rajasekar, 2013) and does not have enough knowledge and information about the working of Mutual Funds (Padmaja, 2013). The sixth position is occupied by insurance followed by fixed income products. Insurance products are never a sought-after products in the eyes of the investors. They are often pushed-in by the insurance agents and investors feel distrust towards the intentions of insurance companies (Uma & Uma, 2015). The eight and ninth position is occupied by advisory services and estate planning services respectively. Hung et al. (2008) in their report outlined that investors are confused between the roles of brokers-dealers and investment advisors and therefore, they have no inclination to seek advisory services. Furthermore, the factor that contributed to the least preference for estate planning services is lack of knowledge about estate planning (Ismail et al., 2013).

4.2 Analysis - Section II of the Questionnaire

The demographic characteristics of the respondents along with their investment pattern and preferred Wealth Management Service have been analyzed in the previous section. Investment preference with respect to wealth Management service has also been observed. The need of the study now was to determine the important factors influencing the behavior of investors towards Wealth Management because these factors play a important role in explaining the behavior of investors.

In order to determine the influence of these factors, the proposed research model has been tested for its goodness of fit to the data and consequently the model will enable Wealth Management practitioners in understanding of how investor psychology impacts investment outcomes and thereby benefitting Wealth Management advisory relationship.

The study also investigated the impact of moderators on the determinants of Investor Behavior. The moderator variable includes risk appetite, whose interaction effect will be examined on financial literacy, beliefs and subjective norms. The determinants of the Wealth Management Behavior were extracted using Factor Analysis: Exploratory Factor Analysis. The data was first tested for its suitability using KMO and Barlette's test. Kaiser-Meyer-Olkin Measure of Sampling Adequacy (KMO) has been employed to examine the factorability in the samples. KMO is a sampling adequacy index, which lie between 0 to 1, with higher values stand between

0.6 and 1.0 inferring that Exploratory Factor Analysis is relevant and suitable (Tabachnick & Fidell, 2007). Bartlett's test of Sphericity attempts to access the hypothesis that the correlation matrix represents an identify matrix where all diagonal elements are characterized as1 and all off-diagonal elements are represented by 0, signifying that all of the research variables are uncorrelated. If the Significant value for this analysis is below 0.05, we reject the null hypothesis that the population matrix is an identity matrix (Field, 2013). The Significant value for this analysis leads us to reject the null hypothesis and conclude that there are correlations in the data set that are appropriate for factor analysis. The global implication of correlation matrices is examined with Bartlett's Test of Sphericity, if it provides support for the reliability of the factor analysis of the data samples. The results of the two statistical measures are shown in the table 4.4 below:

Table 4.4: KMO and Bartlett's Test

Kaiser-Meyer-Olkin Measure of Sampling Adequacy.		**.897**
Bartlett's Test of Sphericity	Approx. Chi-Square	9654.095
	df	861
	Sig.	.000

As seen in the above table, the KMO sampling adequacy obtained from the data samples is significant at 0.897 and the application of Bartlett's Test of Sphericity is relevant as it is below 0.05, thus the results obtained from this test deliver enough evidence to prop the suitability and adequacy of the data.

4.2.1 Exploratory Factor Analysis

After the data was checked for its suitability for factor analysis, Exploratory Factor Analysis (EFA) was conducted. Exploratory Factor Analysis (EFA) is normally conducted to examine the association between the observed and latent variables which is unknown or uncertain (Byrne, 2010). The analysis extracts the minimum number of factors on the basis of correlation between observed and latent variables (DeCoster, 1998). This correlation is represented by factor loadings where, the item that measures the intended factor will load high on that factor (Byrne, 2010). EFA is also used to develop and validate an instrument in case where measures are assessed by the researcher from literature or other sources (Ruscio & Roche, 2012). The factorial validity helps in confirming whether the data collected for a particular group of variables do or do not represent the latent constructs.

In the context of the study, Principle Axis Factoring, an important technique in the Exploratory Factor Analysis process has been used to examine the factors influencing Wealth Management Behavior and their correlations in the data obtained. Usually, the initial factor extraction doesn't give interpretable factors. Rotation makes larger loading even larger and smaller loadings even smaller. Therefore, process of rotation provides factors that can be named and interpreted. Varimax rotation has been used as it provides clearer separation of factors (Dhillon and Goldstein, 1984).

There were 63 items in the study labeled as V1, V2 ...V63. The variable loading value of above 0.50 is considered significant (Hair et. al., 2010). The Exploratory Factor analysis was run using Principal Axis factoring and Varimax Rotation. The variables with factor loading less than 0.50 were dropped (V). The 63 items scale was then reduced to 61 items. In the extraction process, six factors with *Eigen* values greater than 1.0 collectively explaining 67.15 per cent of variance have been retained. The table 4.5 below shows the factors extracted their items, item's loadings, percentage of variance explained and Cronbach's alpha:

Table 4.5: Summary of Rotated Component Matrix and Cronbach's Alpha and Variance

Factor No.	*Name of the factor*	*Item*	*% of Variance Explained (Cumulative)*	*Factor Loadings*	*Cronbach Alpha*
1.	**Attitude**	V1	30.245 (30.245)	.883	**0.976**
		V2		.845	
		V3		.843	
		V4		.841	
		V5		.835	
		V6		.831	
		V7		.822	
		V8		.816	
		V9		.814	
		V10		.813	
		V11		.797	
		V12		.781	
		V13		.772	
		V14		.770	
		V15		.742	
2.	**Risk Appetite**	V16	12.417 (42.662)	.797	**0.946**
		V17		.794	
		V18		.765	
		V19		.763	
		V20		.760	
		V21		.757	
		V22		.751	
		V23		.745	
		V24		.715	
		V25		.695	
		V26		.690	
		V27		.625	
		V28		.624	

(*Contd...*)

3.	**Subjective Norms**	V29	8.997 (51.659)	.865	0.969
		V30		.861	
		V31		.856	
		V32		.842	
		V33		.838	
		V34		.809	
		V35		.798	
		V36		.797	
		V37		.779	
		V38		.777	
4.	**Beliefs**	V39	8.196 (59.855)	.809	0.942
		V40		.784	
		V41		.781	
		V42		.779	
		V43		.774	
		V45		.758	
		V46		.750	
		V47		.744	
		V48		.731	
		V49		.715	
		V50		.771	
5.	**Investment Behavior**	V51	3.934 (63.789)	.804	0.912
		V52		.801	
		V53		.751	
		V54		.748	
		V55		.654	
		V56		.620	
6.	**Financial Literacy**	V57	3.368 (67.157)	.758	0.935
		V58		.750	
		V59		.665	
		V61		.687	
		V62		.699	
		V63		.664	

The first factor extracted is **Attitude.** Attitude refers to the feelings about a specific object. There are *fifteen* (15) items measuring this factor (V1, V2….V15). The total variance explained by this factor is 30.25% and the factor loadings of the measured variables vary between 0.742 - 0.883. The fifteen items measures the factor on the basis of investor's attitude towards financial products; their perception about the company; the duration of their investment; their behavior in times of uncertainty; their assessment about the future performance of the stock; their perception about the services of the wealth manager; their objective of investment etc.

The second factor extracted is Risk Appetite. Risk Appetite refers to the ability of a person to undertake risk. There are *thirteen* (13) items measuring this factor with total variance of 12.42% and the factor loadings of the variables vary between 0.623 - 0.797. The items measure the mind-sets of the investors in various situations like in times of losses; in times of fluctuations in the economy. It also assesses the thinking of investors towards investment in some companies and stocks.

The third factor extracted is Subjective Norms. Subjective Norms refers to the perception of an individual towards the opinion given by people close to him. The total variance explained by this factor is 8.997%. There are *ten* (10) items measuring this factor and their factor loadings vary from 0.777 - 0.865. The items measure how investors react towards the information/opinion given by their friends, relatives' family, peers, advisors on investment issues. The items also assess the reaction of investors towards the advertisements, publications regarding various financial products. The investors' decisions were also assessed on the basis of their intuition and past experiences.

The fourth factor extracted is Beliefs and it refers to the assumptions of individuals towards something. The total variance explained by this factor is 8.196%. There are *eleven* (11) items measuring this factor with their factor loadings varying between 0.771 - 0.809. The items measure the beliefs of people towards their investment; towards the company they are investing; towards a particular stock; towards the economy; towards their own choice of investment etc.

The fifth factor extracted is Investment Behavior and it refers to the behavior of investor towards the type of investments they make or their investment pattern. The total variance explained by this factor is 3.934%. In all, *six* (6) items measured this factor with factor loadings varying between 0.620 - 0.804. The items measured the behavior of investors by assessing their frequency of availing Wealth Management Services; their attitude towards Wealth Management Service providers; their opinion about the future of wealth management etc.

The sixth factor extracted is Financial Literacy, which indicates the extent of knowledge and awareness an investor possesses about financial matters. The total variance explained by this factor is 3.37%. There were ***six (6)*** items that measured this factor with their factor loadings varying from 0.664 - 0.758. The ***two (2)*** items were dropped because they exhibit low factor loadings. The items assessed the knowledge of investors in financial matters related to knowledge of wealth management services, risk associated with them, institutions that provide wealth management services, investment options available; investor's rights and responsibilities; investment plans etc.

4.2.2 Constructs of the research

The study consists of six (6) latent constructs that are measured by one or more variables (observed variables). Latent variables are factors that cannot be observed directly i.e. they cannot be measured whereas the observed variables are the factors that can be measured directly. The latent variable is thus linked to an observed variable thereby making its measurement possible (Byrne, 2010). The Latent variable in the study are Financial Literacy, Risk Appetite, Beliefs, Subjective Norms, Attitude and Investment Behavior and the Observed Variables are the indicators measuring these constructs.

The observed variables were found on the basis of literature review. Each construct consists of atleast 3 measured variables. For example, Attitude (a Latent Construct) consists of 15 measured variables (A1, A2.....A15). Similarly, Risk Appetite (a Latent Construct) consists of 13 measured or observed variables (R1, R2,........R13). The other constructs along with their variables' coding is shown in the table 4.6 below.

Table 4.6: Constructs in the Research Model

Construct	*Name of the Construct*	*Number of items*	*Coding of Items*
1.	Attitude	15	A1 – A15
2.	Risk Appetite	13	R1-R13
3.	Subjective Norms	10	SN1-SN10
4.	Beliefs	11	B1-B11
5.	Investment Behavior	6	IB1-IB6
6.	Financial literacy	6	FL1-FL6

This part of analysis explains the relationship between variables diagrammatically. The causal relationship between variables (Latent and Observed) has been determined by using Structural Equation Modeling (SEM) (Hair et. al., 2010). SEM assesses the direct and indirect relationships among the studied variables by constructing two models: Measurement Model and Structural Model (Kaplan, 2008). Measurement Model is represented by Confirmatory factor Analysis (CFA) which is concerned only with the extent of relationship between observed variables and their latent constructs. It assumes that the observed variables will fully load on their constructs and will have zero loadings on the other factors (Byrne, 2010). On the other hand, Structural Model represents the relationship between latent constructs i.e., impact of change in one latent variable on another. The proposed hypotheses are tested statistically to determine whether the variables are consistent with the data or not. The adequacy of goodness-of-fit proves the existence of relationship between variables under study. It is believed that, it is highly unlikely to get a perfect-fit between the hypothesized model and the observed data, the discrepancy is known as residual (Byrne, 2010).

The Models are represented using geometric symbols- circle (eclipse; ⬭), a rectangle (▭), single-headed arrow (→), and a double-headed arrow (↔). The circles represent latent constructs whereas rectangles represent observed variables. The correlation between observed and latent factors is represented by single-headed arrows whereas the covariance between the latent factors is represented by double-headed arrows. Each of the observed variables is associated with an error term, which represents measurement error and reveals the capability of observed variable in measuring the underlying factor (Byrne, 2010). Moreover, the latent factor is also associated with residual term which measures the variance in dependent variable which remains unexplained by the predictor variable. In other words, it shows the adequacy of association between predictor variable and dependent variable. The rest of the chapter clarifies the two important aspects of SEM; Measurement Model and Structural Model using the variables under study (Financial Literacy, Risk Appetite, Beliefs, Subjective Norms, Attitude and Investment Behavior). Also, before presenting the models, it is important to understand the measures that reflect whether the data fits the underlying theory or not.

4.2.3 Measures of Model Fit

In order to know whether a model that reflects the data, fits the underlying theory or not, model fit indices are used. There are lots of fit indices available with various opinions as to which model fit should be used and what should be the threshold values of these indices (Hooper, Coughlan & Mullen, 2008). Kaplan (2008) considers assessing the model fit as one of the most important steps in Structural Equation Modelling. The following indices are widely used in examining the model fit:

4.2.3.1 Absolute Fit Indices

An absolute measure of fit presumes that the best fitting model has a fit of zero (Kenny, 2014)). The measures then examine how far the model is from zero. These fit indices are known as 'badness' measures of fit. The lower the value of these indices the better it is. Chi-Squared test, RMSEA, GFI, AGFI, the RMR and the SRMR are some of the indices included in this category (Hooper, Coughlan & Mullen, 2008).

Chi-squared test: The chi-squared test is the traditional fit statistic, which is reported in most of the SEM analysis. It 'assesses the magnitude of discrepancy between the sample and fitted covariance matrices' (Hu and Bentler, 1999). As it is regarded as 'badness' of fit statistic (Kline, 2005; Mulaik et al, 1989), the good model fit shows an insignificant result at 5% confidence interval. But since the fit suffers from some limitations like assuming multivariate normality and its sensitivity to sample size (Hooper, Coughlan & Mullen, 2008), an alternative indices is referred to assess the model fit. The alternative index is Wheaton et al's (1977) relative/normed chi-square ($\chi 2$/df) or Cmin/df. The acceptable threshold of this alternative index is recommended as ranging between 2-5 (Wheaton et al, 1977; Tabachnick and Fidell, 2007).

Root Mean Square Error of approximation (RMSEA): This index or statistic is used to determine how fine the model developed through structural equation modeling (SEM) fits the population covariance matrix with obtained values of the selected variables (Hooper, Coughlan & Mullen, 2008). Since RMSEA is a measure of error of approximation, it is also commonly known as population-based index. This Index is also referred as "badness of fit" index wherein a value of 0 signifies the absolute fit and values higher than or closer to 0.10 signifies a poor fit. Originally, according to MacCallum, Browne and Sugawara (1996), RMSEA values close to 0.01 indicates an , values close to 0.05 indicates good or close approximation fit and the values close to 0.08 indicates reasonable error of approximation with a mediocre fit. Subsequently studies conducted by Hu and Bentler, 1999; Steiger, 2007 observed that the cut-off value of 0.7 or 0.6 or lesser indicates good fit of the model. RMSEA index can be employed in two ways different ways to evaluate the model's fit. First, it can be used descriptively as a standard measure which is not coupled directly to the scale of theoretical constructs (also referred as latent variables) by examining the sample values and comparing it against a particular cut-off values of 0.01, 0.05 and 0.10 as described above. Secondly it can be used inferentially by examining the distributional properties to a) determine confidence intervals and b) conduct hypothesis testing. Since mostly the above mentioned cut-off values of population estimates may differ from sample estimates, confidence intervals can help us to determine and measure that differential element or gap between sample and population values to gain a confidence level over these parametric estimates for their intended use. P of Close Fit (PCLOSE) is use to test the null hypothesis that the value of RMSEA is no greater than 0.05. PCLOSE value greater than 0.05 concludes that RMSEA is less that 0.05 and there is a close or good fit of the proposed or developed model. If the value of PClose is less than 0.05, the model is worst fit model because at significant level of 0.05 the null hypothesis is rejected. Therefore, for mode to be a good fit, the value of PClose should be above 0.05 so as to accept the null hypothesis that RMSEA is close to model fit (Kenny, 2014).

Goodness-of-fit-index (GFI) & Adjusted Goodness-of fit index (AGFI): GFI is a goodness-of-fit index that examines the fit between observed covariance matrix and the covariance accounted for by the model (Hooper, Coughlan & Mullen, 2008). Though the recommended cut-off of the index is 0.90 but in case of low factor loadings and low sample sizes the cut-off of 0.95 is considered suitable (Miles and Shevlin, 1998). Adjusted goodness-of-fit index is another index related to GFI and adjusts GFI based on degrees of freedom (Hooper, Coughlan & Mullen, 2008). The values of AGFI ranges between 0 & 1 and the value above 0.9 is considered appropriate indicating good fit of the model. Moreover, due to the sensitivity of the measures to sample size, it was recommended by Sharma et al (2005) to not to use these index.

4.2.3.2 Relative Fit Indices

Relative fit indices are the group of indices that do not use the value of chi-square for assessing the model fit but rather compare its value to a base model (Hooper, Coughlan & Mullen, 2008). The more is the variance between the overall fit of the two models, the larger the values of these descriptive statistics (Byrne, 2010).

The three significant relative indices used are Comparative Fit Index (CFI), Normed Fit Index (NFI) and Tucker Lewis Index (TLI). All these indices assess the model fit by comparing the chi-square value of the model with the chi-square value of the independence model. NFI & TLI suffers from a limitation that they are sensitive to sample size and does not give reliable result if the sample size is below 200 (Mulaik et al, 1989) though the other indices can indicate good fit. The values of these indices can range from 0 to 1 with the recommended cut-offs of 0.95 or more (Hu and Bentler, 1999) for a well fitted model. CFI is considered to be the revised form of NFI as it gives reliable results even for small sample sizes (Tabachnick and Fidell, 2007). The value of this measure also ranges between 0 and 1 with a recommended cut-off of 0.95 or more (Hu and Bentler, 1999).

Table 4.7: Summary of Model Fit measures used in the research

Fit Measures	Threshold Values
CMIN/DF	Value between 2-5 indicates good model fit.
RMSEA	Value 0.6 or lesser indicates good model fit.Value of 0 indicates exact model fit.
GFI	Value of 0.90 or above recommended as good model fit.

(Contd...)

CFI	The value of this index can range from 0 to 1 with the recommended cut-offs of 0.95 or more indicating good model fit.
TFI	The value of this index can range from 0 to 1 with the recommended cut-off of 0.95 or more indicating well fitted model.
NFI	The value of this index can range from 0 to 1 with the recommended cut-off of 0.95 or more indicating well fitted model.

4.2.4 Measurement Model

In order to confirm the factors or the constructs identified in Exploratory Factor Analysis, Confirmatory Factor Analysis (CFA) is conducted as a next step after exploratory factor analysis. To examine the overall model fit, first of all, the model fitness of individual constructs is evaluated i.e., a zero-order CFA is constructed for all latent constructs, which is shown in the diagrams below. Zero-order correlations reflect the bivariate relationships between independent and dependent variables without taking into consideration the effect of other variables in the regression equations (Nathans, Oswald, & Nimon, 2012).

(a) Attitude

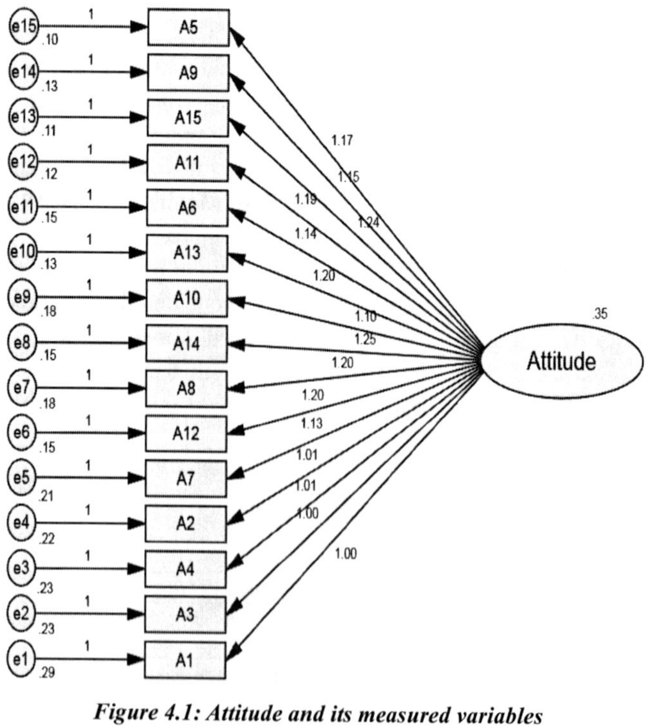

Figure 4.1: Attitude and its measured variables

In the above figure 4.1, Attitude is the latent construct having 15 measured variables. Since a measured variable doesn't explain the latent variable perfectly, an error term is added. The degree to which each of these measured variables is related to latent construct is represented by the variable's loadings or unstandardized estimates which range from 1.00 - 1.25. The unstandardized regression coefficients represent the expected change in the dependent variable associated with a unit change in a given predictor while controlling for the correlated effects of other predictors (Ecological Society of America, 2005); this result suggests that for every single unit of increase in A10, Attitude is increased by 1.25 units. The above figure also shows the error variance which represents the amount of variance unexplained by the observed variable (The University of Texas, 2012); for e.g., the result suggests that e1 is 0.29 which means 29% of the variance is unexplained by A1 in predicting Attitude. The lower the variance, the better it is. The figure also shows the R^2 value which is 0.32 and reflects the degree of variance in the dependent variable determined by all the predictors; the results here shows that 32% of the variances in the Attitude are explained by all the observed variables. The higher the R^2, the better it is. (The University of Texas, 2012). Apart from unstandardized regression coefficients, the output also displays the standardized regression coefficients value as shown in the table 4.8 below:

Table 4.8: Standardized Regression Weights - Attitude

			Estimate
A1	<—	Attitude	.743
A3	<—	Attitude	.779
A4	<—	Attitude	.783
A2	<—	Attitude	.786
A7	<—	Attitude	.829
A12	<—	Attitude	.881
A8	<—	Attitude	.856
A14	<—	Attitude	.888
A10	<—	Attitude	.842
A13	<—	Attitude	.894
A6	<—	Attitude	.865
A11	<—	Attitude	.902
A15	<—	Attitude	.909
A9	<—	Attitude	.885
A5	<—	Attitude	.914

The standardized regression weights signifies the variation in the dependent variable, expressed in standard deviation units, that is attributable to a unit change in the predictor variable keeping all other independent variables constant (Nathans, Oswald, & Nimon, 2012). The standardization of the coefficients based on the standard deviations of the variables is the approach typically used to make coefficients comparable (Ecological Society of America, 2005). In the table above, A5 & A15 have factor loadings of 0.914 and 0.909; this shows that they are best indicators of Attitude. The model fit indices for Attitude is presented in Appendix (Part D).

(b) Risk Appetite

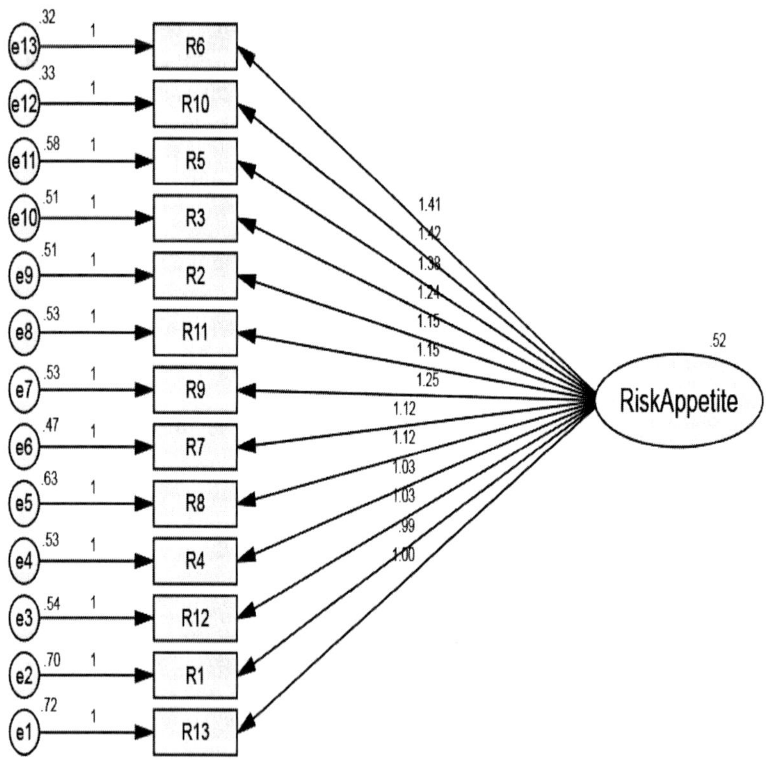

Figure 4.2: Risk Appetite and its measured variables

In the figure 4.2 above, measured variables for the latent construct Risk Appetite are shown. 13 measured variables were found to be related to the construct having loadings or unstandardized estimates ranging from 0.99 - 1.42. The unstandardized regression coefficients represent the expected change in the dependent variable associated with a unit change in a given predictor while controlling for the correlated effects of other predictors (Ecological Society of America, 2005); this result suggests that for every single unit of increase in R10, Risk Appetite is increased by 1.42 units. The above figure also shows the error variance which represents the amount of variance unexplained by the observed variable (The University of Texas, 2012) ; for e.g., the result suggests that e1 is 0.72 which means 72% of the variance is unexplained by R13 in predicting risk Appetite. The lower the variance, the better it is. The figure also shows the R^2 value which is 0.52 and reflects the proportion of variance in the dependent variable explained by all the predictors; the results here shows that 52% of the variances in the Risk Appetite are explained by all the observed variables. The higher the R^2, the better it is. (The University of Texas, 2012). Apart from unstandardized regression coefficients, the output also displays the standardized regression coefficients value as shown in the table 4.9 below:

Table 4.9: Standardized Regression Weights - Risk Appetite

			Estimate
R12	<—	RiskAppetite	.710
R4	<—	RiskAppetite	.715
R8	<—	RiskAppetite	.712
R7	<—	RiskAppetite	.761
R9	<—	RiskAppetite	.776
R11	<—	RiskAppetite	.752
R2	<—	RiskAppetite	.756
R3	<—	RiskAppetite	.782
R5	<—	RiskAppetite	.793
R10	<—	RiskAppetite	.873
R6	<—	RiskAppetite	.875
R1	<—	RiskAppetite	.647
R13	<—	RiskAppetite	.647

The standardized regression weights signifies the variation in the dependent variable, expressed in standard deviation units, that is attributable to a unit change in the predictor variable keeping all other independent variables constant (Nathans, Oswald, & Nimon, 2012). The standardization of the coefficients based on the standard deviations of the variables is the approach typically used to make coefficients comparable (Ecological Society of America, 2005). In the table above, R6 & R10 have factor loadings of 0.875 and 0.873; this shows that they are best indicators of Risk Appetite. Moreover, the variable with low factor loading (below 0.7) will have to be dropped as it might cause concerns in discriminant validity i.e. Average Shared Variance. The model fit indices for Risk Appetite is presented in Appendix (Part D).

(c) Subjective Norms

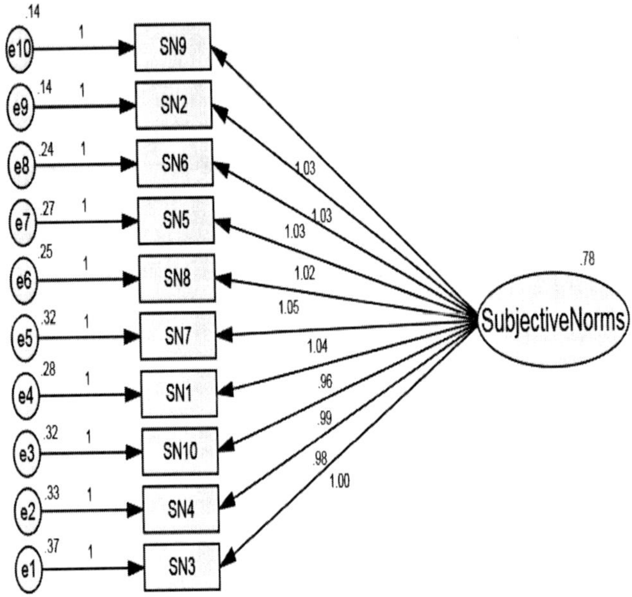

Figure 4.3: Subjective Norms and its measured variables

In the above figure 4.3, measured variables for the latent construct Subjective Norms are shown. 10 measured variables were found to be related the construct having loadings or unstandardized estimates ranging from 0.98 - 1.05. The unstandardized regression coefficients represent the expected variation in the dependent variable associated with a unit change in a given predictor while controlling for the correlated effects of other predictors (Ecological Society of America, 2005); this result suggests that for every single unit of increase in SN8, Subjective Norms is increased by 1.05 units. The above figure also shows the error variance which represents the amount of variance unexplained by the observed variable (The University of Texas, 2012) ; for e.g., the result suggests that e1 is 0.37 which means 37% of the variance is unexplained by SN3 in predicting Subjective Norms. The lower the variance, the better it is. The figure also shows the R^2 value which is 0.78 and reflects the proportion of variance in the dependent variable explained by all the predictors; the results here shows that 78% of the variances in the Subjective Norms are explained by all the observed variables. The higher the R^2, the better it is. (The University of Texas, 2012). Apart from unstandardized regression coefficients, the output also displays the standardized regression coefficients value as shown in the table 4.10 below:

Table 4.10: Standardized Regression Weights - Subjective Norms

			Estimate
SN3	<—	SubjectiveNorms	.823
SN4	<—	SubjectiveNorms	.834
SN10	<—	SubjectiveNorms	.842
SN1	<—	SubjectiveNorms	.849
SN7	<—	SubjectiveNorms	.849
SN8	<—	SubjectiveNorms	.883
SN5	<—	SubjectiveNorms	.869
SN6	<—	SubjectiveNorms	.881
SN2	<—	SubjectiveNorms	.926
SN9	<—	SubjectiveNorms	.926

The standardized regression weights signifies the variation in the dependent variable, expressed in standard deviation units, that is attributable to a unit change in the predictor variable keeping all other independent variables constant (Nathans, Oswald, & Nimon, 2012). The standardization of the coefficients based on the standard deviations of the variables is the approach typically used to make coefficients comparable (Ecological Society of America, 2005). In the table above, SN2 & SN9 have factor loadings of 0.926 each; this shows that they are best indicators of Risk Appetite. The model fit indices for Subjective Norms is presented in Appendix (Part D).

(d) Beliefs

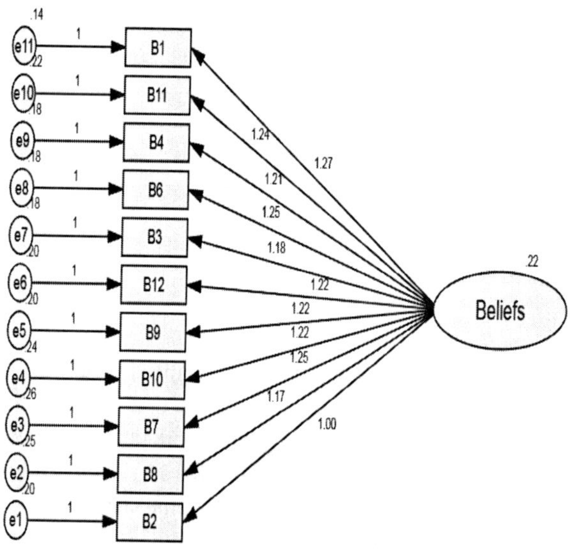

Figure 4.4: Beliefs and its measured variables

In the above figure 4.4, measured variables for the latent construct Beliefs are shown. 11 measured variables were found to be related the construct having loadings or unstandardized estimates ranging from 1.00 - 1.27. The unstandardized regression coefficients represent the expected variation in the dependent variable associated with a unit change in a given predictor while controlling for the correlated effects of other predictors (Ecological Society of America, 2005); this result suggests that for every single unit of increase in B1, Beliefs is increased by 1.27 units. The above figure also shows the error variance which represents the amount of variance unexplained by the observed variable (The University of Texas, 2012); for e.g., the result suggests that e1 is 0.20 which means 20% of the variance is unexplained by B2 in predicting Beliefs. The lower the variance, the better it is. The figure also shows the R^2 value which is 0.22 and reflects the proportion of variance in the dependent variable explained by all the predictors; the results here shows that 22% of the variances in the Subjective Norms are explained by all the observed variables. The higher the R^2, the better it is. (The University of Texas, 2012). Apart from unstandardized regression coefficients, the output also displays the standardized regression coefficients value as shown in the table 4.11 below:

Table 4.11: Standardized Regression Weights - Beliefs

			Estimate
B8	<—	Beliefs	.741
B7	<—	Beliefs	.757
B10	<—	Beliefs	.765
B9	<—	Beliefs	.795
B12	<—	Beliefs	.790
B3	<—	Beliefs	.799
B6	<—	Beliefs	.817
B4	<—	Beliefs	.803
B11	<—	Beliefs	.781
B1	<—	Beliefs	.851
B2	<—	Beliefs	.730

The standardized regression weights signifies the variation in the dependent variable, in standard deviation units, that is attributable to a unit change in the predictor variable keeping all other independent variables constant (Nathans, Oswald, & Nimon, 2012). The standardization of the coefficients based on the standard deviations of the variables is the approach typically used to make coefficients comparable (Ecological Society of

America, 2005). In the table above, B1 & B6 have factor loadings of 0.851 and 0.817; this shows that they are best indicators of Beliefs. The model fit indices for Beliefs is presented in Appendix (Part D).

(e) Investment Behavior

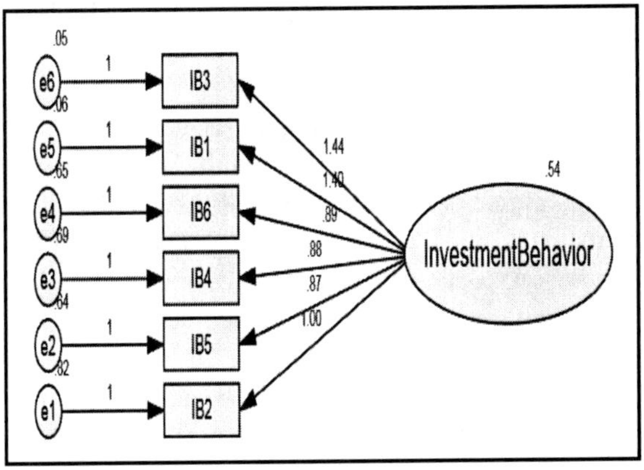

Figure 4.5: Investment Behavior and its measured variables

In the figure 4.5 above, measured variables for the latent construct Investment Behavior are shown. 6 measured variables were found to be related the construct having loadings or unstandardized estimates ranging from 0.87-1.44. The unstandardized regression coefficients represent the expected variation in the dependent variable associated with a unit variation of a given predictor while controlling for the correlated effects of other predictors (Ecological Society of America, 2005); this result suggests that for every single unit of increase in IB3, Investment Behavior is increased by 1.44 units. The above figure also shows the error variance which represents the amount of variance unexplained by the observed variable (The University of Texas, 2012); for e.g., the result suggests that e1 is 0.82 which means 82% of the variance is unexplained by IB2 in predicting Investment Behavior. The lower the variance, the better it is. The figure also shows the R^2 value which is 0.54 and reflects the degree of variation in the dependent variable determined by all the predictors; the results here shows that 54% of the variances in the Investment Behavior are explained by all the observed variables. The higher the R^2, the better it is. (The University of Texas, 2012). Apart from unstandardized regression coefficients, the output also displays the standardized regression coefficients value as shown in the table 4.12 below:

Table 4.12: Standardized Regression Weights - Investment Behavior

			Estimate
IB5	<—	InvestmentBehavior	.625
IB4	<—	InvestmentBehavior	.612
IB6	<—	InvestmentBehavior	.628
IB1	<—	InvestmentBehavior	.975
IB3	<—	InvestmentBehavior	.978
IB2	<—	InvestmentBehavior	.630

The standardized regression weights signifies the variation in the dependent variable, in standard deviation units, that is attributable to a unit change in the predictor variable keeping all other independent variables constant (Nathans, Oswald, & Nimon, 2012). The standardization of the coefficients based on the standard deviations of the variables is the approach typically used to make coefficients comparable (Ecological Society of America, 2005). In the table above, IB3 & IB1 have factor loadings of 0.978 and 0.975; this shows that they are best indicators of Investment Behavior. The variable with low factor loading (below 0.7) will have to be dropped as it might cause concerns in discriminant validity i.e. Average Shared Variance. The model fit indices for Investment Behavior is presented in Appendix (Part D).

(f) Financial Literacy

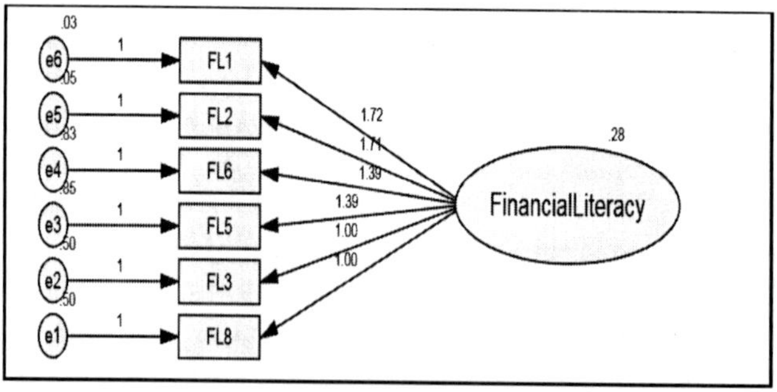

Figure 4.6: Investment Behavior and its measured variables

In the figure 4.6 above, measured variables for the latent construct Financial Literacy are shown. 6 measured variables were found to be related the construct having loadings or unstandardized estimates ranging from 1.00-1.72. The unstandardized regression coefficients represent the expected variation in the dependent variable associated with a unit variation in a given predictor while controlling for the correlated effects of other predictors

(Ecological Society of America, 2005); this result suggests that for every single unit of increase in FL1, Financial Literacy is increased by 1.72 units. The above figure also shows the error variance which represents the amount of variance unexplained by the observed variable (The University of Texas, 2012) ; for e.g., the result suggests that e1 is 0.50 which means 50% of the variance is unexplained by FL8 in predicting Financial Literacy. The lower the variance, the better it is. The figure also shows the R^2 value which is 0.28 and reflects the degree of variation in the dependent variable determined by all the predictors; the results here shows that 28% of the variances in the Investment Behavior are explained by all the observed variables. The higher the R^2, the better it is. (The University of Texas, 2012). Apart from unstandardized regression coefficients, the output also displays the standardized regression coefficients value as shown in the table 4.13 below:

Table 4.13: Standardized Regression Weights - Financial Literacy

			Estimate
FL3	<—	FinancialLiteracy	.597
FL5	<—	FinancialLiteracy	.620
FL6	<—	FinancialLiteracy	.626
FL2	<—	FinancialLiteracy	.972
FL1	<—	FinancialLiteracy	.981
FL8	<—	FinancialLiteracy	.595

The standardized regression weights signifies the variation in the dependent variable, in standard deviation units, that is attributable to a unit change in the predictor variable keeping all other independent variables constant (Nathans, Oswald, & Nimon, 2012). The standardization of the coefficients based on the standard deviations of the variables is the approach typically used to make coefficients comparable (Ecological Society of America, 2005). In the table above, FL1 & FL2 have factor loadings of

Table 4.14: Summary of Model Fit Indices of each Construct

	MODEL FIT INDICES						
Constructs	**CFI**	**TLI**	**NFI**	**GFI**	**RMSEA**	**P-CLOSE**	**CMIN/df**
Attitude	0.992	0.983	0.989	0.97	0.059	0.078	3.305
Risk Appetite	0.992	0.983	0.989	0.968	0.056	0.062	4.2
Subjective Norms	0.998	0.996	0.997	0.989	0.038	0.851	1.966
Beliefs	0.989	0.982	0.983	0.975	0.052	0.382	2.81
Investment Behavior	0.999	0.991	0.998	0.997	0.059	0.305	3.336
Financial Literacy	0.997	0.993	0.997	0.987	0.052	0.079	4.509

0.981 and 0.972; this shows that they are best indicators of Financial Literacy. The variable with low factor loading (below 0.7) will have to be dropped as it might cause concerns in discriminant validity i.e. Average Shared Variance. The model fit indices for Financial Literacy is presented in Appendix (Part D).

The table 4.14 above shows the model fit indices of all constructs namely, attitude, risk appetite, subjective norms, beliefs, investment behavior and financial literacy. In case of Attitude, all indices values are above the cut-off level and imply a good model fit; the GFI (0.97), CFI(0.992), NFI (0.989) and TLI (0.983) value are above the cut-off point, RMSEA (0.059) is close to cut-off point and P-CLOSE (0.078) is in acceptable range. CFI, TLI, NFI and GFI are goodness of fit indices whereas RMSEA is badness of fit index, therefore, the lesser it is the better the model fit is. The value of CMIN/df is also close to cut-off, which means that overall model, is not a bad fit model.

In case of Risk Appetite construct, the goodness of fit indices- CFI, TLI, NFI and GFI are within the acceptable range, RMSEA is close to cut-off with PCLOSE value of 0.062 which is above the 0.05. The CMIN/df value is little more than the threshold but permissible. Thus, the model seems to be fairly a good fit model. In case of Subjective Norms, the goodness of fit indices; CFI, TLI, NFI and GFI are above the cut-off and RMSEA is good enough to be below 0.05 indicating good model fit with a PCLOSE value fairly above the threshold. The CMIN/df is very good as it is below the cut-off value of 3. Thus, overall the model is a good fit. In case of Beliefs also, the goodness of fit indices- CFI, TLI, NFI and GFI are above threshold, RMSEA is close to cut-off point but acceptable with PCLOSE value far above the threshold; CMIN/df value is also within acceptable range indicating a good model fit. In case of Investment Behavior, the CFI, TLI, NFI & GFI are within the acceptable range, RMSEA just near to cut-off with a good PCLOSE value of 0.382. Also, the CMIN/df value indicates good model fit. In case of Financial Literacy also, the CFI, TLI, NFI & GFI are above the cut-off and RMSEA is good enough to be close to 0.05 indicating marginally good model fit with a PCLOSE value fairly above the threshold. The CMIN/df is high though within permissible limits giving marginally good model fit.

After assessing the zero-order correlation of constructs, the next step is to examine the correlation between all six (6) constructs. Before measuring the model fit, it is important to examine the reliability and validity of the model. A reliability analysis has been done to determine the internal consistency of the variables, whereas validity refers to the accuracy of the variables. Both these measures serve different purposes and if a measure is found to be consistent, it does not mean that it will be accurate and vice versa.

4.2.5 Construct Reliability

Reliability indicates the degree to which the measures produce consistent results (Malhotra, 2010). The measure is widely applicable as it can be employed for latent variables or theoretical constructs of a model developed by the researcher using confirmatory factor analysis or path analysis or any other measurement model (Holmes-Smith, Cunningham & Coote, 2009). The three commonly used measures of reliability are Squared Multiple Correlations (SMC), Item-total correlations and Cronbach's Alpha (Hair et al, 2010).

Cronbach's Alpha and SMC has been used in the study to measure the Construct Reliability. Cronbach's Alpha has already been discussed in the section 4.2.1 where all constructs were identified as reliable as the value of Cronbach's Alpha was greater than 0.7. SMC refers to the correlation between a single measured variable and the underlying construct. It is the square of standardized factor loading. SMC value exceeding 0.50 is considered acceptable (Holmes-Smith, Cunningham & Coote, 2009). Any variable exhibiting SMC value less than 0.50 should be deleted for further analysis. The following table 4.15 highlights the SMC values of measured variables. Most of the variables exhibited values greater than 0.05. The variables **(as highlighted in bold)** were considered for deletion to improve the model fit.

Table 4.15: Squared Multiple Correlation (SMC) of 61 measured variables

	Estimate
FL8	**.358**
FL3	**.360**
FL5	.789
FL6	.895
FL2	.943
FL1	.961
IB2	.895
IB5	.984
IB4	**.359**
IB6	**.379**
IB1	.949
IB3	.962
B2	.531
B8	.547

	Estimate
SN2	.989
SN9	.990
R13	**.464**
R1	**.463**
R12	.536
R4	.540
R8	.522
R7	.571
R9	.610
R11	.612
R2	.617
R3	.628
R5	.611

(Contd...)

B7	.572
B10	.584
B9	.633
B12	.624
B3	.639
B6	.669
B4	.643
B11	.607
B1	.726
SN3	.514
SN4	.574
SN10	.546
SN1	.591
SN7	.597
SN8	.675
SN5	.604
SN6	.642

R10	.633
R6	.635
A1	.568
A3	.622
A4	.628
A2	.635
A7	.690
A8	.734
A12	.760
A10	.718
A14	.763
A13	.787
A6	.759
A11	.806
A9	.785
A15	.806
A5	.841

4.2.6 Construct Validity

'Construct validity refers to the degree to which inferences can legitimately be made from the operationalizations in your study to the theoretical constructs on which those operationalizations were based' (Trochim, 2006). In other words, it means whether the scale measures what it claims to measure. Construct validity includes convergent validity, discriminant validity and nomological validity (Malhotra, 2010). For the current study, convergent validity and discriminant validity will be determined. Both these validities should be determined together in order to produce the evidence for construct validity (Trochim, 2006). When there are multiple constructs in a survey study, it is important to satisfy convergent and discriminant validities in order to satisfy construct validity (Agarwal, 2011).

4.2.6.1 Convergent Validity

Convergent validity shows the degree to which the measures of a construct are positively related to each other (Malhotra, 2010). Convergent validity is determined by comparing Cronbach alpha of the construct with Average Variance Explained by the measures (Hair et.al, 2010). The Average Variance Explained by the measures is nothing but the square of average of the factor loadings. The construct is said to be valid as far as convergent validity is concerned if the following conditions are satisfied (Hair et al., 2010):

(1) Cronbach Alpha co-efficient is greater than 0.7

(2) Cronbach Alpha co-efficient> Average Variance Explained

(3) Average Variance Explained > 0.5

4.2.6.2 Discriminant Validity

Discriminant validity shows the extent to which the constructs differ from each other. It is assessed by comparing the squared correlation (R^2) of the paired constructs with the AVEs of each construct (Fornell & Larcker, 1981). For this, Maximum of the two correlation coefficients is taken and squared. This is called Maximum Shared Variance (MSV). Discriminant validity can be said to be satisfactory if MSV of a pair of constructs is less than the AVE for each corresponding construct (Hair et.al, 2010).

Discriminant Validity: MSV < AVE

The Validity of the model was assessed using Stats tool package where the correlations and standardized regression weights were input into the excel sheet and the following result was achieved:

Table 4.16: Validity Results

	CR	AVE	MSV	ASV	Investment Behavior	Attitude	RiskAppetite	Subjective Norms	Beliefs	Financial Literacy
InvestmentBehavior	0.885	0.670	0.154	0.054	0.818					
Attitude	0.975	0.727	0.165	0.103	0.271	0.853				
RiskAppetite	0.942	0.598	0.206	0.086	0.093	0.324	0.773			
SubjectiveNorms	0.953	0.672	0.165	0.083	0.392	0.406	0.172	0.820		
Beliefs	0.946	0.616	0.087	0.063	0.175	0.280	0.287	0.195	0.785	
FinancialLiteracy	0.885	0.669	0.206	0.084	0.073	0.306	0.454	0.164	0.295	0.818
No Validity Concerns - Wahoo!										

The above table 4.16 shows that there were no Validity concerns. After investigating the reliability and validity issues the overall model was assessed for fitness. The following figure indicates the relationship between measured variables and their underlying constructs. The fit indices generated by the model are within the acceptable range indicating that the model fits the data. CMIN/df= 1.983; CFI= 0.916; NFI= 0.946; TLI= 0.917; GFI=0.961; RMSEA=0.047; PCLOSE= 0.927) (see Appendix C for references to fit measures)

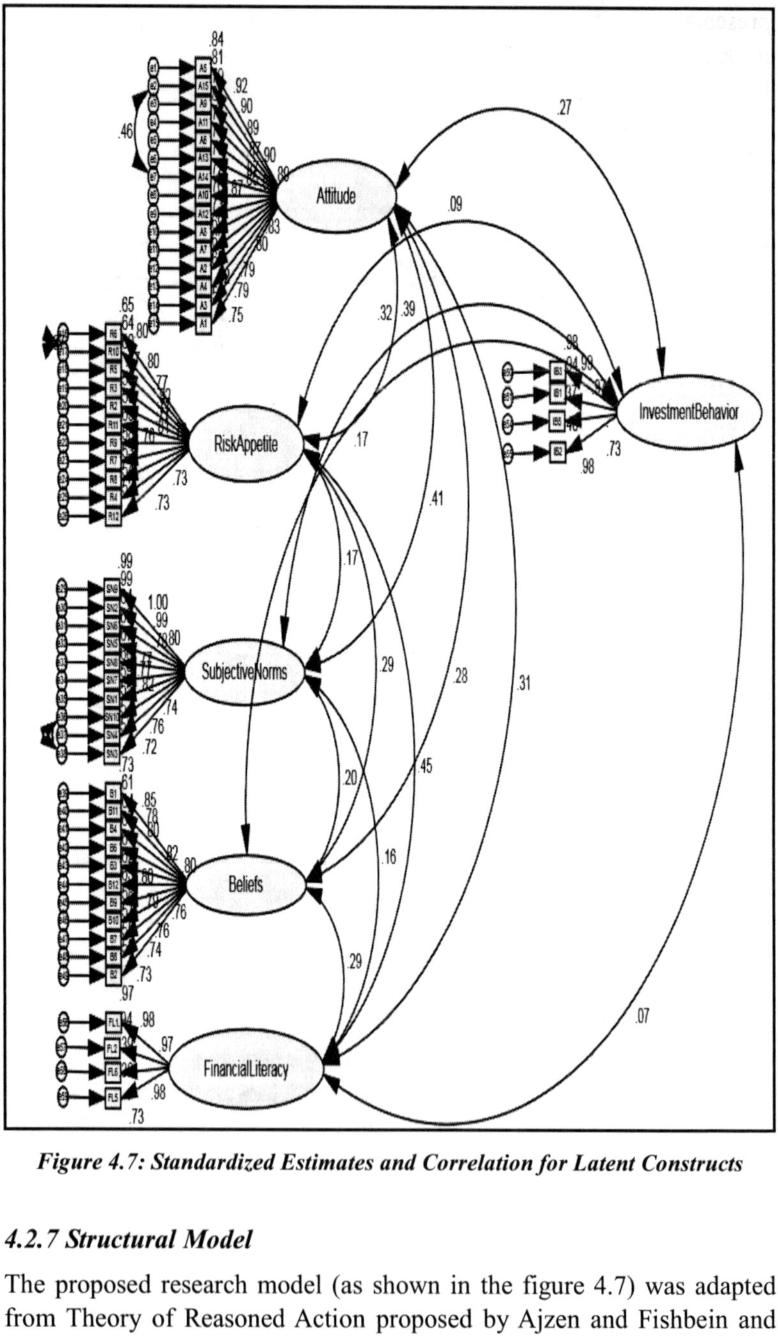

Figure 4.7: Standardized Estimates and Correlation for Latent Constructs

4.2.7 Structural Model

The proposed research model (as shown in the figure 4.7) was adapted from Theory of Reasoned Action proposed by Ajzen and Fishbein and presents the influence of five (5) exogenous variables (Financial Literacy, Risk Appetite, Beliefs and Subjective Norms) on investors Attitude (endogenous variable) and the influence of Attitude on Investment Behavior (endogenous variable). This model in this study is called as 'Wealth Management Behavior Model'.

Exogenous latent variables are those variables whose values change due to change in the values of external variables which are not included in the model whereas; endogenous variables are those variables that are directly or indirectly influenced by the exogenous variables included in the model (Byrne, 2010).

In the path analysis, both standardized and unstandardized estimates of the model have been presented. For parameter estimation, maximum likelihood method is adopted. In an unstandardized estimate; the regression weights, co-variances, intercepts and variances are presented in the model (Byrne, 2010). In case of standardized estimates; the standardized regression weights, correlations, squared multiple correlations will be presented (Byrne, 2010). The regression weights tell the magnitude of change in the dependent variable due to a unit change in the single independent (observed) variable. Squared Multiple Correlation (SMC) tells the percentage of variance accounted by or explained by the predictor (observed) variable in the underlying latent (dependent) variable. The fit measures on the other hand tell about the overall fit of the model with the data.

4.2.7.1 Proposed Research Model

The SEM analysis has been carried out in three (3) steps to test the proposed model:

Step 1: Testing the proposed model by investigating the determinants (Financial Literacy, beliefs, Risk Appetite and Subjective Norms) and their influence on Endogenous variables (Attitude and Investment Behavior). This model does not take into consideration the influence of moderators (Age, Gender, Income, Occupation and Education).

Step 2: Testing the mediating effect of Attitude on the relationship between Financial Literacy, Risk Appetite, beliefs, Subjective Norms and Investment Behavior. This model does not take into consideration the influence of moderators (Age, Gender, Income, Occupation and Education).

Step 3: Testing the proposed model by evaluating the effect of Moderators on determinants by using multiple regression analysis.

The hypotheses to be tested in the first step are:

H1a: Financial Literacy has a significant influence on Investors' Attitude to invest.

H1b: Risk Appetite has a significant influence on Investors' Attitude to invest.

H1c: Beliefs have a significant influence on Investors' Attitude to invest.

H1d: Subjective Norms have a significant influence on Investors' Attitude to invest.

H1e: Attitude has a significant influence on Investors' Attitude to invest.

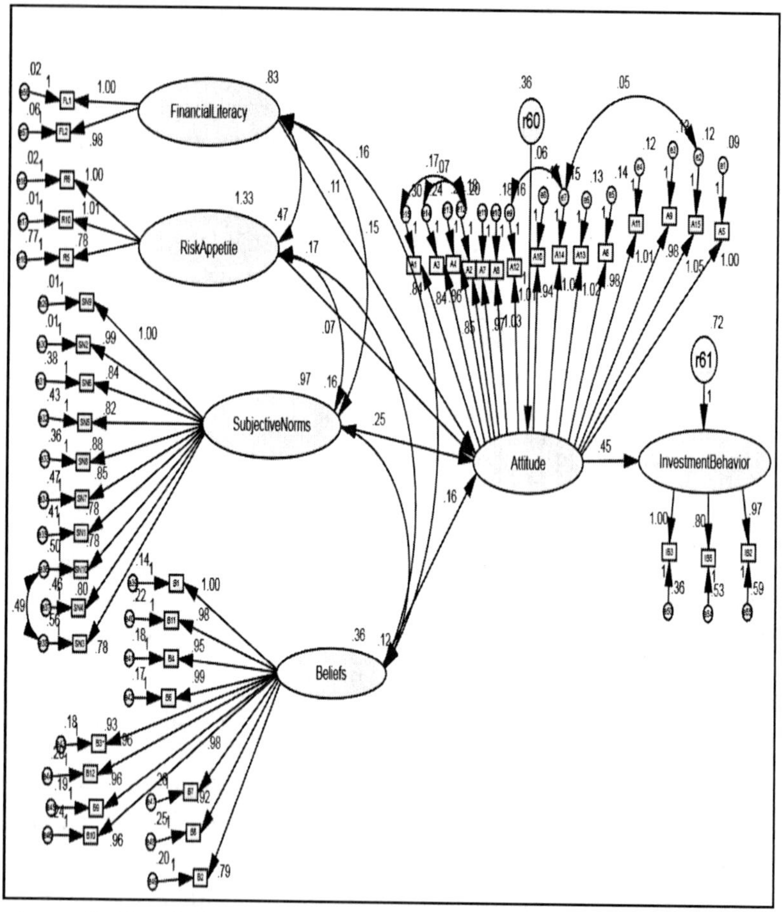

Figure 4.8: Wealth Management Behavior Model with Unstandardized Estimates

The initial model after modifications has been presented in figure 4.8 with unstandardized estimates and in figure 4.9 with standardized estimates. The model fit has been improved by examining the modification indices. Also, some of the items (predictors) were deleted (F5, R3, R2, R8, R4 and R12) as these items exhibited strong sample correlation (greater than 0.8) and thus indicates the presence of multi-collinearity (Holmes-Smith, Cunningham & Coote, 2006). In addition, some items (F6, IB1, R11, R9, R7) were also deleted while examining standardized residual covariance. Standardized residual co-variances (SRCs) with values greater than 2 decreases the model fit and shows the discrepancy between proposed and estimated model fit (Gaskin, 2015) therefore, it is important to remove those items in order to address the problem of SRCs. After these deletions the model fits are obtained (See figure 4.8 and 4.9).

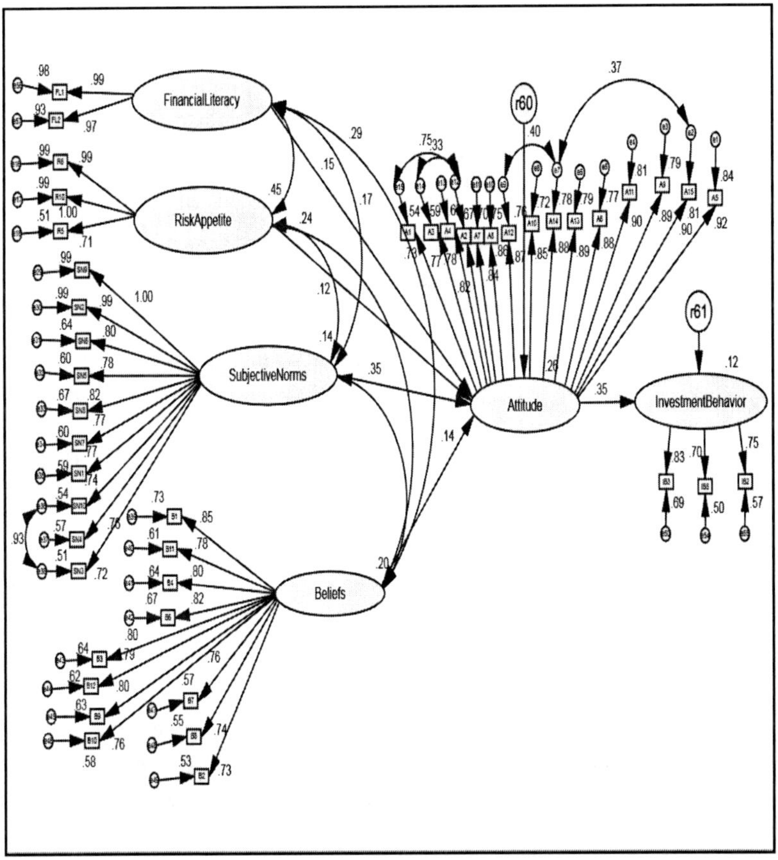

Figure 4.9: Wealth Management Behavior Model with Standardized Estimates

The initial SEM model is tested and modified and explains the relationship between predictors and their underlying factors. Figure 4.8 shows the unstandardized estimates of the model depicting regression weights, co-variances, and variances. Figure 4.9 shows standardized estimates of the model depicting standardized regression weights, correlations and Squared Multiple Correlations (SMC). The model generates fit measures that indicates goodness-of fit of the model to the data (CMIN/DF= 3.387; RMSEA=0.054 with PCLOSE= 0.634; TLI =0.893; NFI=0.870; CFI=0.905; GFI=0.981); although relative indices do not meet the threshold limit but looking at the overall measures, the values are acceptable (see Appendix E for reference to fit measures).

The model also shows the path analysis between determinants and dependent variables. The paths between the variables are statistically significant at 0.05 level of significance i.e., the p-value as shown in the table 4.17 is less than 0.05.

Table 4.17: Regression Weights for the Initial Model

			Estimate	*S.E.*	*C.R.*	*P*	*Label*
Attitude	<---	Financial Literacy	0.111	0.03	3.675	***	par_43
Attitude	<---	Risk Appetite	0.073	0.023	3.125	0.002	par_44
Attitude	<---	Subjective Norms	0.246	0.025	9.801	***	par_45
Attitude	<---	Beliefs	0.157	0.043	3.625	***	par_46
Investment Behavior	<---	Attitude	0.454	0.055	8.302	***	par_47

P-value is statistically significant at 0.05 level of significance.

The significant paths shown in the table – leads to the acceptance of hypotheses developed between predictors and dependent variables. In other words, the hypotheses H1a-H1e are accepted. This means that Financial Literacy, beliefs, risk Appetite, Subjective norms influence Attitude. Concurrently, Attitude influence Investment Behavior.

Table 4.18: Squared Multiple Correlations

Research Constructs	*Estimate*
Attitude	0.255
Investment Behavior	0.123

The results also show the amount of variance explained by the predictors in dependent variables which is depicted by the Squared Multiple Correlation of variables. The values show reasonable explanation for Attitude and Investment Behavior (see table 4.18). The determinants (Financial Literacy, Risk Appetite, Beliefs and Subjective Norms account for only 25.5% variance in Attitude and 12.3% variance in Investment Behavior.

The strength of the relationship between factors and behavior is reflected in the standardized regression weights. The standardized regression weights are used as it enables a researcher to compare the relative effect of each independent variable on dependent variable (Hair et al, 2010). The table 4.19 shows the standardized regression weights between factors and behavior. Since, the paths are statistically significant, the stronger one being between Subjective Norms and Attitude (0.347) and between Attitude and Investment Behavior (0.351), the rest are relatively weaker but statistically significant. This implies that greater the social pressure to engage or not to engage in a behavior, the greater will be the attitude towards investment which in turn will lead to strong influence on investment behavior. In addition, the higher the financial literacy of an investor the more favorable will be his attitude towards investment.

Table 4.19: Standardized Regression Weights for Research Constructs and Mediate Variables

Research Constructs		*Mediate Variables*	*Estimate*
Attitude	<—	FinancialLiteracy	0.145
Attitude	<—	RiskAppetite	0.120
Attitude	<—	SubjectiveNorms	0.347
Attitude	<—	Beliefs	0.136
InvestmentBehavior	<—	Attitude	0.351

The results also show covariance between the predictors/observed variables. The determinants are significantly related to each other as can be seen in the table 4.20. The financial literacy is highly associated with risk appetite which means that the more financially literate an investor is, more will be his tolerance to bear risk.

Table 4.20: Covariance Between the Predictor Variables

			Estimate	*S.E.*	*C.R.*	*P*	*Label*
RiskAppetite	<-->	FinancialLiteracy	0.470	0.045	10.481	***	par_38
SubjectiveNorms	<-->	FinancialLiteracy	0.148	0.035	4.179	***	par_39
Beliefs	<-->	FinancialLiteracy	0.159	0.023	6.913	***	par_40
RiskAppetite	<-->	SubjectiveNorms	0.157	0.044	3.541	***	par_41
SubjectiveNorms	<-->	Beliefs	0.115	0.024	4.803	***	par_42
RiskAppetite	<-->	Beliefs	0.166	0.029	5.825	***	par_54

In nutshell, it can be said that the determinants significantly explain Investment Behavior though their capability in explaining the variance of investment behavior is not much strong. The most important determinant influencing attitude is found to be subjective norm with stronger standardized regression weight. The determinants, in total, account for 25.5% of the variance in Attitude and Attitude account for only 12.3% of the variance in Investment Behavior.

A further analysis on the model has been performed to find out the impact of interaction between independent variables on investors' attitude which in turn influence behavior.

4.2.8 Moderation

A model shows causal relationships between variables and represents direct effects, moderating effects, mediating effects and reciprocal effects. Moderation effect or interaction is said to take place between a predictor variable and an outcome when a third variable (moderating variable) interferes and changes the relationship between predictor and dependent variable (Baron and Kenny, 1986). The moderating variables can be categorical, interval, continuous or ratio level and depending on the type of variable, the appropriate statistical tests are used like multiple regression analysis, analysis of variance or structural equation modeling (Baron and Kenny, 1986). A moderator variable is normally considered in the relationship when there is enough evidence that the moderator may enhance or reduce the nature of relationship between the predictor and outcome variable (Lindley and Walker, 1993).

In order to test the moderating effect, the researcher tests the hypothesis that the dependent variable is predicted by these independent variables. So, when the dependent variable is regressed upon the independent variable, the relationship may be significant or insignificant. The nature of relationship is further tested by introducing an interaction term which is the product of the two predictor variables one of which is considered as moderator variable. If the relationship between dependent variable and the interaction term is found to be significant, the moderator variable is said to have a moderating effect on the relationship between predictor and outcome variable. The study examines the moderating effect of risk appetite on the relationship between financial literacy, beliefs, subjective norms and attitude.

4.2.8.1 Moderating role of Risk Appetite

The research undertaken by various behavioral finance experts proves that the investment behavior is not only affected by physical considerations but also by mental traits (Kannadhasan, 2006). Psychological and behavioral factors to a great extent determine the investor's behavior. Theorists believe that the behavior of investors is governed by their attitude and risk bearing capacity (Eisenhardt, 1989; Wiseman & Gomez-Mejia, 1998; De Long, Shleifer, Summers, & Waldmann, 1990; Weber, Blais, & Betz, 2002; Mohanta & Debasish, 2011). Risk appetite or risk bearing capacity is considered an important aspect in analyzing the investors' attitude (Illing & Aaron, 2005). It is proved to be a key factor driving investor behavior (Kannadhasan, 2006). Shift in risk appetite causes shift in investors' attitude and thus behavior. Being central to the concept of investors' attitude and behavior, it is believed to have a significant impact on other factors influencing attitude (Fung, Tam, & Yu, 2009). It is because of this reason; risk appetite is taken as a moderating variable in this study in order to examine its role in influencing the relationship between financial literacy, beliefs, subjective norms and attitude. Moderation effect has been shown by introducing an interaction term. Interaction Moderation has been chosen because so far, the interaction between other financial literacy, beliefs, subjective norms and risk appetite has rarely been tested. Interactions facilitates more specific clarification of causal relationship by providing a technique that explains not only how predictor variable affects the outcome but also, the circumstances under which the relationship between predictor and dependent will change depending on the influence of moderating variable. Applying regression to interaction moderating is considered essential to draw conclusions with regard to the following proposed hypotheses:

H2a: Risk Appetite moderates the relationship between Financial Literacy and Attitude towards investment.

H2b: Risk Appetite moderates the relationship between Beliefs and Attitude towards investment.

H2c: Risk Appetite moderates the relationship between Subjective Norms and Attitude towards investment.

4.2.8.2 Moderation Interaction Model

The interaction term i.e. the product of predictor variable (independent and moderator variable) is created in SPSS using their standardized values. Standardized value means that the mean of the responses will be 0 and their standard deviation 1. The standardized values are calculated to avoid multicollinearity between the products of predictor variables. In other words, it means isolating the unique effects of that interaction. So, the standardized values of the predictor as well as dependent variable has been calculated and used in the model. The following figure 4.10 and 4.11 shows the

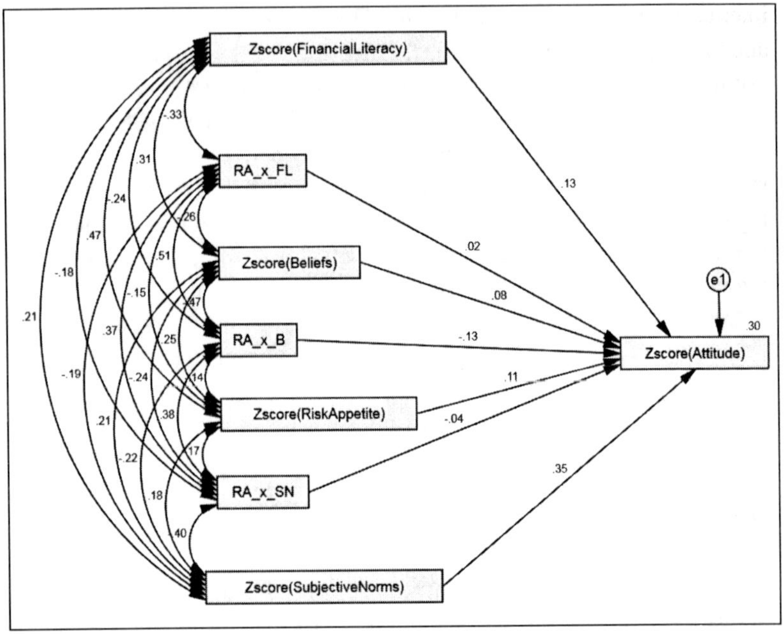

Figure 4.10: Standardized Estimates of Initial Moderation Interaction Model

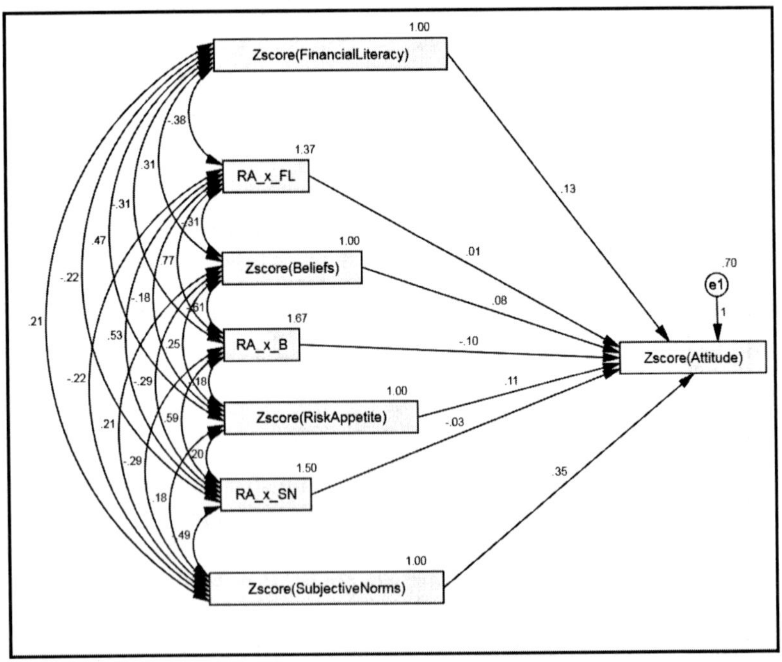

Figure 4.11: Unstandardized Estimates of Initial Moderation Interaction Model

interactive model with indicating the impact of moderating variable (risk appetite) on the relationship between financial literacy, beliefs, subjective norms and attitude.

Table 4.21: Regression Weights for All Variables

			Estimate	*S.E.*	*C.R.*	*P*	*Label*
ZAttitude	<---	ZBeliefs	.077	.038	2.036	.042	par_1
ZAttitude	<---	RA_x_B	-.100	.032	-3.076	.002	par_2
ZAttitude	<---	ZRiskAppetite	.109	.037	2.946	.003	par_3
ZAttitude	<---	ZFinancialLiteracy	.133	.039	3.424	***	par_25
ZAttitude	<---	ZSubjectiveNorms	.351	.036	9.782	***	par_26
ZAttitude	<---	RA_x_FL	.015	.034	.439	.661	par_27
ZAttitude	<---	RA_x_SN	-.029	.031	-.923	.356	par_28

The table 4-21 shows the regression estimates or beta values of interacting variables. The p-value shows that the interacting variable RA_x_FL & RA_x_SN are non-significant which means that risk appetite does not moderate the financial literacy-attitude relationship and subjective norm-attitude relationship. Thus, hypotheses H1 & H3 are not supported. The path showing the interaction relationship is therefore deleted from the model and model fit is assessed. The model with significant interacting variable and other predictor variables is shown in the figure4.12 and 4.13 below:

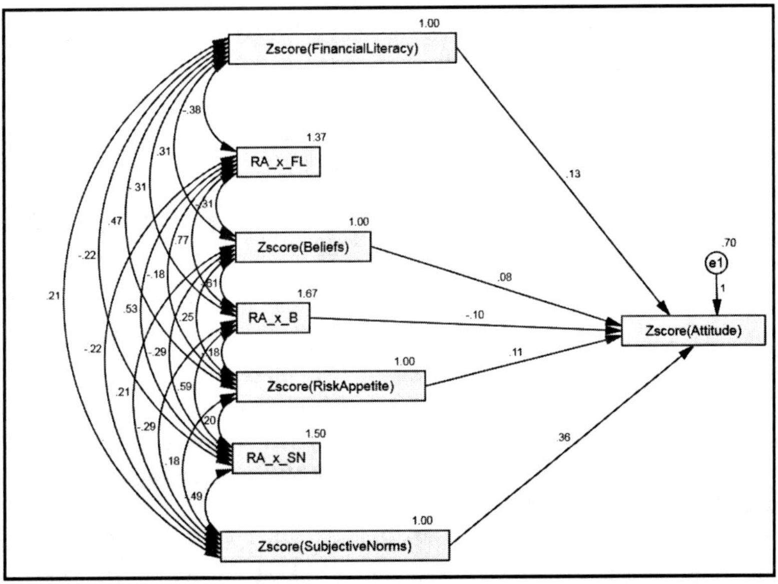

Figure 4.12: Unstandardized Estimates of Initial Interaction Model

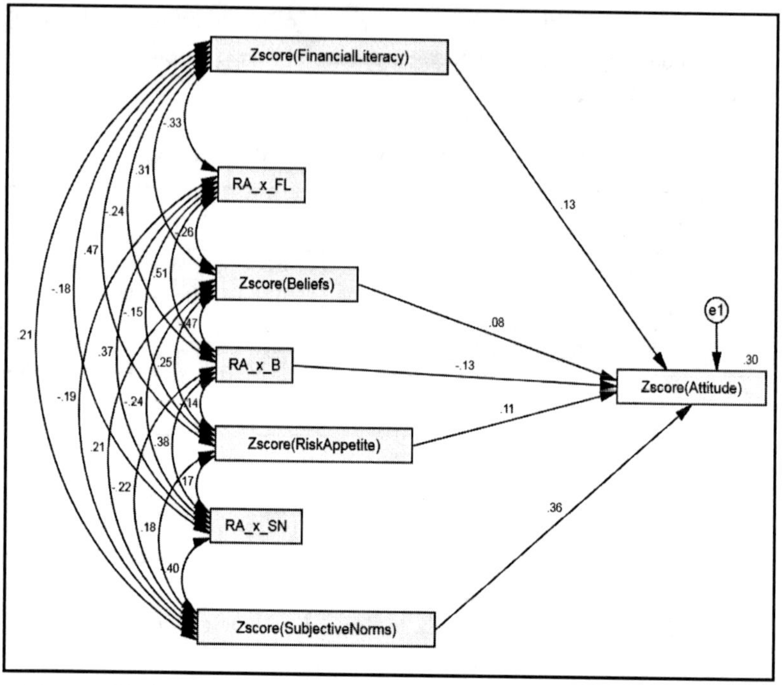

Figure 4.13: Standardized Estimates of Initial Moderation Interaction Model

Table 4.22: Regression Weights all Variables

			Estimate	*S.E.*	*C.R.*	*P*	*Label*
ZAttitude	<---	ZBeliefs	.078	.038	2.062	.039	par_1
ZAttitude	<---	RA_x_B	-.101	.029	-3.518	***	par_2
ZAttitude	<---	ZRiskAppetite	.111	.037	3.014	.003	par_3
ZAttitude	<---	ZFinancialLiteracy	.130	.038	3.424	***	par_25
ZAttitude	<---	ZSubjectiveNorms	.361	.034	10.669	***	par_26

The table 4.22 indicates that the effect of financial literacy, beliefs, risk appetite and subjective norms on attitude are significant ($R^2 = 0.30$, $p<0.05$) and the moderating effect of risk appetite on the relationship between beliefs and attitude is also significant. Thus, the hypothesis H2 is accepted. The model generates fit measures that indicates goodness-of fit of the model to the data (CMIN/DF= 0.459; RMSEA=0.054 with PCLOSE= 0.634; TLI =0.893; NFI=0.870; CFI=0.905; GFI=0.981); although relative indices do not meet the threshold limit but looking at the overall measures, the values are acceptable (see Appendix E for reference to fit measures).

The nature of the interacting relationship is plotted and presented in the figure 4.14 below. The graph was plotted using the statistical tools package available online.

Table 4.23: Unstandardized Regression Coefficients

5	**Variable names:**	
6	Independent variable:	Belief
7	Moderator:	Risk Appetite
8	Dependent variable	Attitude
9	**Unstandardized Regression Coefficients:**	
10	Independent variable:	0.080
11	Moderator:	0.110
12	Interaction:	-0.100
13		
14	Intercept / Constant:	3
15		

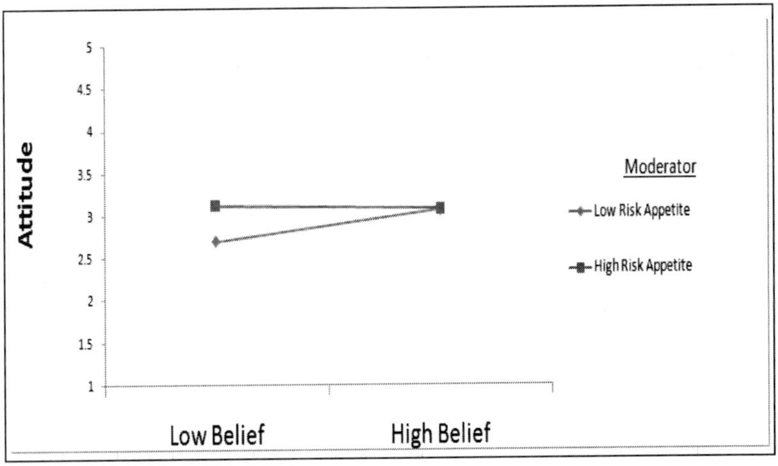

Figure 4.14: Nature of Interaction Relationship

The interaction plots in the figure 4.14 indicates that with positive belief towards investment attitude becomes favorable for people with low risk bearing capacity to exhibit investment behavior. Moreover, higher risk appetite of an investor deteriorates the positive relationship between beliefs and attitude. In other words, higher is the risk tolerance of a person; less significant is the impact of belief on attitude towards investment.

The results show the interaction effect of each of the predictors with risk appetite. In other words, the interaction moderation effect shows the influence of risk appetite on the relationship between financial literacy, beliefs, subjective norms and attitude. Risk Appetite does not seems to influence the relationship between financial literacy and attitude and subjective norms and attitude. On the other hand, risk appetite negatively influences the relationship between beliefs and attitude. Thus, the results support H3b which hypothesized that risk appetite moderates the relationship between beliefs and attitude but does not support H3a and H3c which hypothesize that risk appetite moderates the relationship between financial literacy and attitude and subjective norms and attitude.

4.2.9 Mediation

Mediation is a form interrelationship between variables that describes causation. It is normally used to provide a more precise explanation to the causal relationship between a predictor and outcome (Hair et al., 2010). The mediation effect can be examined through path analysis and SEM. Path analysis is a chain of regression equations that explores the direct and indirect paths between predictor and dependent (or outcome) variables. SEM is based on maximum likelihood analysis and is advantageous to use because it simplifies the complex mediation models involving multiple predictors, mediators and outcomes. Also, SEM analysis provides information whether the hypothesized model fits the data or not (Gunzler et al., 2013). Kim, Kaye & Wright (2001) highlighted that SEM analysis becomes necessary when the model includes latent variables that are represented by numerous indicator variables.

A mediator corresponds to a dominant variable through which an independent variable influences a dependent variable (Baron & Kenny, 1986). According to Baron and Kenny (1986), a variable is said to be a mediator if it fulfills the given conditions: (a) variation in scale of the independent variable considerably results in variations in the assumed mediator, (b) changes in the level of mediator considerably result in changes in the dependent variable and (c) while determining and evaluating the relationships between the independent variable and the mediator and for the relationship between the mediator and the dependent variable, the previous observed relationship between the independent and dependent variables is no longer relevent, with the significant exhibition of mediation arising when this path is zero. They added that, in order to test for mediation, the following three regression equations should also be assessed: first, regressing the mediator on the independent variable; second, regressing the dependent variable on the independent variable and third, regressing the dependent variable on both the independent variable and the mediator. Individual coefficients for each separate equation need to be evaluated and tested (Baron and Kenny 1986).

However, the Baron and Kenny or causal steps approach suffers from various limitations (Hayes, 2009). The researches asserts that the causal steps approach, cannot detect the indirect effect of predictor variable on dependent variable through an intervening or a mediator variable (Fritz & MacKinnon, 2007; MacKinnon, Lockwood, Hoffman, et al., 2002). Therefore, the mediation analysis should be based on contemporary approach familiarized by Preacher and Hayes (2004, 2008) and Hayes (2013). The most well-known approach to that tests the indirect effect and its significance is *Bootstrapping* (Bollen & Stine, 1990; Shrout & Bolger, 2002; Hayes, 2009). Bootstrapping is a non-parametric method that computes the indirect effect of the samples by replacing the samples during the analysis and generating the sampling distribution (Hayes, 2009; Kenny, 2014). The bootstrap procedure generates the size of the indirect effect, a confidence interval, a p-value and a standard error. A zero value is checked for in the lower and upper bound values of confidence interval. If zero is not there, then the researcher can be confident that the indirect effect is different from zero and hence, the relationship is intervened by the mediator variable. Also the p-value can be used to determine the significance of the indirect effect.

One of the objectives of the research is to determine the mediating impact of Attitude on the relationship between financial literacy, risk appetite, beliefs, subjective norms and investment behavior. To examine the mediating effect the following hypotheses were constructed:

H3a: Attitude will mediate the effect of Financial Literacy on Investment Behavior.

H3b: Attitude will mediate the effect of Risk Appetite on Investment Behavior.

H3c: Attitude will mediate the effect of Beliefs on Investment Behavior.

H3d: Attitude will mediate the effect of Subjective Norms on Investment Behavior.

In order to examine the mediating effect, the study used SEM analysis that determines the indirect effect (i.e. with mediator variable) of predictors on the outcome variable. SEM provides the estimates of direct effects, indirect effects and total effects. Gaskin (2014) enumerate three types of mediation viz; partial, full and no mediation. According to him, partial mediation takes place when both direct and indirect effects of the relationship between predictor and outcome are significant. Full or complete mediation takes place when the direct effect becomes insignificant when the mediator variable is included. The relationship has no mediation effect when the indirect effect is insignificant. The mediation analysis for the study has been carried out using Bootstrapping approach. Bootstrapping was performed in AMOS with 1000 iterations and at 95% confidence interval. The zero is considered to be the decision decisive factor as to whether indirect effect is significant or not. It follows that when zero (0) is outside the lower and upper bound values of Confidence Interval, the indirect effect is significant otherwise insignificant (Byrne, 2010; Hayes, 2009). The study involves various steps to establish the mediating relationship.

4.2.9.1 Direct Effects Model

To test the hypothesis H3a-H3d, a structural model with direct relationships between financial literacy, beliefs, risk appetite, subjective norms and investment behavior was assessed first. The regression weights, p-value are presented in the table 4.23.

Table 4.24: Standardized Estimates (Without Mediator)

Endogenous Variables		*Exogenous Variables*	*Estimate*	*P*
InvestmentBehavior	<—	FinancialLiteracy	0.069	0.079
InvestmentBehavior	<—	RiskAppetite	0.055	0.15
InvestmentBehavior	<—	Beliefs	0.091	0.011
InvestmentBehavior	<—	SubjectiveNorms	0.462	***

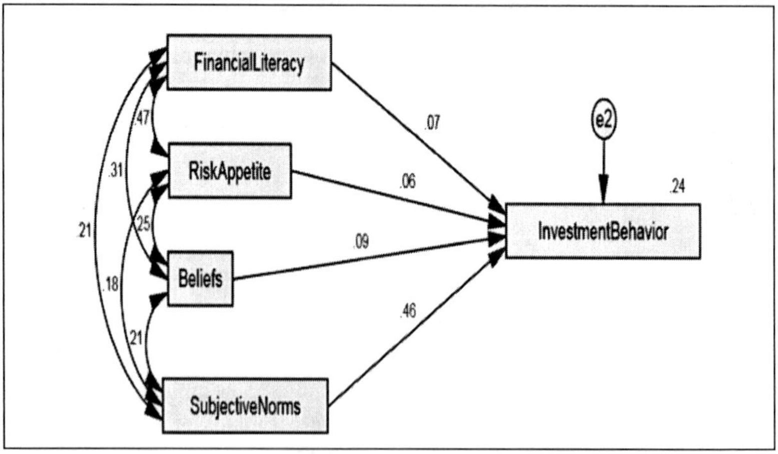

Figure 4.15: Mediation - Direct Effects Model

The above table 4.23 display the results of path between predictors and outcome variables without the influence of mediator variable. The direct path between financial literacy and investment behavior is weak and non significant (0.069, p-value = 0.079), the path between risk appetite and investment behavior is also weak and non-significant (0.055, p-value = 0.15). Furthermore, the path between beliefs and investment behavior is weak but significant at 95% confidence level i.e. p < 0.05 (0.091, p-value= 0.011). The path between subjective norms and investment behavior is strong and highly significant (0.462, p-value <0.01).

4.2.9.2 Indirect Effects Model

The next step is to assess the indirect effects of the relationship between predictors and the dependent variable when a mediator is added in the model. The regression weights, p-values are presented in the table 4.24.

Table 4.25: Standardized Path Estimates (with mediator variables)

Endogenous Variables		*Exogenous Variables*	*Estimate*	*P*
Attitude	<—	Financial Literacy	0.143	***
Attitude	<—	Risk Appetite	0.107	0.004
Attitude	<—	Beliefs	0.134	***
Attitude	<—	Subjective Norms	0.377	***
Investment Behavior	<—	Attitude	0.084	0.034
Investment Behavior	<—	Financial Literacy	0.081	0.041
Investment Behavior	<—	Risk Appetite	0.046	0.229
Investment Behavior	<—	Beliefs	0.08	0.027
Investment Behavior	<—	Subjective Norms	0.43	***

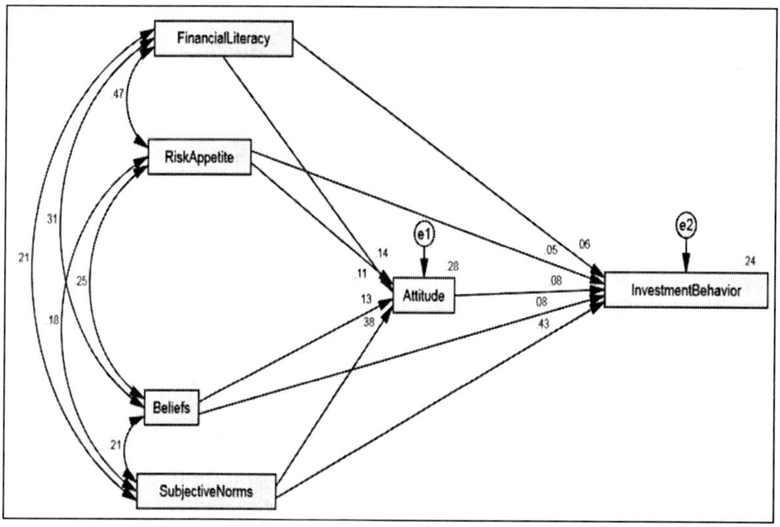

Figure 4.16: Mediation - Indirect Effects Model

The path coefficients between independent variables and mediator are strong and significant [0.143 (p-value < 0.01); 0.107 (p-value = 0.004); 0.134 (p-value < 0.01); 0.377 (p-value < 0.01)]. Moreover, the path coefficient between mediator and dependent variable is also significant (0.084, p-value 0.034). All the independent variables have positive influence on the mediator variable and mediator variable is also has positive influence on the dependent variable. However, in order to assess whether the mediating variable accounts for full mediation, partial mediation or no mediation, the direct effect of independent variables on dependent variables has been considered in the mediation model. The table 4.25 and 4.26 below shows the standardized direct and indirect effects associated with the variables in the study calculated by bootstrapping approach. The regression weights, standard error, confidence intervals (lower bound & upper bound) and their significance values are shown below:

Table 4.26: Results of Standardized Indirect Effect Test on Investment Behavior through Attitude

			Bootstrap Bias-Corrected 95% CI		
Constructs	*Std Indirect Effect*	*Standard Error*	*Lower Bound*	*Upper Bound*	*P-value*
Subjective Norms	0.32	0.018	0.003	0.062	0.061
Beliefs	0.011	0.007	0.001	0.026	0.042
Risk Appetite	0.009	0.006	0.001	0.022	0.037
Financial Literacy	0.012	0.008	0.003	0.03	0.029

Table 4.27: Results of Standardized Direct Effect Test on Investment Behavior through Attitude

			Bootstrap Bias-Corrected 95% CI		
Constructs	*Std Direct Effect*	*Standard Error*	*Lower Bound*	*Upper Bound*	*P-value*
Subjective Norms	0.43	0.048	0.327	0.517	0.003
Beliefs	0.08	0.037	0.009	0.158	0.031
Risk Appetite	0.046	0.046	0.043	0.135	0.28
Financial Literacy	0.081	0.047	0.181	0.012	0.08

The bootstrap estimates, as presented in table 4.24 & table 4.25 above, are based on 1000 bootstrap samples. The output shows significant indirect relationship between subjective norms, beliefs, risk appetite, financial literacy and investment behavior through attitude. As can be seen from the table above the mean indirect effect was in the range 0.009-0.32 and the 95% confidence interval lies between .003 and .262 for all variables. This means that since zero is outside the CI, the indirect effect is significant.

The findings of this study can be further explained by examining that if the relationship between independent variables and dependent variable which was significant in the direct effects model is no longer significant in the mediation model, though the indirect relationship is significant, full mediation is said to have taken effect (Hair et al., 2010). Further, if the relationship between independent variables and dependent variable which was significant in the direct effects model is still significant in the mediation model but is reduced and the indirect relationship is also significant, partial mediation is said to have taken effect (Hair et al., 2010). On the other hand, if the relationship between independent variables and dependent variable which was significant in the direct effects model is no longer significant through indirect effect, no mediation is said to have taken effect. There may be sometimes a case, where the relationship between independent and dependent variables is not significant in the direct effects model but still it is believed to have some indirect effect (Hair et al., 2010). This relationship is further assessed through mediating model and if indirect effect is found to be significant, the relationship is said to be fully mediated by the mediator variable.

Bearing in mind the above mentioned considerations, on comparing direct and indirect effects, the following results were obtained:

Table 4.28: Summary of Mediation Results

			Direct Effect Without Mediator	***Indirect Effect With Mediator***	***Direct Effect With Mediator***	
DV		***IV***	***Standardized Estimates (Significance value)***	***Standardized Estimates (Significance value)***	***Standardized Estimates (Significance value)***	***Mediation***
Investment Behavior	<---	Financial Literacy	0.069 (*0.079*)	0.012 (*0.029*)	0.058 (*0.08*)	Full Mediation
Investment Behavior	<---	Risk Appetite	0.055 (*0.15*)	0.009 (*0.037*)	0.046 (*0.229*)	Full Mediation
Investment Behavior	<---	Beliefs	0.091 (*0.011*)	0.011 (*0.042*)	0.08 (*0.031*)	Partial Mediation
Investment Behavior	<---	Subjective Norms	0.462 (***)	0.32 (*0.061*)	0.43 (***)	No Mediation

4.2.9.3 Mediation Results

The table 4.26 above, shows the direct and indirect effects with and without mediator. For the path Financial Literacy → Attitude → Investment Behavior the direct effect without mediator is small and insignificant (0.069, p-value= 0.079) but the indirect effect though small is significant (0.012, p-value = 0.029) whereas the direct effect is further reduced and remains insignificant. Thus, this shows that attitude full mediates the path between financial literacy and investment behavior. The p-value of the direct path associated with the path Risk Appetite à Attitude à Investment Behavior is > 0.05 (0.15) and regression coefficient is small (0.055), the indirect effect on the other hand is significant but small (0.009, p-value=(0.037) whereas the direct effect in the mediation model remains insignificant (0.229). Thus, Attitude fully mediates the relationship between risk appetite and investment behaviour. For the path Beliefs → Attitude → Investment Behavior, the p-value associated with indirect effect is < 0.05 (0.042) and the p-value associated with direct effect is also < 0.05 (0.031) and direct effect without mediation being significant (0.011). Therefore, this is an evidence of 'Partial Mediation'. In other words, Attitude partially mediates the path between Beliefs and Investment Behavior. Similarly, the p-value associated with indirect path Subjective Norm → Attitude → Investment Behavior is > 0.05 (0.061). Thus this shows that the relationship between subjective norm and investment behavior is not interceded by attitude and hence, no mediation.

The results show that the effect of predictor variables was interceded by attitude, with financial literacy and risk appetite being mediated fully, belief being mediated partially and subjective norms being not mediated at all. Subjective Norms may therefore, have direct positive relationship with Investment behavior. The results support H4a-c, which hypothesized that Attitude would mediate the effects of Financial Literacy, Risk Appetite and Beliefs on Investment Behavior but does not support H4d which hypothesized that Attitude mediates the effect of Subjective Norms on Investment Behavior. The table 4.27 summarizes the results of our hypothesis testing conducted in this part of the analysis.

Table 4.29: Summary of Hypothesis Testing

No.	*Hypothesis*	*Supported?*
H1a	Financial Literacy has significant influence on investor's attitude.	**Yes**
H1b	Risk Appetite has significant influence on investor's attitude.	Yes
H1c	Beliefs have significant influence on investor's attitude.	Yes
H1d	Subjective Norms have significant influence on investor's attitude.	Yes
H2	Investor's Attitude has significant influence on investor's Investment Behavior.	Yes
H3a	Risk Appetite moderates the relationship between Financial Literacy and Attitude towards investment.	No
H3b	Risk Appetite moderates the relationship between Beliefs and Attitude towards investment.	Yes
H3c	Risk Appetite moderates the relationship between Subjective. Norms and Attitude towards investment.	No

(Contd...)

H4a	Attitude mediates the effect of Financial Literacy on Investment Behavior.	Yes
H4b	Attitude mediates the effect of Risk Appetite on Investment Behavior.	Yes
H4c	Attitude mediates the effect of Beliefs on Investment Behavior.	Yes
H4d	Attitude mediates the effect of Subjective Norms on Investment Behavior.	No

4.3 Summary

The chapter investigates the reliability of the instrument by assessing the Cronbach Alpha coefficient value for each variable in the study viz. financial literacy, risk appetite, beliefs, subjective norms, and attitude and investment behavior. The alpha coefficient for all the variables was sufficiently high and acceptable (above 0.9) which confirms that the designed questionnaire is valid. The analysis corresponding to the descriptive statistics of demographic variables reveals that the significant proportion of respondents in the above survey (about 76.8%) are male. A large number of investors are in the age group 41-50 years (42.5%), 31-40 years (28.2%), 20-30 years (12%). It was also observed that, majority of the investors are either graduate (48%) or post-graduate (27%). The occupational characteristics revealed that the majority of investors in the study were either a private company employee (40.6%) or self-employed (26.1%). Also, it was noticed that majority of the investors being offered Wealth Management Services lie in the income group 30,00,001-40,00,000 (30.7%) and 20,00,000-30,00,000 (21%).

In addition, the study examined the wealth management services' preference of the investors and found that the investment inclinations are dynamic due to the introduction of new investment avenues and the personal beliefs of the investors. The results show that private equity followed by loan/credit services is the most preferred investment services among the HNI investors. Portfolio Management Services is the third preferred choice followed by investment in real estate. Mutual Funds occupy the fifth position. The sixth position is occupied by insurance followed by fixed income products. The eighth and ninth position is occupied by advisory services and estate planning services respectively.

Further, in order to assess the relationship between predictors and investment behavior, which is the central part of this research study, was analyzed using SEM with AMOS. In the context of the study, Principle Axis Factoring, an important method in the Exploratory Factor Analysis process has been used to explore the factors influencing Wealth Management Behavior and their correlations in the data gathered. The 68 items scale was then reduced to 61 items and in the extraction process, six factors with Eigen values higher than 1.0 collectively exhibiting 67.15 per cent of variance was retained. The six factors identified were Financial Literacy, Risk Appetite, Beliefs, Subjective Norms, Attitude and Investment behavior.

Before measuring the model fit, it was important to examine the reliability and validity of the model. A reliability analysis was done to check the internal consistency of the variables, whereas validity refers to the accuracy of the variables. Cronbach's Alpha and Squared Multiple Correlation (SMC) was used in the study to measure the Construct Reliability. SMC refers to the correlation between a single measured variable and the underlying variable. It is the square of standardized factor loading. Some of the indicators were deleted exhibiting small values of SMC to improve the model fit. The validity of the model has also been measured using Stats tool package where the correlations and standardized regression weights were input into the excel sheet and as a result, no validity concerns were found.

Further, the causal relationship between variables (Latent and Observed) was then determined using SEM. Two steps of SEM data analyses has been presented and discussed along the results of testing hypothesis. The 1st step of the SEM data analysis includes investigating the model fitness of the measurement model. The model fit statistics generated by the model were found to be within the acceptable range indicating that the model fits the data. (CMIN/df= 1.983; CFI= 0.916; NFI= 0.946; TLI= 0.917; GFI=0.961; RMSEA=0.047; PCLOSE= 0.927).

The 2nd step in the SEM data analyses includes testing the proposed research model which was adapted from Theory of Reasoned Action proposed by Ajzein and Fishbein and presents the influence of five (5) exogenous variables (Financial Literacy, Risk Appetite, Beliefs and Subjective Norms) on investors Attitude (endogenous variable) and the influence of Attitude on Investment Behavior (endogenous variable). The model was tested with modifications and a good model fit was obtained. This model in this study is called as 'Wealth Management Behavior Model'.

The fit indices generated by the model were CMIN/DF= 3.387; RMSEA=0.054 with PCLOSE= 0.634; TLI =0.893; NFI=0.870; CFI=0.905; GFI=0.981. Two groups of hypotheses were tested. Group 1 of hypothesis includes testing the relationship between exogenous variables (Financial Literacy, Risk Appetite, Beliefs and Subjective Norms) on investors Attitude (endogenous variable) and group 2 includes testing the hypotheses of influence of Attitude on Investment Behavior (endogenous variable). The hypotheses, H1a-H1d were accepted. It indicated that Financial Literacy (H1a), Risk Appetite (H1b), Beliefs (H1c) and Subjective Norms (H1d) significantly influence investor's attitude. In addition, the hypothesis H2 was also accepted and it indicated that investor's attitude to invest influences investor's investment behavior. Moreover, the predictors (Financial Literacy, Risk Appetite, Beliefs, and Subjective Norms) account for 25.5% variance in Attitude and Attitude accounts for 12.3% variance in Investment Behavior.

A further analysis on the model was performed to find out the impact of interaction between independent variables on investors' attitude which in turn influence investment behavior. The model shows causal relationships between variables and represents direct effects, moderating effects, mediating effects and reciprocal effects. Moderation effect or interaction is said to take place between a predictor variable and an outcome when a third variable (moderating variable) interferes and changes the relationship between predictor and dependent variable. The study evaluates the moderating effect of risk appetite on the relationship between financial literacy, beliefs, subjective norms and attitude. Introducing an interaction term has showed moderation effect. Interaction Moderation was chosen because so far, the interaction between other financial literacy, beliefs, subjective norms and risk appetite has rarely been tested. Interaction moderation tests a group of hypotheses, H3a-H3c, which includes testing the impact of interacting moderator on the relationship between predictors and attitude. The moderation hypothesis was tested by analyzing the impact of interaction term on the relationship between predictors (financial literacy, beliefs and subjective norms) and attitude. After testing the paths that were not significant have been removed from the model and model fit was assessed. The p-value showed that the interacting variable RA_x_FL & RA_x_SN are non-significant which means that risk appetite does not moderate the financial literacy-attitude relationship and subjective norm-attitude relationship. Thus, hypotheses H3a & H3c were rejected which means risk appetite does not influence the relationship between financial literacy and attitude and subjective norms and attitude. But the interaction was found to have a significant influence on the relationship between beliefs and attitude. Thus, the hypothesis H3b was accepted which indicated that risk appetite moderates the relationship between beliefs and attitude.

Furthermore, one of the objectives of the research is to determine the mediating effect of Attitude on the relationship between financial literacy, risk appetite, beliefs, subjective norms and investment behavior. The mediation analysis for the study has been carried out using Bootstrapping approach. Bootstrapping was performed in AMOS with 1000 iterations and at 95% confidence interval. The zero is considered to be the decision decisive factor as to whether indirect effect is significant or not. It follows that when zero (0) is outside the lower and upper bound values of Confidence Interval, the indirect effect is significant otherwise insignificant. To test mediation, a group of hypothesis H4a – H4d was proposed which includes examining the effect of attitude on the relationship between financial literacy, risk appetite, beliefs, subjective norms and investment behavior. On testing the direct and indirect effects of the Wealth Management behavior Model, the hypotheses H4a-H4c were accepted. It indicated that Financial Literacy (H4a) & Risk Appetite (H4b) were fully mediated by attitude. Beliefs (H4c) were partially mediated by attitude. The hypothesis H4d was rejected which means Subjective Norms (H4d) were not mediated by attitude at all.

Chapter - 5

Findings & Discussions

This chapter provides discussions on the results obtained from data analysis on the conceptual model proposed. The model has been evolved for wealth management behavior on the basis of evidence from the literature review. The model involves variables which are the major influencers of investment behavior and investor's attitude. The results of the relevant hypotheses testing have been discussed and their consistency with the literature has also been reviewed in this chapter.

5.1 Preliminary Findings

- ***Investment Behavior changes with the gender of investor:*** The significant proportion of respondents in the survey (about 76.8%) is male. This shows the investing habits of men and women. It is interesting to note that men are more inclined towards investing and trading than women. Men are found to be more confident about investing whereas; women are found to be more goal-focused and less interested in trading. Women consider safety of their investment first rather than return and therefore, they associate money with security, independence and quality of their life and their family's lives and thus are least concern about investment. On the other hand, men thrive for short-term returns on their portfolios and always look for avenues of investment. The results of the study are consistent with the findings of Boston Consulting Group (2010) and Jasen (2015), where the researcher examined that women are more inclined to focus on long-term horizon planning whereas; men are inclined towards short-term returns from their portfolio.
- ***Investment Behavior changes with the age of investor:*** A significant number of investors are in the age group 41-50 years

(42.5%), 31-40 years (28.2%), 20-30 years (12%). It is noted here that more people have started investing at the young age because of their concern towards dynamic economic conditions in place along with the availability of various sources of investment education. These young investors believe that saving alone in a bank is not sufficient to be at par with the increasing standard of living and therefore, they need to secure their future by investing in various other potential avenues. On the other hand, the number of older investors in the age group 51-60 years (9.8%) and 61 and above (6.9%) are already leading a stable lifestyle and are less inclined towards exploring new investment options and have comparatively less risk-appetite. The findings were consistent with the study of Leong (2015), who observed the differences in their investment behavior with the age of the investor. The study is analogous to the findings of Bigda (2013) and Chin (2014), who claims that since young investors have more time to retirement, they are more willing to take risk and therefore invest in different avenues. On the other hand, some other researchers (Grable and Lytton, 1999; Wang and Hanna, 1997) found that older investors have more tolerance of risk and therefore are more inclined to undertake investment.

- ***Change in the investment behavior with the level of financial literacy***: The study classifies investors into different education levels; undergraduate, graduate and postgraduate. It has been observed that, majority of the investors are either graduate (48%) or post-graduate (27%) and the increase in education level of an individual significantly influences his investment behavior. Education brings more awareness and higher acumen of the economic factors, which steers them to adopt sophisticated and complex investment options. Moreover, an educated individual will be able to trade-off between cost-benefit while analyzing various investment options. These results are similar to the findings of Hira, 2009 and Bongini and Colombo, 2014 that in the past few years' education has attained a lot of consideration in many different applications and broader scope in different industries especially the government companies, consumer industry, banking institutions, marketing and advertising industry. The findings are consistent with the results of Chen and Volpe, 1998 as individuals with higher education tend to make more appropriate judgment and often make more prudent investment decisions for their saving and more wisely utilize the credit available to them.

- ***Change in the investment behavior with the occupations of the investors***: The study also tries to build an association between occupation and investment behavior. The occupation of investors in the study is classified into private company employee, self-employed, government employee and others (professionals like lawyers, doctors, architectures etc.). The majority of investors in this study were either a private company employee (40.6%) or self-employed (26.1%). Different occupation holders have different objectives in mind while taking investment decisions.
- ***Change in the investment behavior with the level of income and earning***: With the increasing income level in the private sector, the employees in private sector have more wealth at their disposal to invest. The increasing wealth makes them inclined towards exploring investment options and thus broadens their financial goals. The results of the study are in line with the findings of Roszkowski et al. (2005) as it was observed that occupational status is also affecting the level of investment, which is also influenced by risk taking ability. According to them, people with higher-ranking occupational status are more risk seeker as compare to low ranking occupational status. It was also found in the research that Wealth Management services are offered to people whose account deposits are above a certain defined limit by the banks or financial institutions and which varies from one bank to another. However, the amount of deposits depends on the income level of an individual. Therefore, the study classifies the respondents on the basis of their income. It is apparent from the above table that majority of the investors being offered Wealth Management Services lie in the income group 30,00,001-40,00,000 (30.7%) and 20,00,000-30,00,000 (21%). The results are similar to the study conducted by Barberis and Thaler (2003) where they observed that higher income creates the ability of tolerating the loses and hence, people with high income prefer taking higher risk in anticipation of higher returns Income level of investor is also affects its behavior toward investment. Finding were inline with the study conducted by Barber and Odean (2001) where it was found that person with greater wealth assumes greater risk.
- ***Investor's preferences and diversification of investment:*** The turbulent economic environment has enabled investors to diversify their risk by not putting all their eggs in one basket rather explore more avenues to park their funds. The results of investor's

preference towards wealth management services shows that private equity followed by loan/credit services are the most preferred investment services among the HNI investors. Portfolio Management Services is the third preferred choice followed by investment in real estate. Mutual Funds occupy the fifth position because some investors find mutual funds a non-reliable avenue for investment (Dr. Rajasekar, 2013) and do not have enough knowledge and information about the working of Mutual Funds . The sixth position is occupied by insurance followed by fixed income products. Insurance products are never sought-after products in the eyes of the investors. They are often pushed-in by the insurance agents and investors feel distrust towards the intentions of insurance companies (Uma & Uma, 2015). The eight and ninth position is occupied by advisory services and estate planning services respectively. Hung et al. (2008) in their report outlined that investors are confused between the roles of brokers-dealers and investment advisors and therefore, they have no inclination to seek advisory services. Furthermore, the factor that contributed to the least preference for estate planning services is lack of knowledge about estate planning (Ismail et al., 2013).

- ***Factors directly influencing the Investment behavior***: In the context of the study, Principle Axis Factoring, a key method in the Exploratory Factor Analysis process was used to explore the factors influencing Wealth Management Behavior and their correlations in the data obtained. The 68 items scale was then reduced to 61 items and in the extraction process, six factors with Eigen values greater than 1.0 collectively explaining 67.15 per cent of variance was retained. The six factors identified were Financial Literacy, Risk Appetite, Beliefs, Subjective Norms, Attitude and Investment Behavior.

5.2 Relationship Between Variables

The causal relationship between variables was determined using SEM. Two steps of SEM data analyses have been presented and the relevant hypotheses have been tested.

- The 1st step of the SEM data analysis includes investigating the model fitness of the measurement model. The model fit statistics generated by the model were found to be within the acceptable range indicating that the model fits the data (CMIN/df= 1.983; CFI= 0.916; NFI= 0.946; TLI= 0.917; GFI=0.961; RMSEA=0.047;

PCLOSE= 0.927). This is a Measurement Model and is represented by Confirmatory factor Analysis (CFA) which is concerned only with the extent of relationship between observed variables and their latent constructs. It assumes that the observed variables will fully load on their constructs and will have zero loadings on the other factors (Byrne, 2010).

- In the 2nd step of SEM analysis, the proposed Wealth Management Behaviour model has been tested for its fitness. The model was adapted from the Theory of Reasoned Action proposed by Ajzen and Fishbein (1980) and presents the influence of five (5) exogenous variables (Financial Literacy, Risk Appetite, Beliefs and Subjective Norms) on investors Attitude (endogenous variable) and the influence of Attitude on Investment Behavior (endogenous variable). The hypotheses relevant to the model has been tested and presented. The model has been tested by examining the influence of financial literacy, beliefs, risk appetite and subjective norms on investor's attitude and investment behavior without considering the impact of demographics on these variables.
- The results of the model testing and various issues related to the variable have been presented in the table below:

Table 5.1: Results of Model Testing

Variable	*Predictors*	*Main Issues for Wealth Managers*	*Remarks*
Financial Literacy	FL 1 FL 2	In order to boost financial literacy among investors, the wealth managers should give emphasis on effective educational programmes and spread the finance related information and awareness to the existing as well as potential investors.	Identified as a key variable in influencing investor's attitude.
Risk Appetite	R5 R6 R10	The risk appetite of every individual investor is unique. It is important for an investor to consider its appropriate risk level based on his individual financial goals. Moreover, the financial advisors or wealth managers can also help an investor in assessing his risk appetite by providing a risk assessment framework. The mangers can examine the risk	Identified as a key variable in influencing investor's attitude.

(*Contd...*)

		appetite by using structured set of questionnaires, interviews and thus evaluating their financial needs and desires which in turn will help him in determining investor's attitude.	
Subjective Norms	SN1 SN2 SN3 SN4 SN5 SN6 SN7 SN8 SN9 SN10	Behavior of an individual to invest or not to invest is based on the information provided by friends, peers, colleagues, family etc. The piece of information that an investor receives from any of these group member may not be suitable to his circumstances. The role of financial advisors is to evaluate such information and organize financial awareness campaigns so that strong normative information is imparted in the society.	Identified as a key variable in influencing investor's attitude.
Beliefs	B1 B2 B3 B4 B6 B7 B8 B9 B10 B11 B12	Beliefs are the ideas that are transformed to opinions and finally became beliefs. Beliefs are the perceptions of an individual that impede him from performing a particular action. The financial advisors or wealth managers can help an individual in overcoming these limiting beliefs by assessing their beliefs, giving them counter references and providing them sufficient evidence and experience to transform their limiting belief into positive beliefs.	Identified as a key variable in influencing investor's attitude.
Attitude	A1 A2 A3 A4 A5 A6 A7 A8 A9 A10 A11 A12 A13 A14 A15	Keeping in mind the selective nature of today's investors, the financial advisors or wealth managers have to perform their role of being a moderator who transforms an unfavorable investor's attitude to a favorable one. Educating the investor is one way. Apart from education and creating awareness, it is imperative for a manager to build confidence in the client by giving him efficient and valuable services.	Identified as a key variable in influencing investor's behavior.

5.2.1 Financial Literacy

- On analyzing the relationship between variables it was found that Financial Literacy influence Attitude but the strength of the relationship is small (0.145). Financial Literacy is defined as a set of skills and knowledge that enables an individual to take informed judgments (Lodhi, 2014; Lusardi & Mitchell 2014; Baker et al, 2014; Bernheim et al., 2011; Cole and Shastry, 2009).
- The results of the study are consistent with the findings of Maditinos et al., 2007. He examined in his research that the level of financial literacy has a significant relation with the attitude towards asking their investment. Investors with higher knowledge of financial matters generally adopt a different approach while investment as compared to investors with investors with less financial literacy.
- In a similar study conducted by Al-Tamimi and Kalli, 2009; Lusardi and Mitchell, 2007; Mirshekary and Saudagaran, 2005, it was found that financial literacy is associated with the individual's ability of efficiently saving money and making sound investment decisions. If a person with low financial knowledge will make a mistake he will have to pay a significant price for his mistake.
- These researchers examined how the investors use the annual reports, financial statements and other sources of information of different organizations to make their investment decisions which transformed their attitude towards investment. It was identified that investors with high financial literacy level use their knowledge when developing their own portfolio and which would be influenced by behavioral factors (Muller and Weber, 2010 and Doran et al, 2010).
- This study is contrary to the findings of Perry, 2008; Braunstein and Welch, 2002; Gathergood, 2012; Bodnaruk and Simonov, 2012; who are of the view that knowledge of finance does not influence on the quality of investment decisions.
- The analysis also identified the main issues associated with financial literacy that is lack of awareness among investors. So, in order to boost financial literacy among investors, the wealth managers should give emphasis on effective educational programmes and spread the finance related information and awareness to the existing as well as potential investors.

5.2.2 Risk Appetite

- Additionally, the analysis also examined the positive relation between risk appetite and investor's attitude though the strength of the relationship is small. Risk appetite refers to the ability and willingness of an individual to undertake risk (Walia and Dr. Kiran, 2009; Hui, Zheng and Wang, 2013; Gai and Vause, 2006; Kim, Kaye and Wright, 2001; Wang and Jing, 2009). The results are aligned with the findings of Bennet and Selvam, 2011; Alanko, 2009; Halko and Kaustia 2009; Sehgal, Sood and Rajput, 2009; Froot and O'Connell, 2003; Baker and Jeffrey, 2006; Fisher and Meir, 2000 and Eichengreen and Mody,1998 who opined that one of the important factors influencing investor's attitude is their tolerance for risk.
- Prevailing sentiments in the financial markets predominantly drives the economy and influences the stock prices in the market, which in turn have the significant influence on the investor's behavior and attitude. Wang and Jing, 2009 also examined that risk aversion is a combination of multiple economic and psychological theories, which indicates the investor's attitude in the situation of uncertainty. Risk aversion is the essential element of the investor's behavior towards risky investments. Tversky and Kahneman (1974) reveal that predicting and forecasting under uncertainty do not usually follow probability rules.
- The prospect theory by Tversky and Kahneman claims that people tend to be risk averse in the "profitable zone" and risk seeking in the "losing zone" (Tversky and Kahneman 1992). Therefore, deviating from the standpoint of standard finance, behavioral finance also examines subjective factors, where observed risks include both emotional and perceptional aspects. Two main attitudes toward risk are risk aversion and risk seeking, both could manifest in one individual under different circumstances (Olsen 2007, Olsen 2008). It was proved that one of the important factors influencing investing attitude is investors' tolerance for risk (Bennet and Selvam, 2011).
- The main issue associated with risk appetite examined in the study was that since the risk appetite of every individual investor is unique, it is important for an investor to consider its appropriate risk level based on his individual financial goals. Moreover, the financial advisors or wealth managers can help an investor in assessing his risk appetite by providing a risk assessment

framework. The mangers can examine the risk appetite by using structured set of questionnaires, interviews and thus evaluating their financial needs and desires which in turn will help him in determining investor's attitude.

5.2.3 Subjective Norms

- The positive relationship between subjective norms and attitude is also established in the study. Subjective norms are related to the influence of society such as friends, relatives, peers and other influential members on the behavioral intention of the decision-maker. In case of investment decision-making two major influences are the influence of close friends or relatives and the influence of the advisors who recommend various policies to the decision-maker.
- According to the Theory of Reasoned Action, an individual investor will most likely have an intention to perform a certain behavior if a person who is important to him thinks that he should perform such behavior. The findings of the study are in line with the results of Venkatesh and Davis, 2000; Sharma and Gupta, 2011; Croy, Paul, & Craig, 2010; Hussein, Hassan and Al-Anood, 2009; Hong, Kubik & Stein, 2010 who pointed out that even though an individual has no inclination towards a particular behavior, he may still conduct such behavior under the social influence and pressure.
- The investors with less knowledge about the financial system rely extensively on the suggestions and opinion of close relatives, colleagues, friends, peers and family and take their advice before making any investment related decisions. Further, Septyanto and Adhikara, 2014; Listyarti and Suryani, 2014; Gain et al., 2012 also found out that subjective norms positively influence investment intentions. They also observed that financial information particularly accounting information and intentions of investors has a positive significant effect on investment decisions.
- The main issue identified with respect to subjective norms is that the behavior of an individual to invest or not to invest is based on the information provided by friends, peers, colleagues, family etc. The piece of information that an investor receives from any of these group member may not be suitable to his circumstances. The role of financial advisors is to evaluate such information and organize financial awareness campaigns so that strong normative information is imparted in the society. Also, the financial advisor

may assess that information and guide the investor properly as to how to use the information in his best interest.

5.2.4 Beliefs

- Concurrently, financial beliefs of an individual are also assessed to have a positive relationship with investor's attitude. Beliefs are the ideologies of an individual which turns into opinion after some point of time and eventually becomes beliefs supported by substantial evidence. Morris and Shin, 2002 reported that Belief is an important determining element of the average public opinion about the prevailing financial situation in an economy.
- In another similar study, Karpoff, 1986;Varian, 1985 observed that the primitive, traditional and fundamental beliefs of individuals influences their interpretation of the information which in turn effects their perspectives and any changes in their belief subsequently leads to a significant change in their trading patterns. The studies are consistent with the results of Tim, Ken and Gene, 1996; Dolan et al., 2012 who reviewed the determinants that play a significant role in changing the financial attitude of an individual and found beliefs to be positively influencing the individual's attitude.
- On the other hand, Agle and Buren, 1999 observed that conventional and religious beliefs had a very minute connection with individual's attitude and therefore opined that it is extremely important to explore more on this front to understand the influence of personal belief on the investor's attitude and examine the behavior of an investor considering belief as the ground element.
- The main issue identifies in the context of beliefs is that since beliefs are the perceptions of an individual that impede him from performing a particular action. The financial advisors or wealth managers can help an individual in overcoming these limiting beliefs by assessing their beliefs, giving them counter references and providing them sufficient evidence and experience to transform their limiting belief into positive beliefs.

5.2.5 Attitude

- Attitude is also identified as an important influence of Investment Behaviour. It is observed to be a driving element of the individual's exhibited behavior. In simple words, attitude predicts behavior. As described in the theory of reasoned action, attitude is considered as a significant factor influencing the behavior of an individual. Attitude is described as a psychological and cognitive tendency, which is exhibited by assessing any particular element with some degree of favour or disfavour (Eagly and Chaiken, 1993).

- Attitude of an investor towards risk taking involved in an investment plays an important role not only affects his investment behavior but also influences the economic growth and development (Kisaka and Mwewa, 2014). A lot of research has been conducted in this field to claim that an attitude has a considerable influence on the intention and behavior of an individual (Michael, 2011; Ramayah and Suki, 2006; Teo and Pok, 2003; Shih and Fang, 2004; Mathieson 1991).
- The main issue associated with Attitude is that keeping in mind the selective nature of today's investors, the financial advisors or wealth managers have to perform their role of being a moderator who transforms an unfavourable investor's attitude to a favourable one. Educating the investor is one way. Apart from education and creating awareness, it is imperative for a manager to build confidence in the client by giving him efficient and valuable services. Service is the only differentiator that guides a client to choose amongst varied advisors/managers.
- So if an investor wants to grab the opportunity, he will have to focus on providing efficient and valuable service to the clients. The service is said to be valuable in the eyes of the client if a manager is able to actively take interest in the financial goals of the clients and integrates his personal goals with the overall financial goals of the client. Being flexible towards the needs of the investors and providing customized services is another key to success that helps in building investor's confidence and transforms investor's attitude.
- In nutshell, it can be said that the determinants significantly explain Investment Behavior though their capability in explaining the variance of investment behavior is not much strong. The most important determinant influencing attitude is found to be subjective norm with stronger standardized regression weight. The determinants, in total, account for 25.5% of the variance in Attitude and Attitude account for only 12.3% of the variance in Investment Behavior. The final Wealth Management Behavior Model expressing the relationship the variables under study is as follows:

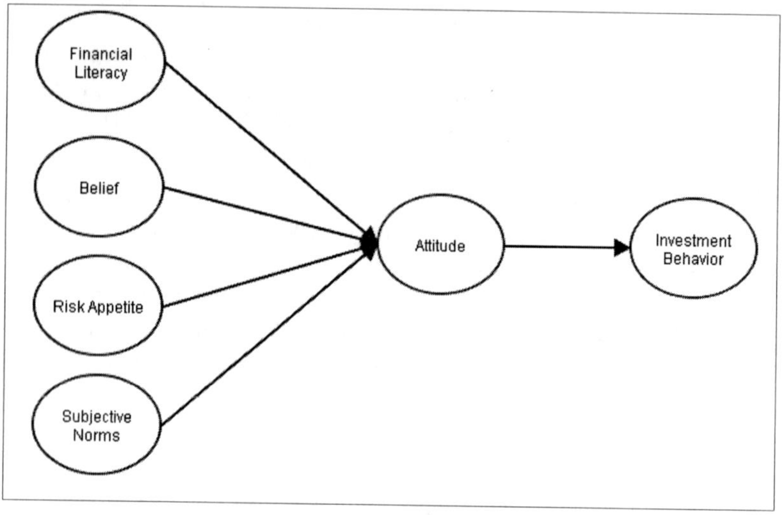

Figure 5.1: Wealth Management Behavior Model

- A further analysis on the model has been performed to find out the impact of interaction between independent variables on investors' attitude which in turn influence behavior. Moderation effect or interaction is said to take place between a predictor variable and an outcome when a third variable (moderating variable) interferes and changes the relationship between predictor and dependent variable (Baron and Kenny, 1986). A moderator variable is normally considered in the relationship when there is enough evidence that the moderator may enhance or reduce the nature of relationship between the predictor and outcome variable (Lindley and Walker, 1993).

5.3 Moderating Role of Risk Appetite

- The dynamic economic environment places much prominence on estimating the risk appetite of individuals across different fields. Understanding the importance of risk appetite on investor's attitude is increasing because of the prevalent situations. Risk appetite not only impacts investor's attitude but also other components of attitude which in turn influence overall attitude of an investor. Influence of risk on attitude has various implications for economic decisions made across the entire economy.
- The interaction term i.e. the product of predictor variable (independent and moderator variable) are created in SPSS using

their standardized values. The following model has been tested to analyze the interaction between predictors and risk appetite and their influence on attitude:

- The results revealed that the interacting variable RA_x_FL & RA_x_SN were non-significant which means that risk appetite does not moderate the financial literacy-attitude relationship and subjective norm-attitude relationship. The results are contrary to the findings of Wang and Jing, 2009 ; Edmiston and Gillett-Fisher 2006 ; Siegal and Hoban, 1982 who derived insight to the relationship between the financial literacy and taking risk while making investment decisions. These studies examined that financial knowledge and personality of an individual has positive influence on the risk taking behavior and investment decision-making.
- On the other hand, a significant moderating interaction effect was found between beliefs and risk appetite. In a similar study conducted by Filbeck, Hatfield and Horvath (2005), determined the risk tolerance of an individual relates to the individual's personal traits and beliefs. Several other studies are also consistent with the results and investigate the relationship between individual's personal characteristics, beliefs and the degree of risk he can bear.
- The studies concluded that the level of risk tolerance in the individual are directly associated with the perception, thinking,

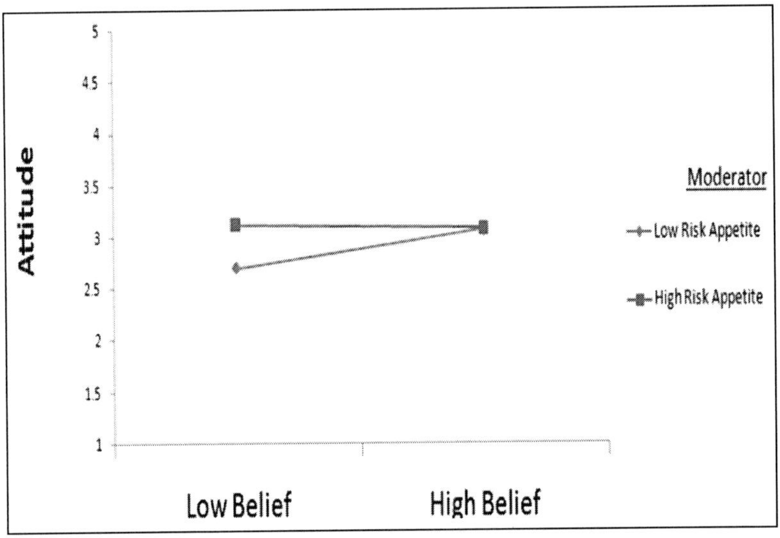

Figure 5.2: Nature of Interaction Relationship

intuition and individual's preferences. Individuals who have higher inclination to their feeling have less risk tolerance and those who are more inclined to listen their minds have high risk-tolerance (Lyons, 2004; Grable and Lytton, 1998; Riley and Chow, 1992; Lusardi and Mitchell, 2011).

- The nature of the interacting relationship between beliefs and risk appetite is plotted and presented in the figure 5.2 above:
- The interaction effect indicates that with positive belief towards investment, attitude becomes favorable for people with low risk bearing capacity to exhibit investment behavior. Moreover, higher risk appetite of an investor deteriorates the positive relationship between beliefs and attitude. In other words, higher is the risk tolerance of a person; less significant is the impact of belief on attitude towards investment. Finally the interacting model that evolved, exhibiting relationship between predictors and outcome shown below:

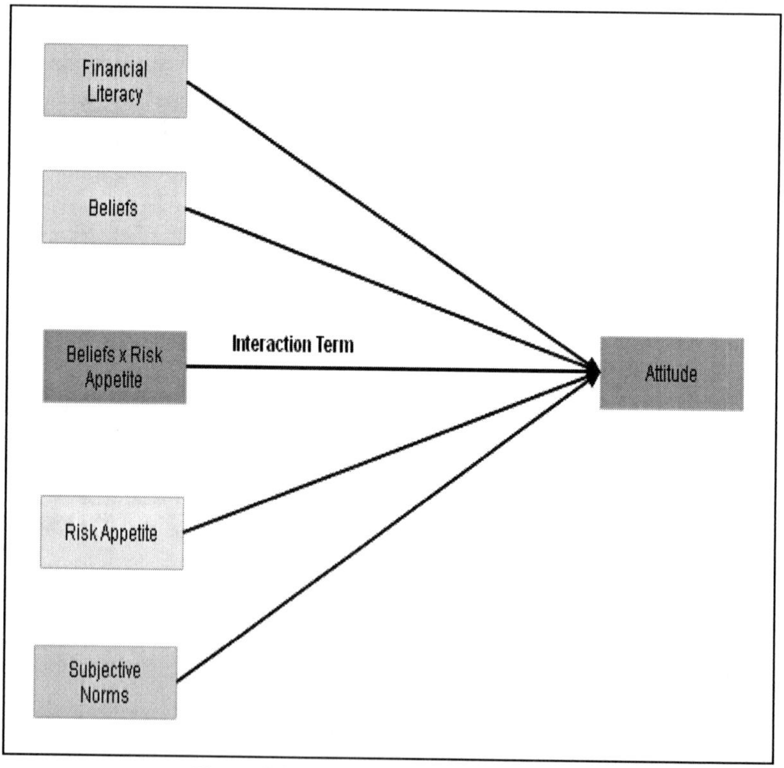

Figure 5.3: Moderation Interation Model

- The interaction moderation effect shows the influence of risk appetite on the relationship between financial literacy, beliefs, subjective norms and attitude. Risk Appetite does not seems to influence the relationship between financial literacy and attitude and subjective norms and attitude. On the other hand, risk appetite negatively influences the relationship between beliefs and attitude.

5.4 Mediation Effect of Attitude

- Mediation is a form interrelationship between variables that describes causation. It is normally used to provide a more precise explanation to the causal relationship between a predictor and outcome (Hair et al., 2010). A mediator corresponds to a dominant variable through which an independent variable influences a dependent variable (Baron & Kenny, 1986).
- The most well-known approach to that tests the indirect effect and its significance is Bootstrapping (Bollen & Stine, 1990; Shrout & Bolger, 2002; Hayes, 2009). One of the objectives of the study was to determine the mediating effect of Attitude on the relationship between financial literacy, risk appetite, beliefs, subjective norms and investment behavior. In order to examine the mediating effect, the study used SEM analysis that determines the indirect effect (i.e. with mediator variable) of predictors on the outcome variable. The following Wealth Management Behavior model was constructed to assess the direct impact of predictors on investment behavior.

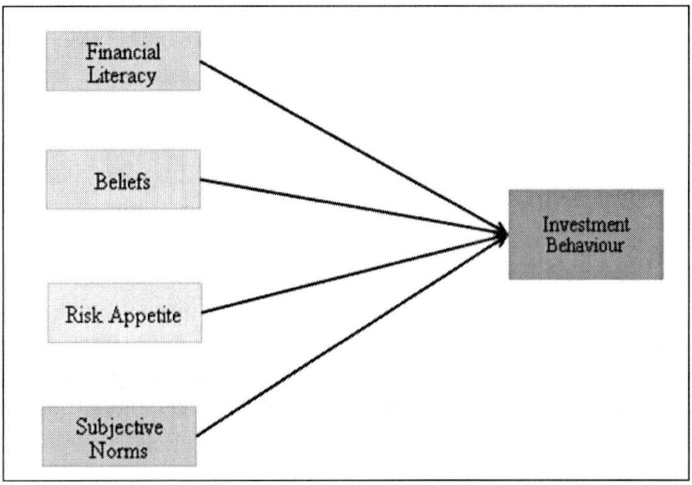

Figure 5.4: Direct Path Relationship

- The findings reveal that the direct path between financial literacy and investment behavior is weak and non-significant (0.069, p-value = 0.079) which does not synchronize with the findings of Park, Mothersbough and Fieck, 1994; Brucks, 1985; Glaser and Walther, 2013; Danes, Casas and Boyce, 1999; Bernheim, Garrett and Maki, 2001; Hira and Loibl, 2005; Borden et al., 2006. The findings of all these researchers show that individuals with higher financial knowledge exhibit more responsible financial behavior. They opined that the level of the knowledge of an investor accounts for the information he possesses and influences his behavior of making decisions. Though the result is contrary to the findings of previous researchers, the present study might find some evidence of mediation between financial literacy and investment behavior.
- On the other hand, the study also revealed that the path between risk appetite and investment behavior is also weak and non-significant (0.055, p-value = 0.15). The results are contrary to the findings of Barsky et al. 1997; Nosic and Weber, 2007; Hui, Zheng and Wang, 2013; Dohmen et al. 2005; Hallahan et al. 2004. These researchers established positive relationship between investor's behavior and their willingness to take risk. According to Alanko, 2009 investor's attitude and decision making related to risky investments plays a vital role in understanding investor's behavior and perception towards risk and this study can provide wealth managers with a deep insight and useful information to improve and focus on investor's demands and customer satisfaction. These results also show some evidence of mediation in the present study.
- However, the path between beliefs and investment behavior is found to be weak but significant at 95% confidence level i.e. $p < 0.05$ (0.091, p-value= 0.011). This outcome is consistent with study of Kelley and Tetlock, 2013; Campbell, 2007; Li and Li, 2014; Egan et al, 2014; Guiso, Sapienza and Zingales, 2008; Glaser and Walther, 2013. These researchers examined that the personal beliefs and perception of an individual significantly influences his thinking and can change his mind which in turn can drive a change in his financial behavior. Another piece of evidence was founded by Ben, 2012; Morris and Shin, 2002; Karpoff, 1986; Varian, 1985; Patton and Timmermann, 2010; Dolan et al., 2012; Tim, Ken and Gene, 1996 who says that individual investor's decisions are primarily motivated by their beliefs rather than their preferences.

- Additionally, the path between subjective norms and investment behavior is also found to be strong and highly significant (0.462, p-value <0.01). The findings are homogeneous with the findings of Sharma and Gupta, 2011; Croy, Paul & Craig, 2010; Hussein, Hassan and Al-Anood, 2009; Cole and Shastry, 2009; Septyanto and Adhikara, 2014; Listyarti and Suryani, 2014; Gain et al., 2012; Chiou, 1998. All these researchers concluded that that the investors with less knowledge about the financial system rely extensively on the suggestions and opinion of close relatives, colleagues, friends, peers and family and take their advice before making any investment related decisions. The perspective of peers and other close referents are considered essential factors in the investment decision-making. They also observed that financial information particularly accounting information and intentions of investors has a positive significant effect on investment decisions.
- Further, in order to assess the indirect effects of the relationship between predictors and the dependent variable a mediator is added in the model and results were examined. The following diagram shows the Wealth Management Behavior model when a mediator is added.

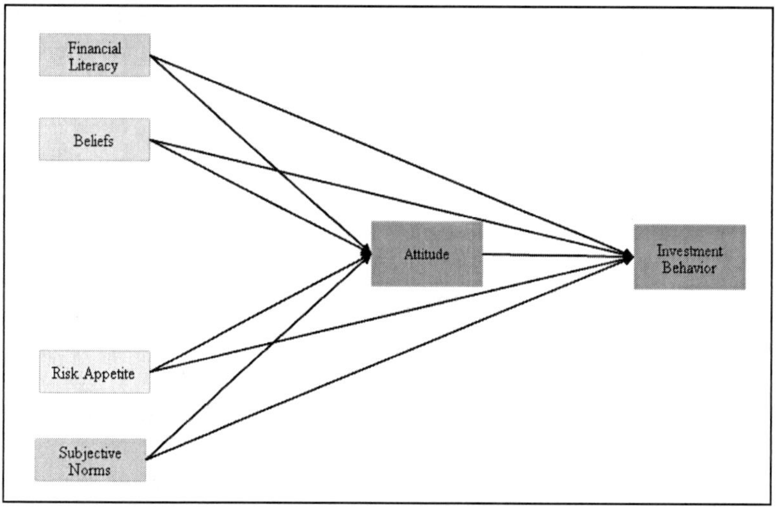

Figure 5.5: Indirect Path Relationship

- The path coefficients between independent variables and mediator were found to be strong and significant [Financial Literacy: 0.143 (p-value < 0.01); Risk Appetite: 0.107 (p-value = 0.004); Beliefs:

0.134 (p-value < 0.01); Subjective Norms: 0.377 (p-value < 0.01)]. Moreover, the path coefficient between mediator and dependent variable is also significant (Attitude: 0.084, p-value 0.034).

- All the independent variables are positively related to the mediator variable and mediator variable is also positively related to the dependent variable. The consistency of the results has already been verified in the previous section of this chapter.
- However, in order to assess whether the mediating variable accounts for full mediation, partial mediation or no mediation, the direct & indirect effect of independent variables on dependent variables was considered in the mediation model.
- The findings of the study revealed that, the direct path between Financial Literacy and Investment Behavior without mediator is small and insignificant (0.069, p-value= 0.079) but the indirect effect though small is significant (0.012, p-value = 0.029) whereas the direct effect is further reduced and remains insignificant. Thus, this shows that attitude fully mediates the path between financial literacy and investment behavior. Also, the direct path associated with the path Risk Appetite and Investment Behavior is non-significant and regression coefficient is small (0.055), the indirect effect on the other hand is significant but small (0.009, p-value = (0.037) whereas the direct effect in the mediation model remains insignificant (0.229). Thus, Attitude fully mediates the relationship between risk appetite and investment behavior.
- Further, the path between Beliefs and Investment Behavior mediated by attitude i.e. indirect path is significant along with the direct path between beliefs and investment behavior. Therefore, this is an evidence of 'Partial Mediation'. In other words, Attitude partially mediates the path between Beliefs and Investment Behavior.

4 On the other hand, the indirect path associated with Subjective Norm and Behavior mediated by attitude is non-significant. Thus demonstrating that the relationship between subjective norm and investment behavior is not mediated by attitude and hence, no mediation. The table below summarizes the major findings of the mediation effect:

Table 5.2: Mediation Effects Results

			Direct Effect Without Mediator	***Indirect Effect With Mediator***	***Direct Effect With Mediator***	
DV		***IV***	***Standardized Estimates (Significance value)***	***Standardized Estimates (Significance value)***	***Standardized Estimates (Significance value)***	***Mediation***
Investment Behavior	<---	Financial Literacy	0.069 (*0.079*)	0.012 (*0.029*)	0.058 (*0.08*)	Full Mediation
Investment Behavior	<---	Risk Appetite	0.055 (*0.15*)	0.009 (*0.037*)	0.046 (*0.229*)	Full Mediation
Investment Behavior	<---	Beliefs	0.091 (*0.011*)	0.011 (*0.042*)	0.08 (*0.031*)	Partial Mediation
Investment Behavior	<---	Subjective Norms	0.462 (***)	0.32 (*0.061*)	0.43 (***)	No Mediation

Chapter - 6

Conclusions, Implications & Suggestions

The main purpose of this research is to evaluate investors' behavior with reference to Wealth Management. The learning from the research is discussed in this chapter in the context of wealth management. The results and findings are summarized and recommendations are made for wealth managers and investors. Further, implications for wealth managers and practitioners, limitations of the study and the future directions of the research are outlines.

6.1 Conclusion

As discussed, the theory of behavioral finance has many significant applications. Understanding the investor's psychology to provide him customized products and services is associated with a field of study which is known as Behavioral Finance. It is important for a finance manager or advisor to understand the intentions and behavior of his client so as to design appropriate customized business model to serve his requirements. Therefore, the financial institutions identify the most influencing factor that determines that behavior which in turn will affect its financial policies and strategies. Irrespective of how much an investor is well-aware, or explored profoundly the various investment options, he behaves reasonably before investing because of the fear about future.

The primary aim of this investigation was to uncover and discover the fundamental factors that impact on the use of wealth management services amongst investors in Delhi/NCR. Research on investment behavior has indicated that investors' attitude is an important element that drives investment behavior. Also, there are various components that influence attitude. Therefore, the current study intended to evaluate the impact of financial literacy, risk appetite, personal beliefs, and subjective norms on attitude and further the influence of attitude on investor's investment behavior in the context of wealth management. Apart from these, this research intends to assess the significant association between attitude, beliefs, financial literacy, risk appetite and investment behavior.

In order to fulfill the above mentioned objectives, structural equation modeling was applies using AMOS. The statistical findings indicated significant positive influence of all components on attitude and significant positive influence of attitude on investment behavior. In order to appraise financial literacy of an investor, the items focused on investors' knowledge and awareness of investment instruments, his basis for selection of investment avenues and his approach towards investment. On the basis of the proposed model, the findings suggest that with the increase in investor's financial knowledge, his attitude towards investment increases i.e. more knowledgeable an investor is more positive his attitude towards investment will be. The items that measure attitude are investor's opinion towards benefits in investing wealth management services, perception about wealth management products, preferences to avail wealth management services and his concern about the financial environment.

Further to determine the beliefs of an investor, items focused on investor's opinion about wealth management industry, his opinion about companies offering wealth management services, and overall belief about the financial market. The research revealed that as the beliefs of an investor towards the wealth management increases, his attitude towards investing in wealth management services also increases.

Additionally, subjective norms involve the influence of friends, peers, colleagues, and family on the investor's decision-making. Items that measure subjective norms included influence of family, friends, colleagues, and media on investors' attitude to invest. Results outlines that as the influence of these people increases, the attitude towards investment becomes positive and thus increases.

Moreover, the items used to measure risk appetite included investor's perception of fluctuations in the market, perceived benefits of diversification, performance of funds and perception on returns. Findings revealed that risk appetite has positive influence on attitude to invest. As the individual's appetite or tolerance for risk increases, his attitude towards investment also increases.

Finally, items judged the investment behavior of an investor that measure investor's investment activities, his frequency of investment and search for various wealth management services. The respondents were also assessed on the basis of their efforts they put in while investing in wealth management services. Research revealed that as the attitude of investors towards wealth management increases or becomes positive, they inclined towards availing the wealth management service.

These results outline a positive relationship between financial literacy, risk appetite, beliefs, subjective norms and attitude and also between attitude and investment behavior. The results of the study are significant and in cohort with the literature. Out of all the factors influencing attitude namely; financial literacy, beliefs, risk appetite and subjective norms, subjective norms is found to have a great influence on attitude followed by beliefs, financial literacy and risk appetite.

The study on the pervasive nature of risk appetite revealed that the interacting variable risk appetite-financial literacy and risk appetite-subjective norms were non-significant which means that risk appetite does not moderate the financial literacy-attitude relationship and subjective norm-attitude relationship. On the other hand, a significant moderating interaction effect was found between beliefs and risk appetite. The moderation effect was undertaken in the study because the turbulent financial environment gives much importance on assessing risk appetite of individuals across different fields. Risk appetite or risk bearing capacity is considered an important aspect in analyzing the investors' attitude. Shift in risk appetite causes shift in investors' attitude and thus behavior. Being central to the concept of investors' attitude and behavior, it is believed to have a significant impact on other factors influencing attitude.

Furthermore, the research on mediating effect of Attitude on the relationship between financial literacy, risk appetite, beliefs, subjective norms and investment behavior discovered that Financial Literacy & Risk Appetite were fully mediated by attitude. Beliefs were partially mediated by attitude and Subjective Norms were not mediated by attitude at all. In other words, since it was proved earlier that financial literacy, risk appetite, beliefs and subjective norms influence investor's attitude which in turn influence investment behavior, so it was apparent that that attitude has a mediating effect and might explain the relationship between predictors and investment behavior.

6.2 Implication

The application of behavioral finance is gaining importance in the financial economy and thus its implications are becoming wider. The behavioral elements i.e. the factors that govern an individual's behavior intrinsically exist within each individual without his awareness. The aim of the study was to identify the factors that influence investor's attitude and ultimately his behavior towards wealth management services. The study has various implications for financial practitioners especially wealth managers as well as investors.

6.2.1 Implications for wealth managers

It will assist wealth managers in becoming more effective by understanding their clients' psychology. It will facilitate them in building a portfolio which is behaviorally personalized and meets clients' long-term goals. Further, the keeping in mind the behavioral biases of the client, the wealth manager can adopt a systematic approach to advise his client and delivering him what is expected. If the client gets what he expects, he will appreciate the efforts, be happier and contended thus, making the advisory relationship successful. By getting an insight of the clients' motives, the manager can make him understand the reasons for designing a customized portfolio for him irrespective of the financial market environment. Furthermore, understanding the various behavioral biases, a manager can recommend strategies to an investor to overcome that bias. For example, an investor might face belief bias which means an investor might have a wrong belief about a stock and may want to invest in that stock. The manager in that situation may advice or demonstrates the stock's performance overtime and helps an investor to review his investment decision. Also, a manager can help an investor overcome subjective norm bias by evaluating such information and organizing financial awareness campaigns so that strong normative information is imparted in the society.

6.2.2 Implications for investors

Sometimes investors have a wrong belief about a company or product as a potential investment. They may trade excessively on such products or may hold an undiversified portfolio of such products assuming that they have enough knowledge without verifying the past performance statistics of that investment product. Moreover, they often ignore the downside risk associated with this belief and this leads to poor performance of their portfolio thus incurring heavy losses to the investor. The study might enable an investor to review the stock or the investment product by seeking advice from a wealth manager and assess the performance of the investment over a period of time to avoid making such mistakes.

Man being a social animal; choose investments based on the information available or provided by friends, family, colleagues or media. He usually does not engage in diligent research to verify whether the information or investment will be fruitful or not. Therefore, the results of the study will enable an investor to consider the effect of subjective norms on his decision-making and he might engage in finding accurate and sufficient information based on multiple opinions.

6.3 Recommendation

Financial and investment institutions are becoming more promising by delivering more effective solutions to the investors to manage their wealth (Walia and Dr. Kiran, 2009). It is thus necessary for these institutions to explore more about the expectation and perception of the investors to understand their behavior. This will not only help them to discover some crucial information that can support them to make their investment decisions more prudently but will also help them to generate ideas to drive new innovations with modern technology which will essentially steer them towards developing strategies and designing efficient financial products. Financial institutions need to invest more in research and development to study investor's behavior and their investment pattern from a wide perspective to identify and unveil such parameters that account for the investor's satisfaction and simultaneously design a portfolio in accordance with the need of the customers. Financial advice provided by wealth managers must be based on thorough understanding of the customer's requirements and their exhibited behavior patterns. (Kahneman and Riepe, 1998)

Financial service providers must follow the segmentation approach to specifically address the needs of the particular segments of their customers and attract more customers by exhibiting a more professional approach. With this approach financial managers can attain more customer satisfaction at reduced price as the focus remains at a specific segment. Instead of offering same product to the entire client base, portfolios and services should be customized in accordance to the needs and desires of an individual customer. It is necessary for the wealth managers to identify which cluster or category an investor belongs to in order to directly addresses their specific requirements.

A clear understanding of the various determinants of the investor's investment behavior and financial attitude helps the wealth managers to be more effective and client centric. It has been observed that the psychological factors significantly influence the attitude and behavior of an investor, which in turn impacts their decision-making. Hence studying the influence of these cognitive factors on behavior is becoming quite crucial for the interest of the wealth managers in predicting investor's behavior. Understanding the relative importance of attitude, subjective norms and perceived behavior in predicting the customer's intention has strong implications for the wealth managers. It can help them to design more efficient marketing and financial products according to the customer's investment intentions under different situations.

6.4 Scope for Future Research

The suggestions of future research on determining the factors influencing investor's wealth management behavior are as follows:

- The study might include High Net worth Individuals residing in other parts of the country to generalize the results for India as a whole.
- The researcher could undertake other factors that have influence on investor's attitude and thus investment behavior.
- The impact of macro environmental factors can also be undertaken in the research to examine the impact of these factors on investor's behavior.
- The factors influencing investor's behavior from the standpoint of financial practitioners or wealth managers can be studied, which will give a broader, view about investor's psychology.
- The research model can be based on Theory of Planned behavior which is a revised version of theory of reasoned action and includes perceived behavioral control as a predictor of investor's intention and thereby affecting investor's behavior.
- Furthermore, the relationship between investment behavior and factors affecting attitude can be examined using qualitative research methods such as focus groups, interviews etc.
- In addition, longitudinal studies may be undertaken to examine the change in investor's attitude and investment behavior with regard to wealth management.
- Impact of demographic variables like age, gender, education, income etc., as moderators can be examined in the Wealth Management Behavior Model. Demographic variables can influence the investor's attitude and their investment behavior. Various studies have proved this influence.

- Incorporating the behavioral intention and assessing its mediation effect on the relationship between investor's attitude and investment behavior can examine the same model.

Bibliography

1. Ackert, L. & Deaves, R., 2010. Behavioral Finance: Psychology, Decision-Making, and Markets. 1st ed. Mason, USA: South-Western Cengage Learning.
2. Agarwal, N. K., 2011. Verifying survey items for construct validity: A two-stage sorting procedure for questionnaire design in information behavior research. Proceedings of the American Society for Information Science and Technology. Available at: http://www.asis.org/asist2011/proceedings/submissions/166_FINAL _ SUBMISSION.pdf (Accessed on 21st January, 2015)
3. Agle, B.R. & Van Buren III, H.J., 1999. God and Mammon: The Modern Relationship. Business Ethics Quarterly, 9(4), pp. 63-582.
4. Ajzen, I & Driver, BL 1992, 'Application of the theory of planned behavior to leisure choice.', Journal of Leisure Research, vol 24, no. 1, pp. 207-224.
5. Ajzen, I. & Fishbein, M., 1980. Understanding attitudes and predicting social behavior. 1st ed. Englewood Cliffs, NJ: Prentice-Hall.
6. Ajzen, I., 1991. The Theory of Planned Behavior: Organizational Behavior and Human Decision Processes. Academic Press. Inc, 50(2), pp. 179-211.
7. Ajzena, I. & Fishbeinb, M., 2000. Attitudes and the Attitude-Behavior Relation: Reasoned and Automatic Processes. European Review of Social Psychology, 11(1), pp. 1-33.
8. AlTamimi, HAH & Kalli, AAB 2009, 'Financial literacy and investment decisions of UAE investors', The Journal of Risk Finance, vol 10, no. 5, pp. 500-516.
9. Alanko, Elias, 2009. What drives investors' risk appetite - Empirical evidence from private Finnish investors.Ph.D thesis, Department of Accounting and Finance, Helsinki School Of Economics. pp. 1-70.
10. Alba, J.W. & J. Wesley, H., 1987. Dimensions of Consumer Expertise. Journal of Consumer Research, 13(4), pp. 411-54.
11. Ali.I and Waheed.S., 2013. Determinants of Small Equity Investor's Risk Assumption Attitude.2nd International Conference on Humanities, Economics and Geography (ICHEG'2013) June 17-18, 2013 London (UK).
12. Allianz 2014, Allianz Global Welath Report. Available at: https://www.allianz.com/en/press/news/studies/140923_allianz-global-wealth-report.html/ (Accessed on 2nd Dec 2014).
13. Amenc et al., 2010. Edhec-risk European private wealth management survey.France: EdhEc-Risk Institute Publication.

14. Amenc, N., Martellini, L., Milhau, V. & Ziemann, V., 2009. Asset-liability management in private wealth management. Journal of Portfolio Management , 36(1), pp. 100-20.
15. Anand, S. & Murugaiah, V., 2004. Marketing of financial services: strategic issues. SCMS Journal of Indian Management, 2(4), pp. 32-39.
16. Ananda, J. & Herath, G., 2008. Multi-attribute preference modelling and regional land-use planning. Ecological Economics, 65(1), pp. 325-35.
17. Arbuckle, James L. 1995, Amos ™ 18 User's Guide, Available at: http://www.sussex.ac.uk/its/pdfs/Amos_18_Users_Guide.pdf (Accessed on 6th Dec 2013).
18. Armitage, C.J. & Conner, M., 2001. Efficacy of the Theory of Planned Behaviour: A Meta-analytic Review. British Journal of Social Psychology, 40(4), pp. 471-99.
19. Asia-Pacific Wealth Report 2014, Asia-Pacific Wealth Report 2014 from Capgemini and RBC Wealth Management. Available at: https://www.capgemini.com/thought-leadership/asia-pacific-wealth-report-2014-from-capgemini-and-rbc-wealth-management (Accessed on 2nd Dec 2014).
20. Azam, M.S., Quaddus, M. & Lubna, N., 2013. Behavioral Modeling of the Individual's Acceptance and use of Internet in Bangladesh: An Analysis Using an Integrated Approach. Journal of International Technology and Information Management, 22(1), pp. 123-42.
21. Bahbah, A., 2009. Wealth Management in Any Market: Timeless Strategies for Building Financial Security. 1st ed. New Jersey, USA: John Wiley and Sons.
22. Bahl, S.D., 2012. A Study of advanced Financial Literacy among the working women in Punjab. ZENITH International Journal of Business Economics & Management Research, 2(12), pp. 176-90.
23. Baillot, P., 2009. Directeur de Bred Banque privée. La Banque privée pousse à la créativitéau lendemain de la crise, Agefi.Available at: http://www.agefi.fr/articles/la-banque-priveepoussee-a-la-creativite-au-lendemain-de-la-crise-1112380.html (Accessed: 03 March 2013).
24. Baker, M. & Jeffrey, W., 2006. Investor sentiment and the crosssection of stock returns. The Journal of Finance, 61(1), pp. 1645-80.
25. Baker.H et al.,2014. Financial Literacy and Education in Investor Behavior: The Psychology of Financial Planning and Investing. New Jersey, USA:John Wiley and Sons, Inc.
26. Bandura, A., 1982. Self-efficacy: Mechanism in Human Agency. American Psychologist, 37(2), pp. 122-47.
27. Barber, B.M. & Odean, T., 2001. Boys will be boys: gender, overconfidence, and common stock investment. The Quarterly Journal of Economics, 116(1), pp. 261-92.
28. Barberis, N., & Thaler, R., 2003. A Survey of behavioral finance. Amsterdam, North-Holland: Handbook of the Economics of Finance. ISBN-13: 978-0444513625.
29. Barnewall M., 1987. Psychological Characteristics of the Individual Investor in Asset Allocation for the Individual Investor.Charlottsville, Va: The Institute of Chartered Financial Analysts.

30. Baron, RM & Kenny, DA 1986, 'The Moderator-Mediator Variable Distinction in Social Psychological Research: Conceptual, Strategic, and Statistical Considerations', Journal of Personality and Social Psychology, vol 51, no. 6, pp. 1173-1182.

31. Barsky, R.B., Juster, T.F., Kimball, M.S. & Shapiro, M.D., 1997. Preference Parameters and Individual Heterogeneity: An Experimental Approach in the Health and Retirement Study. Quarterly Journal of Economics, 112(2), pp. 537-79.

32. Basu, A.K. & Drew, M.E., 2009. Portfolio size effect in retirement accounts: What does it imply for liecycle asset allocation funds. The Journal of Portfolio Management, 35(3), pp. 61-72.

33. Bayer et al., 1996. The effects of financial education in the workplace: Evidence from a survey of employers.Cambridge, MA: National Bureau of Economic Research (NBER).

34. Bearddsley et al., 2015. Global Wealth 2015: Winning the growth Game. Available at: https://www.bcgperspectives.com/content/articles/financial-institutions-growth-global-wealth-2015-winning-the-growth-game/ (Accessed on: 20 August 2015).

35. Becchetti, L, Caiazza, S & Coviello, D 2013, 'Financial education and investment attitudes in high schools: Evidence from a randomized experiment', Applied Financial Economics, vol 23, no. 10, pp. 817-836.

36. Beinhocker, ED 2006, The origin of Wealth: Evolution, complexity and the radical remaking of Economics, 1st edn, Harvard Business School Press, USA.

37. Ben, I., 2012. Beliefs Drive Investors More than Preferences. Avialable at: http://researchnews.osu.edu/archive/dispeffect.htm (Accessed on: 12th August 2015)

38. Bennet, E. & Selvam, M., 2011. Investor's perception towards the influence of SPERTEL risks on the value of equity shares. International Journal of Research in Computer Application and Management, 1(2), pp. 61-65.

39. Bennet, E. et al., 2011. Investors' attitude on stock selection decision. International Journal of Management & Business Studies, 1(2), pp. 7-15.

40. Bennet, E., Selvam, M., Vivek, N. & Shalin, E.E., 2012. The impact of investor's sentiment on the equity market: Evidence from Indian stock market. African Journal of Business Management, 6(32), pp. 9317-25.

41. Bentler, P.M. & Speckart, G., 1979. Models of Attitude-Behavior Relations. Psychological Review, 86(5), pp. 452-64.

42. Bernheim, B.D., Garrett, D.M. & Maki, D.M., 2001. Education and saving: The long-term effects of high school financial curriculum mandates. Journal of Public Economics, 80(3), pp. 435-65.

43. Bernheim, B.D., Skinner, J. & Weinberg, S., 2001. What Accounts for the Variation in Retirement Wealth among U.S. Households? American Economic Review, 91(4), pp. 832-57.

44. Biais, B., Hilton, D., Mazurier, K. & Pouget, S., 2005. Judgmental overconfidence, selfmonitoring and trading performance in an experimental financial market. Review of Economic Studies, 72(2), pp. 287-312.

45. Bigda, Carolyn 2013, Young investors shift their sentiment on risk, Available at: http://articles.chicagotribune.com/2013-01-08/business/sc-cons-0103-started-investor-sentiment-20130108_1_young-investors-meir-statman-portfolio-in-stock-funds (Accessed on: 20th December 2014).

46. Bodnaruk, A. & Simonov, A., 2014. Do financial experts make better investment decisions. Journal of Financial Intermediation, 23(4), pp. 1-48.

47. Bollen, Kenneth A. & Stine, Robert 1990, Direct and indirect Effects: Classical and Bootstrap Estimates of Variability. Available at: http://www.odum.unc.edu/content/pdf/Bollen%20(1990%20SM).pdf (Accessed on; 5th August 2015).

48. Bongini, P, Colombo, L & Iwanicz-Drozdowska, M 2015, 'Financial Literacy: Where Do We Stand?', Journal of Financial Management, Markets and Institutions, vol 2015 , no. 1, pp. 3-12.

49. Borden, L.M., Lee, S.A., Serido, J. & Collins, D., 2008. Changing college students' financial knowledge, attitudes, and behavior through seminar participation. Journal of Family Economic Issues, 29(1), pp. 23-40.

50. Boyd, W.L., 1994. Customer preferences for financial services: An analysis. International Journal of Bank Marketing, 12(1), pp. 9-15.

51. Brandmeir et al., 2014. Allianz Gobal Wealth Report 2014. Available at: https://www.allianz.com/v_1411376219000/media/economic_research/publications/specials/en/AGWR14e.pdf (Accessed on: 12th December 2014)

52. Braunstein, S. & Welch, C., 2002. Financial Literacy: An Overview of Practice, Research, and Policy. Federal Reserve Bulletin, 1 November. pp. 445-57.

53. Brennan, M. & Xia, Y., 2002. Dynamic asset allocation under inflation. The Journal of Finance, 57(3), pp. 1201-38.

54. Brimble, M., Vyvyan, V. & Ng, C., 2013. Belief and Investing: Preferences and Attitudes of the Faithful Australasian. Accounting, Business and Finance Journal, 7(1), pp. 23-41.

55. Brubaker, R.G. & Fowler, C., 1990. Encouraging college males to perform testicular self-examination: Evaluation of a persuasive message based on the revised theory of reasoned action. Journal of Applied Social Psychology, 20(1), pp. 1411-22.

56. Brucks, M., 1985. The Effects of Product Class Knowledge on Information Search Behavior. Journal of Consumer Research, 12(1), pp. 1-16.

57. Brunel, J.L.P., 2002. Integrated Wealth Management: The New Direction for Portfolio Managers. 2nd ed. London: Institutional Investor Books.

58. Budge, G.S., 2007. Continuing Challenges to Delivering Integrated Wealth Management Services to Business Owners. The Journal of Wealth Management, 10(2), pp. 51-62.

59. Bursztyn, et al., 2012. Understanding peer effects in financial decisions: Evidence from a field experiment. Available at: http://www.nber.org/papers/w18241.pdf (Accessed on: 14 November 2014).

60. Byrne, B.M., 2010. Structural Equation Modeling with AMOS: Basic Concepts, Applications and Programming. 2nd ed. Ney York: Routledge.

61. Byrne, K., 2005. How do consumers evaluate risk in financial products? Journal of Financial Services Marketing, 10(1), pp. 21-36.

62. Çabuk, S., Tanrikulu, C. & Gelibolu, L., 2014. Understanding organic food consumption: attitude as a mediator. International Journal of Consumer Studies, 38(4), pp. 337-45.

63. Camerer, C.F., Loewenstein, G. & Rabin, M., 2004. Behavioral Economics: Past, Present, Future. In C.F. Camerer, G. Loewenstein & M. Rabin, eds. Advances in Behavioral Economics. New York: Princeton University Press. pp. 3-51.

64. Campbell, J. & Viceira, L., 2005. The term structure of the risk-return trade-off. Financial Analysts Journal, 61(2), pp. 34-44.

65. Campbell, John, 2007. Who are the noise traders.Economist's View. Available at: http://economistsview.typepad.com/economistsview/2007/08/households-inst. html61 (Accessed on 21st January 2015).

66. Capgemini and RBC Wealth Management, 2014. Asia-Pacific Wealth Report 2014. Available at: https://www.capgemini.com/thought-leadership/asia-pacific-wealth-report-2014-from-capgemini-and-rbc-wealth-management (Accessed on: 4th January 2015).

67. Cavazosa, C., 2013. Entering into strategic alliances: an empirical test of the direct and interaction effects of managers' attitudes, subjective norms, and perceived behavioral control. Journal of Strategic Marketing, 21(1), pp. 3-24.

68. Ceru, D., 2004. Strategy and Technology for the New Wealth Management. The Journal of Wealth Management, 8(1), pp. 81-91.

69. Chacko, G. & Viceira, L.M., 2005. Dynamic Consumption and Portfolio Choice with Stochastic Volatility in Incomplete Markets. The Review of Financial Studies, 18(4), pp. 1369-402.

70. Chan, C. & Chan, ., 2011. Attitude toward wealth management services: Implications for international banks in China. International Journal of Bank Marketing, 29(4), pp. 272-92.

71. Chandra, A. & Kumar, R., 2011. Determinants of individual investor behaviour: An orthogonal linear transformation approach. Munich Personal RePEc Archive. Available at: https://mpra.ub.uni-muenchen.de/29722/1/MPRA_paper_29722.pdf (Accessed on: 2nd November 2014).

72. Chen, H. & Volpe, R.P., 1998. An analysis of personal financial literacy among college students. Financial Services Review , 7(2), pp. 107-28.

73. Chin, Hui leong 2014, The Biggest Investing tragedy you should avoid, Available at: https://www.fool.sg/2014/12/10/the-biggest-investing-tragedy-you-should-avoid/ (Accessed on: 25th December 2014).

74. Chiou, J.-S., 1998. The Effects of Attitude, Subjective Norm, and Perceived Behavioral Control on Consumer's Purchase Intentions: The Moderating Effects of Product Knowledge and Attention to Social Comparison Information. Proceedings of the National Science Council, Republic of China, 9(2), pp. 298-308.

75. Chiu, Y.-J. & Chen, Y.-W., 2007. Using AHP in patent valuation. Mathematical and Computer Modelling, 46(7), pp. 1054-62.

76. Choi, et al., 2004. For Better or For Worse: Default Effects and 401(k) Savings Behavior. Available at: http://scholar.harvard.edu/files/laibson/files/for_better_or_for_worse_default_effects_and_401k_savings_behavior.pdf?m=1360042880 (Accessed on: 7th January 2014).

77. Christelis, D., Jappelli, T. & Padula, M., 2010. Cognitive abilities and portfolio choice. European Economic Review, 1 January. pp. 18-38.
78. Clark, Robert L., 2012. Financial Literacy and Retirement Decisions: The Choices Facing Older Workers. Available at: http://www.cael.org/pdfs/tmt_financial_literacy (Accessed on: 12th April 2014).
79. Clercq, B.d., Venter, J.M.P. & Aardt, C.J.V., 2012. An analysis of the inter-relationship between savings product usage and satisfaction using a servqual framework. Southern African Business Review, 16(2), pp. 120-38.
80. Cocco, J.F., Gomes, F.J. & Maenhout, P.J., 2005. Consumption and Portfolio Choice over the Life Cycle. The Review of Financial Studies, 18(2), pp. 491-533.
81. Cognizant Report,2011. Wealth Management in India. Avialable at: http://www.cognizant.com/InsightsWhitepapers/Wealth-Management-in-India-Challenges-and-Strategies.pdf (Accessed on: 27th Nov 2014)
82. Cohen, J., 1988. Statistical Power Analysis for the Behavioral Sciences. 2nd ed. New Jersey: Lawrence Erlbaum Associates Publishers.
83. Cole, S. & Shastry, G. K., 2009. Smart money: The effect of education, cognitive Ability, and Financial Literacy on Financial Market Participation. Available at: http://www.thefiscaltimes.com/sites/default/files/pdf/Harvard%20-%20Effect%20of%20Education%20-%20Feb%202009.pdf (Accessed on: 3rd July 2014).
84. Companies in India 2014, 'Top 20 Wealth Management Companies in India'. Available at: http://companiesinindia.in/wealth-management-companies-in-india/ (Accessed on 1st June 2014).
85. Cooper, D.R. & Schindler, P.S., 2014. Business Research Methods. 12th ed. Singapore: McGraw-Hill Education.
86. Corter, J.E. & Chen, Y.-J., 2006. Do Investment Risk Tolerance Attitudes Predict Portfolio Risk? Journal of Business and Psychology, 20(3), pp. 369-81.
87. Cronbach, L.J., 1951. Coefficient alpha and the internal structure of tests. Psychometrika, 22(3), pp. 297-334.
88. Crosby, S., Jensen, J., & Ong, J., 2011. Anticipating a new age in wealth management. Global Private Banking and Wealth Management Survey 2011, USA: PWC Limited. Available at: https://www.pwc.com/gx/en/private-banking-wealth-mgmt-survey/pdf/global-private-banking-wealth-2011.pdf (Accessed on: 26th March 2014).
89. Crotty, M 1998, The Foundations of Social Research , 2nd edn, Sage Publications, New Delhi.
90. Croy, G., Paul, G. & Craig, S., 2010. Injunctive social norms primacy over descriptive social norms in retirement savings decisions. The International Journal of Aging and Human Development, 71(4), pp. 259-82.
91. Danes, S.M., Huddleston-Cases, C. & Boyce, L., 1999. Financial planning curriculum for teens: Impact evaluation. Financial Counseling and Planning Education, 10(1), pp. 25-37.
92. Das, B., 2008. Mutual Fund Vs. Life Insurance Behavioural Analysis of Retail Investors. International Journal of Business and Management, 3(10), pp. 89-95.

93. Das, B., Mohanty, S. & Shil, N.C., 2008. Mutual Fund vs Life Insurance: Behavioral Analysis of Retail Investors. International Journal of Business and Management, 3(10), pp. 89-103.

94. Das, S., 2012. Small Investor's Perceptions on Mutual Funds in Assam: An Empirical Analysis. Abhinav National Monthly Refereed Journal of Research in Commerce and Management, 1(8), pp. 11-27.

95. Das, S.K., 2012. Semi urban investors attitude and preferences in Mutual Funds Investment: A Case Study of Nagaon Districts of Assam. International Journal of Marketing, Financial Services & Management Research , 1(9), pp. 70-90.

96. Das.G., n,d. A to Z of Mutual Funds- An Ideal Investment Option for Investors. Available at:http://manupatra.com/ roundup/349/Articles/A%20to%20Z%20of%20MUTUAL%20FUNDS.pdf (Accessed on:15th July 2015)

97. Datamonitor 2011, 'Insight on Wealth Management and Private Banking', Annual, Banking, Datamonitor Informa Company, n.d., Datamonitor, n.d.

98. De Long, JB, Shleifer, A, Summers, LH & Waldmann, RJ 1990, 'Noise Trader Risk in Financial Markets', The Journal of Political Economy, vol 98, no. 4, pp. 703-738.

99. Debono, K.G. & Omoto, A.M., 1993. Individual Differences in Predicting Behavioral Intentions from Attitude and Subjective Norm. The Journal of Social Psychology, 133(6), pp. 825-31.

100. Debono, KG & Omoto, AM 1993, 'Individual Differences in Predicting Behavioral Intentions from Attitude and Subjective Norm', The Journal of Social Psychology, vol 133, no. 6, pp. 825-831.

101. DeCoster, Jamie 1998, Overview of Factor Analysis, Available at: http://www.stat-help.com/factor.pdf (Accessed on 23rd November 2014).

102. Deposits, 2014. High Net Worth Individuals. Available at: http://www.deposits.org/dictionary/term/high-net-worth-individuals/ (Accessed: 20 October 2014).

103. Dhivya, R. & Dr. Sekar, C., 2010. Investor's preference towards Financial Investments-Some survey evidence. Indian Journal of Finance, 4(7), pp. 39-53.

104. Diaz-Serrano, L. & D. O'Neill, 2004. The Relationship Between Unemployment and Risk-Aversion. IZA Discussion Paper No. 1214. Available at: http://repec.iza.org/dp1214.pdf (Accessed on: 5th November 2014).

105. Dickson, M., 2000. Personal Values, Beliefs, Knowledge, and Attitudes Relating to Intentions to Purchase Apparel from Socially Responsible Businesses. Clothing Textiles and Research Journal, 18(1), pp. 19-30.

106. Dohmen, et al., 2005. Individual Risk Attitudes : New Evidence from a Large, Representative, Experimentally-Validated Survey. IZA Discussion Papers No. 1730. Available at: http://ftp.iza.org/dp1730.pdf (Accessed on: 13th July 2015).

107. Dolan, P., Elliott, A., Metcalfe, R. & Vlaev, I., 2012. Influencing financial behavior: from changing minds to changing contexts. Journal of Behavioral Finance, 13(2), pp. 126-42.

108. Donkers, B., Melenberg, B. & Soest, A.V., 2001. Estimating Risk Attitudes Using Lotteries: A Large Sample Approach. Journal of Risk and Uncertainty, 22(2), pp. 165-95.

109. Doran, J.S., Peterson, D.R. & C, W., 2010. Confidence, opinions of market efficiency and investment behavior of finance professors. Journal of Financial Markets, 13(1), pp. 174-95.
110. Dr. Kukreja, G., 2012. Investor's Perception for Stock Market: Evidences from National Capital Region of India. Interdisciplinary Journal of Contemporary Research in Business, 4(8), pp. 712-26.
111. Dr. Mehta, S.K. & Aggarwal, N., 2011. The effect of demographies on investment choice: an empirical study of investors in Jammu. Indian Journal of Finance, 5(10), pp. 43-55.
112. Dr. Palaneeswari, T. & Kaleeswari, J., 2011. Investor's perception towards capital market: An empirical study with reference to Sivakasi, Tamil Nadu. Indian Journal of Finance, 5(11), pp. 34-50.
113. Dr. Rajasekar, D., 2013. A study on investor‘s preference towards mutual funds with reference to reliance private limited, chennai - An Empirical Analysis. International Research Journal of Business and Management, 3(1), pp. 38-44.
114. Driga, I., Nita, D. & Cucu, I., 2009. Private Banking and Wealth Management Services Offered by Banks. Annals of the University of Petro°ani, Economics, 9(1), pp. 231-40.
115. Driga, I..N.D.a.C.I., 2009. Private Banking and Wealth Management Services Offered by Banks. Annals of the University of Petro°ani, Economics, 9(1), pp. 231-40.
116. Dun & Bradstreet 2009, Wealth Management, 1st edn, Tata McGraw Hill, New Delhi.
117. Dwivedi et al., 2008. Wealth Management in India: Issues & Concerns. Available at: http://www.indianmba.com/faculty_column/fc859/fc859.html (Accessed on: 24th May 2015).
118. Eagly, A.H. & Chaiken, S., 1993. The Psychology of Attitudes. 1st ed. New York: Wadsworth Publishing.
119. Ecological Society of America 2005, Interpreting the Results from Multiple Regression and Structural Equation Models, Available at: http://www.esapubs.org/bulletin/backissues/086-4/pdf_web/comm1_86_4.pdf (Accessed on 13th July 2015).
120. Edmiston, K. D., & Gillett-Fisher, M. C., 2006. Financial education at the workplace: Evidence from a survey of Federal Reserve Bank employees. Community Affairs Research Working Paper #2006-02. Available at: https://www.kansascityfed.org/publicat/cap/gillettfisher_edmiston_financial_education_april_2006.pdf (Accessed on 23rd July 2015).
121. Edward, L. D., & Richard, M. R., 1997. Intrinsic Motivation and Self-determination in Human Behavior. USA: Springer Science & Business Media.
122. Egan, D., Merkle, C. & Weber, M., 2014. Second-order beliefs and the individual investor. Journal of Economic Behavior & Organization, 107(B), pp. 652-66.
123. Eichengreen, B. & Mody, A., 1998. Interest Rates in the North and Capital Flows to the South: Is There a Missing Link? International Finance, 1(1), pp. 35-58.
124. Eisenhardt, K.M., 1989. Agency Theory: An Assessment and Review. Academy of Management, 14(1), pp. 57-74.

125. Elliehausen, G.E., Lundquist, C. & Staten, M.E., 2007. The Impact of Credit Counseling on Subsequent Borrower Behavior. Journal of Consumer Affairs, 41(1), pp. 1-28.

126. Elmiger, G. & Kim, S., 2003. Risk Grade your investments: Measure your risk & create wealth. 1st ed. Hoboken, NJ: John Wiley & Sons.

127. Emory, C.W., 1994. Business Research Methods. 5th ed. New York, USA: Richard d Irwin.

128. Essvale, M 2008, Business Knowledge for It in Private Wealth Management By Essvale Corporation Limited, 1st edition.

129. Evensky, H, Horan, SM & Robinson, TR 2011, The New Wealth Management: The Financial Advisors Guide to Managing and Investing Client Assets, 1st edn, John Wiley and Sons, New York.

130. Evensky, H.R., 1997. Wealth management: the financial advisor's guide to investing and managing Clients Assets. 1st ed. USA: TheMacGraw-Hill Company.

131. Felicia, O.O., 2014. Attitude of Investors to Capital and Money Market Investments Before and After Financial Crisis. International Journal of Sustainable Economies Management, 3(1), pp. 53-64.

132. Field, A., 2013. Discovering Statistics using IBM SPSS Statistics. Los Angeles: SAGE Publications Ltd.

133. Filbeck, G., Hatfield, P. & Horvath, P., 2005. Risk Aversion and Personality Type. Journal of Behavioral Finance, 6(4), pp. 170-80.

134. Financle Connect, n,d. Minimize Risk, Win in the Flat World. Available at: http://www.infosys.com/finacle/finacle connect/Documents/Wealth-Management-15th-Issue.pdf (Accessed on: 27th Nov 2014).

135. Finkelstein, A. & Poterba, J., 2004. Adverse Selection in Insurance Markets: Policyholder Evidence from the U.K. Annuity Market. Journal of Political Economy, 112(1), pp. 183-208.

136. Fischer, B., Jensen, M. & Sholes, M., 1972. Studies in the theory of Capital Market. 1st ed. New York: Praeger Publishers Inc.

137. Fisher, K.L. & Meir, S., 2000. Investor Sentiment and Stock Returns. Financial Analysts Journal, 56(2), pp. 16-23.

138. Forbes 2012, Forbes World's Billionaires 2012. Available at: http://www.forbes.com/sites/luisakroll/2012/03/07/forbes-worlds-billionaires-2012/ (Accessed on 2nd Dec 2014).

139. Fornell, C. & Larcker, D.F., 1981. Evaluating structural equation models with unobservable variables and measurement error. Journal of Marketing Research, 18(1), pp. 39-50.

140. Friestad, M. & Wright, P., 1994. The Persuasion Knowledge Model: How People Cope With Persuasion Attempts. Journal of Consumer Research, 21(1), pp. 1-31.

141. Fritz, MS & MacKinnon, DP 2007, 'Required Sample Size to Detect the Mediated Effect', Psychological Science, vol 18, no. 3, pp. 233-239.

142. Froot, Kenneth A.; O'Connell, Paul G.J.,2003. The risk tolerance of international investors. Working Paper Series: National Bureau of Economic Research. Available at: http://www.nber.org/papers/w10157.pdf (Accessed on: 27th Cotober 2014).

143. Funfgeld, B. & Wang, M., 2008. Attitude and Behavior in Everyday Finance. International Journal of Bank Marketing, 27(2), pp. 108-28.

144. Fung, L.; Tam, C.-S.; & Yu, I.W., 2009. Changes in Investors' Risk Appetite- An assessment of Financial Integration and Interdependence. IFC Bulletin No. 31. Available at: http://www.bis.org/ifc/publ/ifcb31x.pdf (Accessed on: 27th October 2014).

145. Gai, P. & Vause, N., 2006. Measuring investors' risk appetite. International Journal of Central Banking, 2(1), pp. 167-82.

146. Gali, J., 1994. Keeping Up with the Joneses: Consumption Externalities, Portfolio Choice, and Asset Prices. Journal of Money, Credit and Banking, 26(1), pp. 1-8.

147. Gani, D.V., Ganesh, J. & Dr.Santhi, V., 2012. A Study on the Individual Investor Behavior with Special Reference to Geojit BNP Paribas Financial Service Ltd, Coimbatore. International Journal of Research in Management & Technology, 2(2), pp. 243-52.

148. Garson, D.G., 2012. Testing Statistical Assumptions. 1st ed. North Carolina, USA: Statistical Associates Publishing.

149. Gaskin, J. 2014, Structural Equation Modeling, Available at: http://statwiki.kolobkreations.com/wiki/Structural_Equation_Modeling (Accessed on: 22nd November 2014).

150. Gaskin, J. 2015, Confirmatory Factor Analysis. Available at: http://statwiki.kolobkreations.com/wiki/Confirmatory_Factor_Analysis#Standardized_ Residual_Covariances (Accessed on: 28th January 2015)

151. Gaskin, J., 2012. Exploratory Factor Analysis. Available at: http://statwiki.kolobkreations.com (Accessed on: 28th January 2015).

152. Gathergood, J., 2012. Self-control, financial literacy and consumer over-indebtedness. Journal of Economic Psychology, 33(3), pp. 590-602.

153. Gemes, et al.,2014. Global wealth management outlook 2014–15: New strategies for a changing industry. United States: Booz & Company.

154. Gerrard, P. & Cunningham, J.B., 1997. Islamic banking: a study in Singapore. International Journal of Bank Marketing, 15(6), pp. 204-16.

155. Gervais, S., Heaton, J. & Odean, T., 2002. The Positive Role of Overconfidence and Optimism in Investment Policy. Journal of Financial Economics, 7(2), pp. 695-712.

156. Gill, A. & Biger, N., 2008. Factors that affect Canadian propensity to direct investment abroad: evidence from the Indian real estate market. The Open Business Journal, 1(1), pp. 1-9.

157. Gill, A. & Biger, N., 2009. Gender differences and factors that affect stock investment decision of Western Canadian Investors. International Journal of Behavioral Accounting and Finance, 1(2), pp. 135-51.

158. Gill, A. et al., 2012. Factors that Influence Indian Propensity to Invest in the Real Estate Market. Journal of Finance and Investment Analysis, 1(2), pp. 137-56.

159. Glaser, M & Walther, T 2013, 'Run, Walk, or Buy? Financial Literacy, Dual-Process Theory, and Investment Behavior'. Available at: http://www.cfr-cologne.de/download/kolloquium/2013/GlaserWalther_RunWalkOrBuy.pdf (Accessed on 10th December 2014).

160. Gomes, J.F., 2001. Financing Investment. American Economic Review, 91(5), pp. 1263-85.

161. Grable, J. & Joo, S., 1997. Determinants of risk preference: implication for the family and consumer science professionals. Family Economics and Resource Management, 2(1), pp. 19-24.

162. Grable, J.E. & Lytton, R.H., 1998. Investor risk tolerance: Testing the efficacy of demographics as differentiating and classifying factors. Financial Counseling and Planning, 9(1), pp. 61-73.

163. Grady, B. & Spencer, H.,1990. Managing commercial banks. Englewood Cliffs, NJ: Prentice-Hall.

164. Granberg, D. & Holmberg, S., 1990. The Intention-Behavior Relationship Among U.S. and Swedish Voters. Social Psychology Quarterly, 53(1), pp. 44-54.

165. Gravetter, F.J. & Forzano, L.-A.B., 2012. Research Methods in the Behavioral Sciences. 4th ed. CA, USA: Cengage Learning.

166. Greenfield, T., 1996. Research Methods: Guidance for Postgraduates. 1st ed. London: Wiley.

167. Grinblatt, M., Keloharju, M. & Linnainmaa, J., 2011. IQ and Stock Market Participation. The Journal of Finance, 56(6), pp. 2121-63.

168. Guiso, L., and M. Paiella,2005. The Role of Risk Aversion in Predicting Individual Behavior.Bank of Italy Economic Working Paper. Available at: http://www.researchgate.net/publication/228265818_The_Role_of_Risk_Aversion_in_Predicting_Individual_Behavior (Accessed on 28th January 2015).

169. Guiso, Sapienza & Zingales 2008. Long Term Persistence. NBER Working Paper Series. Available at: http://www.nber.org/papers/w14278.pdf (Accessd on: 23rd July 2013).

170. Gunzler, D., Chen, T., Wu, P. & Zhang, H., 2013. Introduction to mediation analysis with structural equation modeling. Shanghai Archives of Psychiatry, 25(6), pp. 390-94.

171. Gustman, Alan L.; Steinmeier, Thomas L.,2004. What People Don't Know About Their Pensions and Social Security: An Analysis Using Linked Data from the Health and Retirement Study. In William G. Gale, John B. Shoven and Mark J. Warshawsky, editors, Private Pensions and Public Policies. 2004. Washington: D.C., Brookings Institution, pp. 57-125. Available at: http://www.nber.org/papers/w7368.pdf (Accessed on: 29th November 2014).

172. Haarala, A., 2008. How risk attitude of investors is determined. Master's Thesis: University of Vaasa.

173. Hair, J., Black, W., Babin, B. & Anderson, R., 2010. Multivariate data analysis. 7th ed. Upper Saddle River, NJ, USA: Prentice-Hall, Inc.

174. Hallahan, T., Faff, R. & McKenzie, M., 2004. An empirical investigation of personal financial risk tolerance. Financial Services Review, 13(2004), pp. 57-78.

175. Hallman, V.G. & Rosenbloom, J.S., 2009. Private wealth management-The complete reference for the personal financial planner. 8th ed. USA: McGraw Hill Companies.

176. Hamilton, S., 1992. A Second Family Business—Patterns in Wealth Management. Family Business Review, 5(2), pp. 181-88.

177. Handfield, R., Walton, S.V., Sroufe, R. & Melnyk, S.A., 2002. Applying environmental criteria to supplier assessment: A study in the application of the Analytical Hierarchy Process. European Journal of Operational Research, 141(1), pp. 70-87.

178. Harlow, W.V. & Brown, K.C., 1990. Understanding and assessing financial risk tolerance: a biological perspective. Financial Analysts Journal, 46(6), pp. 50-62.

179. Harrison, H., Kubik, J.D. & Stein, J.C., 2010. Social Interaction and Stock Market participation. Journal of Finance, 59(1), pp. 137-63.

180. Harrison, S.,2009. Wealth Management For High Net Worth Individuals. Available at: http://www.financierworldwide.com/article.php?id=5218. (Accessed: 2 December 2012).

181. Harrison, T.,1994. Segmenting the market for retail financial services. A paper presented at the Third ESRC Retailing Seminar: Strategic Issues in Retailing.

182. Hayes, A. F.,2009. Beyond Baron and Kenny: Statistical Mediation Analysis in the New Millennium. Communication Monographs, pp. 408-420.

183. Hilgert, M.A., Hogarth, J.M. & Beverly, S.G., 2003. Household financial management: The connection between knowledge and behavior. Federal Reserve Bulletin, 1 July. pp. 309-22.

184. Hira, T.K. & Loibl, C., 2005. Understanding the Impact of Employer-Provided Financial Education on Workplace Satisfaction. The Journal of Consumer Affairs, 39(1), pp. 173-94.

185. Hira, Tahira K. 2009, Personal Finance: Past, Present and Future, Available at: https://www2.indstate.edu/business/NFI/leadership/briefs/2009-PB-10_Hira.pdf (Accessed on: 2nd January 2015).

186. Hoffmann, A.O., Post, T. & Pennings, J.M., 2013. How investors Perceptions Drive Actual Trading and Risk-taking Behavior. Journal of Behvioral Finance, 16(1), pp. 94-103.

187. Holmes-Smith, P, Cunningham, E & Coote, LV 2009, An Applied Introduction to Structural Equation Modelling, 2nd edn, Sage publications, N.A.

188. Hong, H., Kubik, J.D. & Stein, J.C., 2004. Social Interation and Stock- Market Participation. The Journal of Finance, 59(1), pp. 137-63.

189. Hooper, D., Coughlan, J. & & Mullen, M.R., 2008. Structural Equation Modelling: Guidelines for Determining Model Fit. The Electronic Journal of Business Research Methods, 6(1), pp. 53-60.

190. Hou, K., Peng, L. & Xiong, W., 2009. The Implications of Investor Attention for Price and Earnings Momentum. Journal of Financial Economics, 4(2), pp. 563-602.

191. Hu, L. & Bentler, P.M., 1999. Cutoff criteria for fit indexes in covariance structure analysis: Conventional criteria versus new alternatives. Structural Equation Modeling: A Multidisciplinary Journal, 6(1), pp. 1-55.

192. Hui, E.C.-m., Zheng, X. & Wang, H., 2013. Investor sentiment and risk appetite of real estate security market. Applied Economics, 45(19), pp. 2801-07.

193. Hung, A.A. et al., 2008. Investor and Industry Perspectives on Investment Advisers and Broker-Dealers. 1st ed. Pittsburgh: RAND Corporation.

194. Hung, S.-Y., Lai, H.-M. & Chou, Y.-C., 2010. The determinants of knowledge sharing intention in professional virtual communities: An integrative model. n.d., 2010. PACIS 2010 Proceedings.

195. Hussein, A., Hassan, A.T. & Al Anood, B.K., 2009. Financial literacy and investment decisions of UAE investors. The Journal of Risk Finance, 10(5), pp. 500-16.

196. Iacobucci, D., 2010. Structural equations modeling: Fit Indices, sample size, and advanced topics. Journal of Consumer Psychology , 20(2010), pp. 90-98.

197. Illing, M. & Aaron, M., 2005. A brief survey of risk-appetite indexes. Bank of Canada, Financial System Review, 1 June. pp. 37-43.

198. Investopedia 2015, Variance Inflation Factor, Available at: http://www.investopedia.com/terms/v/variance-inflation-factor.asp (Accessed on 12th October 2014).

199. Isdale, M.H., 2006. Strategies for Simplifying and Increasing the Effectiveness of Wealth Management. The Journal of Wealth Management, 9(2), pp. 14-18.

200. Ismail, S., Hashim, N., Harun, H. & Samad, N., 2013. Determinants of Attitude towards Estate Planning In Malaysia: An Empirical Investigation. Procedia Economics and Finance , 00(2013), pp. 1-9.

201. Jagongo, A. & Mutswenje, V.S., 2014. A survey of the factors in uencing investment decisions: the case of individual investors at the NSE. International Journal of Humanities and Social Science, 4(4), pp. 92-102.

202. Jasen, Georgette 2015, Male Investors vs. Female Investors, Available at: http://www.wsj.com/articles/male-investors-vs-female-investors-how-do-they-compare-1430709406 (Accessed on: 4th July 2015).

203. Johnsson, M., Lindblom, H. and P. Platan,2002. Behavioral finance and the change of investor behavior during and after the speculative bubble at the end of the 1990.Master Thesis, Lund University, Sweden.

204. Jorgenson.W., n.d. Theory of Investment Behavior. Available at:http://www.nber.org/chapters/c1235.pdf (Accessed on: 15th July 2015).

205. Jose, P.E., 2013. Doing Statistical Mediation and Moderation. n.d. ed. New York: Guilford Press.

206. Kabra,., Mishra, P.K. & Dash, M.K., 2010. Factors influencing investment decision of generations in India: an econometric study. Asian Journal of Management Research, 1(1), pp. 308-26.

207. Kadariya, S., 2012. Factors affecting investor decision making: A case of Nepalese capital market. Journal of Research in Economics and International Finance, 1(1), pp. 16-30.

208. Kahneman, D. & Riepe, M.W., 1998. Aspects of Investor's psychology. The Journal Of Portfolio Management, 24(4), pp. 52-65.

209. Kaiser, F., Oerke, B. & Bogner, F., 2007. Behavior-based environmental attitude: Development of an instrument for adolescents. Journal of Environmental Psychology, 27(3), pp. 242-51.

210. Kannadhasan, M. 2006, Role of behavioural Finance in Investment Decisions. Available at: http://dl4a.org/uploads/pdf/52.pdf (Accessed on: 23rd March 2014).

211. Kaplan, D 2008, Structural Equation Modeling: Foundations and Extensions: Foundations and Extensions, 2nd edn, Sage Publications, England.

212. Kaplan, S. & Garrick, B.J., 1981. On the quantitative definition of risk. Risk Analysis, 1(1), pp. 11-27.

213. Karpoff, J.M., 1986. A theory of trading volume. Journal of Finance, 41(5), pp. 1069-87.

214. Karvy Private Wealth, 2014. India Wealth Report ,Hyderabad: Karvy Financials. Available at: http://cafemutual. om/UploadPdf/63554586200181 8750_India-Wealth-Report-2014.pdf. (Accessed on: 22 February 2015).

215. Kaur, M. & Vohra, T., 2012. Understanding individual investor's behavior: A Review of Empirical Evidences. Pacific Business Review International, 5(6), pp. 10-18.

216. Keese, M & Schmitz, H 2010, 'Broke, ill, and obese:The effect of household debt on health', The 2010 Irdes Workshop on Applied Health Economics and Policy Evaluation, University of Duisburg-Essen, Paris.

217. Kelley, E.K. & Tetlock, P.C., 2013. How wise are crowds? insights from retail orders and stock returns. Journal of Finance, 68(n.d.), pp. 1229-65.

218. Kenny, David A. 2015, Measuring Model Fit, Available at: http://davidakenny.net/cm/fit.htm (Accessed on 10th July 2015)

219. Kerlinger, FN 1973, Foundations of Behavioral Research, 3rd edn, Holt, Rinehart and Winston, Inc., American Problem Series, New York.

220. Khanifar, H., N., J. & M., M., 2012. Studying affecting factors on analysts decisions regarding share analysis in Tehran stock exchange: A fundamental analysis approach. European Journal of Economics, Finance and Administrative Sciences, 44(1), pp. 77-86.

221. Khazeh, K. & Decker, W., 1992. How customers choose banks. Journal of Retail Banking, 14(4), pp. 41-44.

222. Khitoliya, P., 2014. Investors Awareness and Perceived Risk Attitude Towards Mutual Fund: An empirical study in Delhi. International Journal of Commerce, Business and Management, 3(3), pp. 450-5+.

223. Kim, J.S., Kaye, J. & Wright, L.K., 2001. Moderating & Mediating Effects in Causal Models. Issues in Mental Health Nursing , 22(1), pp. 63-75.

224. Kisaka, E.S. & Mwewa, N.M., 2014. Effects of Micro-credit, Micro-saving and Training on the Growth of Small and Medium Entreprises in Machakos County in Kenya. Research Journal of Finance and Accounting, 7(2), pp. 43-49.

225. Kline, RB 2005, Principles and Practice of Structural Equation Modeling, 2nd edn, Guilford Press, New York.

226. Kolvereid, L. & Erlend, B., 1996. Growth intentions and actual growth: The impact of entrepreneurial choice. Journal of enterprising Culture, 4(1), pp. 1-17.

227. Kothari, C.R., 2004. Research Methodology Methods & Techniques. 2nd ed. New Delhi: New Age International publisher.

228. Kothari, P. & Mindargi, C., 2013. A Study of Investors Attitude towards Mutual Fund with Special Reference to Investors in Solapur city. International Journal of Accounting and Financial Management Research, 3(2), pp. 1-12.

229. Kroll, 2012. Forbes World's Billionaires 2012. Available at: http://www.forbes.com/sites/luisakroll/2012/03/07/forbes-worlds-billionaires-2012/. (Accessed on 10 July 2013).

230. Kumar & Persaud 2002. Pure Contagion and Investors' Shifting Risk Appetite: Analytical Issues and Empirical Evidence. Working Paper IMF. Available at: https://www.imf.org/external/pubs/ft/wp/2001/wp01134.pdf (Accessed on 23rd June 2014).

231. Kumar, A., & Oswal, K. G. 2012. Holistic Solutions for key Challenges of the Wealth Management Industry. Infosys: Financial Services. Avaialble at: http://www.infosys.com/industries/financial-services/white-papers/Documents/holistic-solutions-key-challenges.pdf. (Accessed on: 3rd July 2014)

232. Kumar, A., 2002. Research Methodolgy in Social Science. 1st ed. New Delhi: Sarup & Sons.

233. Kumar, A., Page, J.K. & Spalt, O.G., 2011. Religious Beliefs, Gambling Attitudes, and Financial Market Outcomes. Journal of Financial Economics, 102(3), pp. 671-708.

234. Lam. K. 2008. Factors Affecting People Investing in Mutual Fund in Malaysia: An Application of the Theory of Planned Behavior. Available at: http://eprints.usm.my/25370/1/Factors_affecting_people_ investing_in_Mutual_Fund.pdf (Accessed on: 12th Feb 2015)

235. Lee, F.S., 2002. Theory creation and the methodological foundation of Post Keynesian economics. Cambridge Journal of Economics, 26(6), pp. 789-804.

236. Leonardo, ., Stefano, C. & Decio, ., 2013. Financial education and investment attitudes in high schools: evidence from a randomized experiment. Applied Financial Economics, 23(10), pp. 817-36.

237. Leong, Grace 2015, Rise in number of young investors, Available at: http://business.asiaone.com/news/personal-finance/rise-number-young-investors (Accessed on: 21st August 2015).

238. Lewis, W., Agarwal, R. & Sambamurthy, V., 2003. Sources of Influence on Beliefs About Information Technology Use: An Empirical Study of Knowledge Workers. MIS Quarterly, 27(4), pp. 657-78.

239. Li & Li 2014. Are Household Investors Noise Traders: Evidence From Belief Dispersion and Stock Trading Volume. Federal Reserve Buletin. Available at: http://www.federalreserve.gov/pubs/feds/2014/201435/201435pap.pdf. (Accessed on 23rd June 2014).

240. Limited, E.C., 2008. Business Knowledge for It in Private Wealth Management. 1st ed. London: Essvale Corporation Limited.

241. Lin, 2004. The empirical study for risk attribute of High Net Worth Individuals & Investment rate of return of Mutual Funds. The Journal of Business, 2(2), pp. 296-333.

242. Lin, C., 2007. Influences of Chinese Elder's Wealth Management Behavior" An Empirical Study. International Journal of Management Studies, 16(2), pp. 97-121.

243. Lindley, P., & Walker, S. N.1993, Theoretical and methodological differentiation of moderation and mediation. Nursing Research, vol. 42, pp. 276–279.

244. Linnainmaa, J., 2011. Why do (some) households trade so much? Review of Financial Studies , 24(1), pp. 1630-66.

245. Listyarti, I. & Suryani, T., 2014. Determinant factors of investors' behavior in investment decision in Indonesian capital markets. Journal of Economics, Business, and Accountancy Ventura , 17(1), pp. 45-54.

246. Liu, F.H.F. & Hai, H.L., 2005. The voting analytic hierarchy process method for selecting supplier. International Journal of Production Economics, 97(3), pp. 308-17.

247. Locke, P. & Mann, S., 2005. Do professional traders exhibit loss aversion? Journal of Financial Economics, 76(1), pp. 401-44.

248. Lodhi, S., 2014. Factors Influencing Individual Investor Behavior: An Empirical Study of City Karachi. IOSR Journal of Business and Management , 16(2), pp. 68-76.

249. Long, J.B.D., Shleifer, A., Summers, L.H. & Waldmann, R.J., 1990. Noise Trader Risk in Financial Markets. The Journal of Political Economy, 98(4), pp. 703-38.

250. Lopes, L.L., 1987. Between Hope and Fear: The Psychology of Risk. Advances in Experimental Social Psychology, 20(1), pp. 255-95.

251. Loucks, J., Waitman, R., & Ericsson, J., 2011. Winning the Battle for the Wealthy Investor:New Cisco IBSG Study Uncovers Significant Opportunity To Address Needs of

252. Lusardi & Mitchell, 2007. Financial Literacy and Retirement Planning: New Evidence from the Rand American Life Panel. Michigan Retirement Research Center Research Paper No. WP 2007-157. Available at: http://papers.ssrn.com/sol3/papers.cfm?abstract_id=1095869 (Accessed on: 3 Dec 2013).

253. Lusardi & Mitchell, 2011. Financial Literacy and Planning: Implications for Retirement Wellbeing. NBER Working Paper Series. Available at: http://www.nber.org/papers/w17078.pdf (Accessed on: 5th Dec 2013).

254. Lusardi, A. & Mitchell, O.S., 2007. Baby Boomer retirement security: The roles of planning, financial literacy, and housing wealth. Journal of Monetary Economics, 54(1), pp. 205-24.

255. Lusardi, A. & Mitchell, O.S., 2014. The Economic Importance of Financial Literacy: Theory and Evidence. Journal of Economic Literature, American Economic Association, 52(1), pp. 5-44.

256. Lyons, A. & Neelakantan, U., 2008. Potential and pitfalls of applying theory to the practice of financial education. The Journal of Consumer Affairs, 42(1), pp. 106-12.

257. Lyons, A., Neelakantan, U. & Scherpf, E., 2007. Gender and marital differences in wealth and investment decisions. Journal of Personal Finance, 6(4), pp. 57-76.

258. Lyons, A.C., 2004. A profile of financially at-risk college students. The Journal of Consumer Affairs, 38(1), pp. 56-80.

259. Lyons, A.C., Palmer, L., Jayaratne, K.S.U. & Scherpf, E., 2006. Are we making the grade? A national overview of financial education and program evaluation. The Journal of Consumer Affairs, 40(1), pp. 208-35.

260. MacKinnon, DP, Lockwood, CM, Hoffman, JM & West, SG 2002, 'A Comparison of Methods to Test Mediation and Other Intervening Variable Effects', Psychological Methods, Vol. 7, no. 1, pp. 83-104.

261. Madhani, P.M., 2007. Wealth Management: Emerging Opportunities. MBA Review, 1(7), pp. 21-24.

262. Maditinos, D., Sevic, Z. & Theriou, N., 2007. Investors' behavior in the athens stock exchange. Studies in Economics and Finance, 24(1), pp. 32-50.

263. Maditinos, D.I., Sevic′, Z. & Theriou, N.G., 2007. Investors' behaviour in the Athens Stock Exchange (ASE). Studies in Economics and Finance: Emerald Group Publishing, 24(1), pp. 32-50.

264. Malhotra, N.K. & Birks, D.F., 2007. Marketing Research: An Applied Approach. 3rd ed. England: Pearson Education Limited.

265. Malhotra, NK 2010, Marketing Research: An Applied Orientation, 6th edn, Pearson education, India.

266. Mandell, L. & Klein, L.S., 2009. The impact of financial literacy education on subsequent financial behavior. Journal of Financial Counseling and Planning Education, 20(1), pp. 15-24.

267. Marcus, Glaser & Walther, 2013. Financial Literacy: Dual Process Theory and Investment Behavior. Available at: http://papers.ssrn.com/sol3/papers.cfm?abstract_id=2167270 (Accessed on: 5th July 2014).

268. Markets, R., 2008. Wealth Management in India. CYGNUS Business Consulting & Research, 1 January. pp. 106-16.

269. Marketsandmarkets.com 2010, 'HNWI of Indian Wealth Management Industry – Trends, Analysis And Forecast (2010-2015)', Market Reports, Finance, Markets and Markets, BFS 1305, marketsandmarkets.com, US.

270. Martínoliver, A & Salasfumás, V 2011, 'IT Investment and intangibles: Evidence from Banks', Review of Income and Wealth, vol 57, no. 3, pp. 513-535.

271. Martz, Eston 2013, Handling Multicollinearity in Regression Analysis, Available at: http://blog.minitab.com/blog/understanding-statistics/handling-multicollinearity-in-regression-analysis (Accessed on 12th January 2014).

272. Mathieson, K., 1991. Predicting user intentions: comparing the technology acceptance model with the theory of planned behavior. Information Systems Research, 2(3), pp. 173-91.

273. Matthew, T.L., Zhu, Z. & Colin, C.C.-C., 2007. Influences of Chinese elder's Wealth Management Behavior: An Empirical Study. International Journal of Management Studies, 16(2), pp. 97-121.

274. Matthias & Schmitz, 2010. The Effect of Household Debt on Health. Available at: http://www.rwi-essen.de/media/content/pages/publikationen/ruhr-economic-papers/REP_10_234.pdf (Accessed on 6th Dec 2013).

275. Maude, D., 2006. Global Private Banking and Wealth Management: The New Realities. 1st ed. England: John Wiley & Sons Ltd.

276. Maydeu-Olivares, A. & Garcý'a-Forero, C., 2010. Goodness-of-Fit Testing. International Encyclopedia of Education, 7(1), pp. 190-96.

277. McCann, RJ & Lavayssiere, B 2008, 'World Wealth Report', Wealth Report, Management, Capgemini & Merrill Lynch, N.D., Merrill Lynch Press, America.

278. McInish, T., 1982. Individual investors and risk-taking. Journal of Economic Psychology, 2(1), pp. 125-36.

279. McKinsey 2014, McKinsey Global Wealth Management Survey 2014. Available at: McKinsey_Global_Wealth_Management_Survey_2014.pdf (Accessed on: 2nd Dec 2014).

280. Michael, L. M., 2011. An examination of the determinants of top management support of information technology projects. Doctoral Thesis. Available at: http://eric.ed.gov/?id=ED530759 (Accessed on 2nd Jan 2014).

281. Miles, J. and Shevlin, M. 1998, 'Effects of sample size, model specification and factor loadings on the GFI in confirmatory factor analysis,' Personality and Individual Differences, vol 25, pp. 85-90.

282. Mindel, M.N. & Sleight, S.E., 2010. Wealth management in the new economy, investor strategies for growing, protecting and transferring wealth. 1st ed. New Jersey: John Wiley & Sons Inc.

283. Mirshekary, S. & Saudagarah, S., 2005. Perceptions and characteristics of financial information users in developing countries: evidence from Iran. Journal of International Accounting, Auditing and Taxation, 14(1), pp. 33-54.

284. Mohamed, E.I. & Alqaydi, F.R., 2013. Financial Literacy, Personal Financial Attitude, and Forms of Personal Debt among Residents of the UAE. International Journal of Economics and Finance, 5(7), pp. 126-38.

285. Mohanta, G. & Dr. Debasish, S.S., 2011. A Study on Investment preferences among urban investors in Orissa. PRERANA Journal of Management Thought and Practice, 3(1), pp. 1-10.

286. Morjaria, 2014. Which is best investment option in India. Available at:http://www.moneycontrol.com/news/investing/which-is-best-investment-optionindia_1179280.html (Accessed on: 25 July 2015)

287. Morris, S. & Shin, H., 2002. Social value of public information. American Economic Review, 92(5), pp. 1521-34.

288. Muehlfeld, K., Weitzel, U. & Witteloostuijn, A.V., 2013. Fight or freeze? Individual differences in investors' motivational systems and trading in experimental asset markets. Journal of Economic Psychology, 34(2013), pp. 195-209.

289. Mulaik, SA, James, LR, Alstine, JV, Bennett, N, Lind, S & Stilwell, CD 1989, 'Evaluation of Goodness-of-Fit Indices for Structural Equation Models ', Psychological Bulletin, vol 105, no. 3, pp. 430-445.

290. Muller, S. & Weber, M., 2010. Financial Literacy and Mutual Fund Investments: Who buys actively managed funds? Schmalenbach Business Review, 62(2), pp. 126-53.

291. Murgea, A., 2008. Investor's psychology cycle on the romanian capital market. Analele Universitãþii "Alexandru Ioan Cuza" Iasi-Stiinte Economice, 55(1), pp. 111-19.

292. Myers, S.C., 2001. Capital structure. Journal of Economic Perspectives, 15(2), pp. 81-102.

293. Nachmias, CF & Nachmias, D 1992, Research Methods in the Social Sciences, 4th edn, St. Martin's Press, New York.

294. Nagy, RA & Obenberger, RW 1994, 'Factors Influencing Individual Investor Behavior', Financial Analysts Journal, Vol. 50, no. 4, pp. 63-68.

295. Nargundkar, R., 2008. Marketing Research Text and Cases. 3rd ed. New Delhi: Tata McGraw Hill.

296. Nathans, L.L., Oswald, F.L. & Nimon, K., 2012. Interpreting Multiple Linear Regression: A guidebook of variable importance. Practical Assessment, Research and Evaluation, 17(9), pp. 1-19.

297. Nosic, A., Weber, M., 2007. Determinants of Risk Taking Behavior: The role of Risk Attitudes, Risk Perceptions and Beliefs. Available at: http://ub-madoc.bib.uni-mannheim.de/1774/1/001_SSRN_ID1027453_code846681.pdf (Accessed on: 26th Nov 2014)

298. Nunnally, J.C. & Bernstein, I.H., 1994. Psychometric Theory. 3rd ed. New York: McGraw-Hill.

299. O'Donoghue, T., Rabin, M.,1998. Procrastination in preparing for retirement. Available at: http://down.cenet.org.cn/upfile/36/200571320257133.pdf (Accessed on: 5th Mar 2014)

300. Obamuyi, T.M., 2013. Factors infuencing investment decisions in capital market: A study of individual investors in Nigeria. Organizations and Markets in Emerging Economies, 4(1), pp. 141-61.

301. Olsen, R.A., 2007. Investors' predisposition for annuities: a psychological perspective. Journal of Financial Service Professionals, 61(5), pp. 51-57.

302. Olsen, R.A., 2008. Perceptions of financial risk: axioms and affect. ICFAI Journal of Behavioural Finance, 5(4), pp. 58-80.

303. Omkarprasad, S.V. & Kumar, S., 2006. Analytic hierarchy process: An overview of applications. European Journal of Operational Research, 169(1), pp. 1-29.

304. Oracle, 2010. Customer Centric Wealth Management. Available at:http://www.oracle.com/us/industries/financial-services/ customer-centric-wealth-mgmt-wp-067632.pdf (Accessed on: 27th Nov 2014)

305. Padmaja, R., 2013. A Study Of Consumer Behavior Towards Mutual Funds With Special Reference To Icici Prudential Mutual Funds, Vijayawada. International Journal of Management Research and Business Strategy, 2(2), pp. 30-41.

306. Pallant, J 2007, SPSS Survival Manual: A Step by Step Guide to Data Analysis using SPSS for Windows, 3rd edn, McGraw Hill Education: Open University Press, England.

307. Pang, G. & Warshawasky, M., 2009. Comparing Strategies for Retirement Wealth Management: Mutual Funds and Annuities. Journal of Financial Planning, 22(8), pp. 36-47.

308. Paola, B., Luca, C.M. & Iwanicz-Drozdowska, 2014. The Importance of being systemically important financial institutions. Journal of Banking & Finance, 17(1), pp. 257-66.

309. Park, C.W., Mothersbaugh, D.L. & Feick, L., 1994. Consumer Knowledge Assessment. Journal of Consumer Research, 21(1), pp. 71-82.

310. Parkinson & Drislane, 2011. Qualitative Research. Online dictionary of the social sciences. Available at: http://bitbucket.icaap.org/dict.pl (Accessed on: 11th May 2013)

311. Patton, A.J. & Timmermann, A., 2010. Why do forecasters disagree? Lessons from the term structure of cross-sectional dispersion. Journal of Monetary Economics, 57(1), pp. 803-20.

312. Perry, V.G & Morris, M.D., 2005. Who is in control? The role of self-perception, knowledge, and income in explaining consumer financial behavior. The Journal of Consumer Affairs, 39(2), pp. 299-313.

313. Perry, V.G., 2008. Is ignorance bliss? Consumer accuracy in judgments about credit ratings. The Journal of Consumer Affairs, 42(2), pp. 189-205.

314. Pompian, M.M., 2012. Behavioral Finance and Wealth Management. 2nd ed. Hoboken, New Jersey: John Wiley & Sons, Inc.

315. Preacher, K. J., & Hayes, A. F. 2004, SPSS and SAS procedures for estimating indirect effects in simple mediation models, Behavior Research Methods, Instruments, and Computers, Vol. 36, pp. 717-731.

316. Preacher, K. J., & Hayes, A. F. 2008, Asymptotic and resampling strategies for assessing and comparing indirect effects in multiple mediator models, Behavior Research Methods, Vol. 40, pp. 879-891.

317. Pui-Wa, L. & Qiong, W., 2007. Introduction to Structural Equation Modeling: Issues and Practical Considerations. Educational Measurement: Issues and Practice, 26(3), pp. 33-43.

318. PWC 2011, Regulations and client expectations change status quo in wealth management industry, finds PwC research. Available at: http://www.pwc.com/gx/en/industries/financial-services/banking-capital-markets/private-banking-wealth-management-survey/global-private-banking-wealth-management-survey-2011.html (Accessed on: 2nd December 2014).

319. Qureshi, A.S., Rehman, K. & Hunjra, I.A., 2012. Factors affecting investment decision making of equity fund managers. Wulfenia Journal Klagenfurt, Austria, 19(10), pp. 280-91.

320. Raheja, S. & Lamba, B., 2013. Behaviour of Investors towards Investment. Indian Journal of Applied Research, 3(10), pp. 12-29.

321. Ramayah & Suki, 2006. Intention to use mobile PC among MBA students: Implications for technology integration in the learning curriculum. UNITAR E-Journal, 7(2), pp. 1-10.

322. Riaz, L., Hunjra, A.I. & Azam, R., 2012. Impact of psychological factors on investment decision making mediating by risk perception: A conceptual study. Middle-East Journal of Scientic Research, 12(6), pp. 789-95.

323. Riley, M. et al., 2000. Researching and writing dissertations in business and management. 3rd ed. London: Thomson Learning.

324. Riley, W.B. & Chow, K.V., 1992. Asset allocation and individual risk aversion. Financial Analysts Journal, 48(6), pp. 32-37.

325. Robinson, J.P., Shaver, P.R. & Wrightsman, L.S., 1991. Criteria for Scale Selection and Evaluation. In J.P. Robinson, P.R. Shaver & L.S. Wrightsman, eds. Measures of Personality and Social Psychological Attitudes. 1st ed. California: Academic Press. pp. 1-16.

326. Roger, B., Griffin, D. & Ross, M., 1994. Exploring the Planning Fallacy: Why People Underestimate Their Task Completion Times. Journal of Personality and Social Psychology, 67(3), pp. 366-81.

327. Rooij, M.V., Lusardi, A. & Alessie, R., 2011. Financial Literacy and Stock Market Participation. Journal of Financial Economics, 101(2), pp. 449-72.

328. Roszkowski, MJ, Davey, G & Grable, JE 2005, 'Insights from Psychology and Psychometrics on Measuring Risk Tolerance', Journal of Financial Planning, vol. 18, no. 4, pp. 66-77.

329. Rousseeuw, PJ & and Van Zomeren, BC 1990, Unmasking Multivariate Outliers and Leverage Points, Journal of the American Statistical Association, 85, 633-639.

330. Ruscio, J & Roche, B 2012, 'Determining the number of factors to retain in an exploratory factor analysis using comparison data of known factorial structure', Psychological Assessment, vol 24, no. 2, pp. 282-292.

331. Sangvinatsos, A. & Wachter, J., 2005. Does the failure of the expectations hypothesis matter for long-term investors? Journal of Finance, 60(1), pp. 179-230.

332. Sashikala, P. & Prasad, R., 2010. A study of the effect of demographics on the choice of investments and ability to take riskin developing countries. International Journal of Applied Accounting and Finance, 1(1), pp. 27-39.

333. Schooley, D. & Deborah, D.W., 1999. Investor's asset allocations versus life-cycle funds. Financial Analysts Journal, 55(5), pp. 37-43.

334. Schuman, H. & Johnson, M.P., 1976. Attitudes and behavior. Annual Review of Sociology, 2(1), pp. 161-207.

335. Schwartz, S.H. & Tessler, R.C., 1972. A test of a model for reducing measured attitude-behavior discrepancies. Journal of Personality and Social Psychology, 24(1), pp. 225-36.

336. Seaberg, B., 2013. Seven Principles of Wealth Planning. White Paper: Morgan Stanley, 1 May. pp. 1-4.

337. Sehgal, M. & Singh, D., 2012. Psychology of investors based on value and life style survey. International Journal of Transformations in Business Management, 2(2), pp. 37-76.

338. Sehgal, S., Sood, G.S. & Rajput, N., 2009. Investor Sentiment in India: A Survey. Vision: The Journal of Business Perspective, 13(2), pp. 13-23.

339. Sekaran, U 2006, Research Methods For Business: A Skill Building Approach, 4th edn, Wiley Publishing, India.

340. Septyanto, D. & Adhikara, A., 2014. Individual Investor's Behaviour in Decision Making on Securities Investment in ISE. Journal of Economics, Business and Accountancy Ventura, 17(2), pp. 187-96.

341. Sewell, M.,2007. Behavioural Finance. Working Paper, Available at: http://www.behaviouralfinance.net/behavioural-finance.pdf. (Accessed: 22 April 2013)

342. Shaikh, .D.A.R. & Kalkundarikar, D.A.B., 2011. Analysis of Retail Investors' Behavior in Belgaum District, Karnataka State. International Journal for Management Research, 1(2), pp. 22-39.

343. Shamsuddoha, M., 2005. Wealth Management Strategies in the Era of E-Commerce. Pakistan Journal of Social Sciences, 3(1), pp. 216-24.

344. Sharma, M. & al., e., 2012. A Study on Factor Influencing Satisfaction of Investors Towards Mutual Funds Industry Using Servqual Model: An Empirical Study. International Journal of Management & Business Studies, 2(4), pp. 52-56.

345. Sharma, M. & Gupta, S., 2011. Role of Subjective Norms in investment decision making of casual investors. The Indian Journal of Finance, 5(11), pp. 39-44.

346. Sharma, S., Mukherjee, S., Kumar, A., and Dillon, W.R. 2005, 'A simulation study to investigate the use of cut-off values for assessing model fit in covariance structure models,' Journal of Business Research, vol 58, no.1, pp. 935-43.

347. Sharpe, W.F., 1966. Security prices, risk and maximal gains from diversification. Journal of Finance, 21(4), pp. 743-44.

348. Shefrin, H & Statman, M 2000, 'Behavioral Portfolio Theory', The Journal of Financial and Quantitative Analysis, vol 35, no. 2, pp. 127-151.

349. Sheppard, B.H., Hartwick, J. & Warshaw, P.R., 1988. The theory of reasoned action: A meta-analysis of past research with recommendations for modifications and future research. Journal of Consumer Research, 15(3), pp. 325-43.

350. Sherraden, M. & Boshara, R., 2008. Learning from Individual Development Accounts. In A. Lusardi, ed. Overcoming the Saving Slump: How to Increase the Effectiveness of Financial Education and Saving Programs. 1st ed. United States of America: The University of Chicago Press Ltd. pp. 280-300.

351. Shih, Y.Y. & Fang, K., 2004. The use of a decomposed theory of planned behavior to study Internet banking in Taiwan. Internet research, 14(3), pp. 213-23.

352. Shim, S. et al., 2010. Financial socialization of first-year college students: The roles of parents, work, and education. Journal of youth and adolescence, 39(12), pp. 1457-70.

353. Shrout, PE & Bolger, N 2002, 'Mediation in Experimental and Nonexperimental Studies:New Procedures and Recommendations', Psychological Methods, vol 7, no. 4, pp. 422-445.

354. Shun-Yao, Tseng & Chyan Yang, 2011. Influence of information search on risky investment preferences. Paper published in 3rd International Conference on Information and Financial Engineering , Singapore. Vol.12 ; IACSIT Press, Singapore

355. Shyan, R. & C.L., 2010. Investor attitudes and behaviour towards inherent risk and potential return in financial products. International Research Journal of Finance and Economics , 44(1), pp. 16-29.

356. Siegel, F.W. & Hoban, J.P., 1982. Relative Risk Aversion Revisited. The Review of Economics and Statistics, 64(1), pp. 481-87.

357. Silverman, D., 1993. Interpreting Qualitative Data. 1st ed. London: Sage publication.

358. Singh, B.K. & Jha, A.K., 2009. An empirical study on awareness & acceptability of mutual fund. Regional Student's Conference, ICWAI, 1(1), pp. 49-55.

359. Singh, J., Chadha, S. & Sharma, A., 2012. Role of Foreign Direct Investment in India: An Analytical Study. International Journal of Engineering and Science, 1(5), pp. 34-42.

360. Sireesha, B.P. & Laxmi, S., 2013. Impact of Demographics on Select Investment Avenues: A Case Study of Twin Cities of Hyderabad and Secunderabad, India. International Journal of Marketing, Financial Services and Management Research, 2(6), pp. 47-55.

361. Slovic, P., 1972. Psychological Study of Human Judgment: Implications for Investment Decision Making. Journal of Finance, 27(4), pp. 779-99.

362. Snyder, M. & Ickes, W., 1985. Personality and social behavior. In S.T. Fiske, D.T. Gilbert & G. Lindzey, eds. Handbook of Social Psychology. 3rd ed. New York: Wiley Publishing. pp. 883-947.

363. Speed, R. & Smith, G., 1992. Retail financial services segmentation. The Service Industries Journal, 12(1), pp. 368-83.

364. Srivastava, A., 2007. An Analysis of Behaviour of Investors in India. ICFAI Journal of Behavioural Finance, 4(2), pp. 43-52.

365. Srivastava, S., 2012. Rational Investment Decisions of Irrational Household Investors. Global Research Analysis, 1(7), pp. 59-61.

366. Stafford, M.R., 1994. How customers perceive service quality. Journal of Retail Banking, 16(2), pp. 29-38.

367. Steiger, J.H. 2007, 'Understanding the limitations of global fit assessment in structural equation modeling,' Personality and Individual Differences, vol 42, no.5, pp. 893-898

368. Stiglitz, J.E., 2002. Information and the change in the paradigm in economics. American Economic Review, 92(3), pp. 460-501.

369. Tabachnick, BG & Fidell, LS 2007, Using Multivariate Statistics, 6th edn, Pearson, New York.

370. Tahira K. Hira, 2009. Personal Finance: Past Present and Future. Available at: https://www2.indstate.edu/business/NFI/leadership/briefs/2009-PB-10_Hira.pdf (Accessed on: 20th August 2014)

371. Talati & Sanghvi, 2011. An Analytical Study on Investor's Awareness and Perception Towards the Hedge Funds in Gujarat. Available at SSRN: http://ssrn.com/abstract=1912313 or http://dx.doi.org/10.2139/ssrn. 1912313 (Accessed on 13th feb 2013)

372. Tarashev, N., Tsatsaronis, K. & Karampatos, D., 2003. Investors' attitude towards risk: What can we learn from options. BIS Quarterly Review, 1 June. pp. 57-65.

373. Taura, A.A., Roslan, M. & Omar, Z., 2014. Self-Regulation as a Mediator in the Relationship between Self-Efficacy, Task Value and Active Procrastination. International Journal of Humanities and Social Science, 4(9), pp. 293-301.

374. Taylor, S. & Todd, P., 1995. Understanding Information Technology Usage: A Test of Competing Models. Information Systems Research , 6(2), pp. 144-76.

375. Teo, T.S.H. & Pok, S.H., 2003. Adoption of WAP-Enabled Mobile Phones Among Internet Users. Omega, 31(6), pp. 483-98.

376. The Boston Consulting Group 2010, Upgrading the Wealth Management Experience for Women, Available at: https://www.bcg.com/documents/file56704.pdf (Accessed on: 5th August 2015).

377. The University of Texas 2012, Structural Equation Modeling Using AMOS: An Introduction, Available at: https://stat.utexas.edu/images/SSC/Site/AMOS_Tutorial.pdf (Accessed on 14th July 2015).

378. Thunderhead, 2013. Rebuilding Trust in Wealth Management.Available at: http://www.thunderhead.com/wp-content/uploads/2013/02/WhitePaper WealthManagement.pdf (Accessed on:28th Nov 2014) .

379. Tim, B., Ken, B. & Gene, B., 1996. Religiosity, Ethical Ideology and Intentions to Report a Peer's Wrongdoing. Journal of Business Ethics, 15(11), pp. 1161-74.

380. Triandis, H. C., 1980. Values, attitudes, and interpersonal behavior. Available at: http://www.cres.gr/behave/pdf/Triandis_theory.pdf (Accessed on 11th May 2015).

381. Trochim, W. M. K., 2006. Introduction to Validity. Social Research Methods. Available at: www.socialresearchmethods.net/kb/introval.php (Accessed on 5th January, 2015).

382. Tversky, A. & Kahneman, D., 1974. Judgment under uncertainty: Heuristics and biases. Science, a publication by American Association for the Advancement of Science, 185(1), pp. 1124-31.

383. Tversky, A. & Kahneman, D., 1992. Advances in prospect theory: Cumulative representation of Uncertainty. Journal of Risk and Uncertainty, 5(1), pp. 297-323.

384. Uma, M.R. & M.Uma, 2015. Customer preference towards the various policies offered by the private insurance companies in Coimbatore city. International Journal of Multidisciplinary Research and Development, 2(2), pp. 653-56.

385. Vaidya, O & Kumar, S 2006, 'Analytic Hierarchy process: An Overview of Applications', European Journal of Operational Research, vol 169, no. 1, pp. 1-29.

386. Van, R.M.C.J., Lusardi, A. & Alessie, R.J.M., 2011. Financial Literacy and Stock Market Participation. Journal of Financial Economics, 101(2), pp. 449-72.

387. Varian, H.R., 1985. Divergence of opinion in complete markets: A note. Journal of Finance, 40(1), pp. 309-17.

388. Venkatesh, V. & Davis, F.D., 2000. A theoretical extension of the technology acceptance model: four longitudinal field studies. Management Science, 46(2), pp. 186-204.

389. Victor, S. & Jonathan, Z., 2007. Fuzzy Math, Disclosure Regulation and Credit Market Outcomes. American Economic Review, 99(2), pp. 06-09.

390. Vincent, F.Y. & Hsiu-I, T., 2011. Identifying Key Factors Affecting Consumer's Choice of Wealth Management Services: an AHP approach. The Service Industries Journal, 31(6), pp. 929-39.

391. Von Gaudecker, H.M., 2011. How Does Household Portfolio Diversification Vary with Financial Literacy and Financial Advice. Available at: (Accessed on: 27th Nov'2014).

392. Wachter, J.A., 2002. Portfolio and Consumption Decisions under Mean-Reverting Returns: An Exact Solution for Complete markets. Journal of Financial and Quantitative Analysis, 37(1), pp. 63-92.
393. Walia, N. & Dr. Kiran, R., 2009. An Analysis of Investor's Risk Perception towards Mutual Funds Services. International Journal of Business and Management, 4(5), pp. 106-20.
394. Walia, N. & Kiran, R., 2009. An Analysis of Investor's Risk Perception towards Mutual Funds Services. International Journal of Business Management, 4(5), pp. 106-20.
395. Wallach, M. & Kogan, N., 1961. Aspects of judgement and decision making: interrelationships and changes with age. Behavioral Science, 6(1), pp. 23-26.
396. Walters, B. & Young, D., 2001. Critical Realism as a basis for economic methodology: a critique. Review of Political Economy, 13(4), pp. 483-501.
397. Wang, F.A., 2001. Overconfidence, investor sentiment and evolution. Journal of Financial Intermediation, 10(2), pp. 138-70.
398. Wang, H. & Hanna, S., 1997. Does risk tolerance decrease with age. Financial Counseling and Planning, 8(2), pp. 27-32.
399. Wang, H.a.H.S., n.d.
400. Wang, J. & Jing, J.X., 2009. Buying Behavior, Social Support and Credit Card Indebtedness. International Journal of Consumer Studies, 33(1), pp. 2-10.
401. Wealthy Under-50 Investors. Available at: http://www.cisco.com/web/about/ac79/docs/Wealth_Management_PoV.pdf (Accessed on: 19th November 2014).
402. Weber, E., Blais, A. & Betz, N., 2002. A domain specific risk attitude scale: Measuring risk perceptions and risk behaviors. Journal of behavioral decision making, 15(1), pp. 263-90.
403. Weinstein, N.D., 1980. Unrealistic optimism about future life events. Journal of Personality and Social Psychology, 39(5), pp. 806-20.
404. Wheaton, B., Muthen, B., Alwin, D., F. & Summers, G. 1977, 'Assessing Reliability and Stability in Panel Models,' Sociological Methodology, Vol. 8, no. 1, pp. 84-136
405. Williams, C.A. & Heins, R.M., 1964. Risk management and insurance. 1st ed. New York: McGraw-Hill Book Co.
406. Wiseman, R. & Gomez-Mejia, L., 1998. A behavioral agency model of managerial risk taking. The Academy of Management Review, 23(1), pp. 133-53.
407. World Wealth Report 2014, 5th Annual world Wealth Report by Merrill Lynch and Capgemini. Available at: https://www.worldwealthreport.com/ (Accessed on 2nd Dec 2014).
408. Xiao, J.J., Tang, C., Serido, J. & Shim, S., 2011. Antecedents and consequences of risky credit behavior among college students: Application and extension of the theory of planned behavior. Journal of Public Policy & Marketing, 30(2), pp. 239-45.

Appendix

Appendix - A

Results of Multivariate Assumptions

Multi-collinearity

Coefficients								
Model		Unstandardized Coefficients		Standardized Coefficients	t	Sig.	Collinearity Statistics	
		B	Std. Error	Beta			Tolerance	VIF
1	(Constant)	1.016	.218		4.667	.000		
	Beliefs	.290	.053	.190	5.482	.000	.908	1.102
	SubjectiveNorms	.098	.034	.098	2.880	.004	.937	1.068
	RiskAppetite	.312	.027	.402	11.680	.000	.920	1.087

a. Dependent Variable: FinancialLiteracy

Coefficients[a]								
Model		Unstandardized Coefficients		Standardized Coefficients	t	Sig.	Collinearity Statistics	
		B	Std. Error	Beta			Tolerance	VIF
1	(Constant)	2.745	.117		23.367	.000		
	SubjectiveNorms	.094	.024	.144	3.892	.000	.946	1.057
	RiskAppetite	.061	.021	.119	2.919	.004	.774	1.292
	FinancialLiteracy	.148	.027	.226	5.482	.000	.764	1.309

a. Dependent Variable: Beliefs

Coefficients[a]								
Model		Unstandardized Coefficients		Standardized Coefficients	t	Sig.	Collinearity Statistics	
		B	Std. Error	Beta			Tolerance	VIF
1	(Constant)	2.298	.234		9.804	.000		
	RiskAppetite	.067	.033	.085	2.009	.045	.769	1.301
	FinancialLiteracy	.125	.044	.124	2.880	.004	.740	1.351
	Beliefs	.236	.061	.153	3.892	.000	.888	1.126

a. Dependent Variable: SubjectiveNorms

Coefficients[a]								
Model		Unstandardized Coefficients		Standardized Coefficients	t	Sig.	Collinearity Statistics	
		B	Std. Error	Beta			Tolerance	VIF
1	(Constant)	.419	.291		1.442	.150		
	FinancialLiteracy	.542	.046	.420	11.680	.000	.880	1.136
	Beliefs	.206	.071	.105	2.919	.004	.880	1.137
	SubjectiveNorms	.090	.045	.070	2.009	.045	.931	1.074
a. Dependent Variable: RiskAppetite								

Appendix - B

Results of Exploratory Factor Analysis

KMO and Bartlett's Test		
Kaiser-Meyer-Olkin Measure of Sampling Adequacy.		.868
Bartlett's Test of Sphericity	Approx. Chi-Square	59932.147
	df	1830
	Sig.	.000

Communalities

	Initial	Extraction
FL1	.945	.714
FL2	.945	.695
FL3	.998	.574
FL5	.971	.614
FL6	.971	.628
FL8	.998	.572
B1	.765	.719
B2	.596	.540
B3	.671	.652
B4	.663	.637
B6	.696	.659
B7	.596	.578
B8	.624	.572
B9	.655	.623
B10	.626	.590
B11	.667	.633
B12	.643	.625
R1	.958	.470
R2	.989	.606
R3	.958	.636
R4	.979	.544
R5	.675	.642
R6	.990	.705
R7	.674	.590

(Contd...)

R8	.644	.536
R9	.957	.623
R10	.990	.698
R11	.989	.600
R12	.979	.540
R13	.959	.471
A1	.889	.672
A2	.925	.732
A3	.882	.697
A4	.866	.695
A5	.867	.839
A6	.846	.758
A7	.816	.689
A8	.857	.729
A9	.821	.776
A10	.793	.727
A11	.875	.807
A12	.899	.757
A13	.887	.782
A14	.902	.776
A15	.907	.823
SN1	.781	.733
SN2	.993	.820
SN3	.962	.713
SN4	.799	.705
SN5	.840	.774
SN6	.857	.793
SN7	.786	.729
SN8	.845	.783
SN9	.993	.823
SN10	.965	.748
IB1	.961	.735
IB2	.558	.493
IB3	.962	.737
IB4	.878	.651
IB5	.530	.527
IB6	.881	.657
Extraction Method: Principal Axis Factoring.		

Total Variance Explained

Factor	Initial Eigenvalues			Extraction Sums of Squared Loadings			Rotation Sums of Squared Loadings		
	Total	% of Variance	Cumulative %	Total	% of Variance	Cumulative %	Total	% of Variance	Cumulative %
1	18.749	30.735	30.735	18.449	30.245	30.245	10.883	17.841	17.841
2	7.905	12.959	43.694	7.574	12.417	42.662	7.852	12.872	30.713
3	5.778	9.472	53.167	5.488	8.997	51.659	7.797	12.782	43.495
4	5.364	8.794	61.961	5.000	8.196	59.855	6.971	11.428	54.923
5	2.739	4.489	66.450	2.400	3.934	63.789	3.848	6.308	61.231
6	2.402	3.937	70.387	2.054	3.368	67.157	3.615	5.927	67.157
7	1.282	2.102	72.489						
8	1.141	1.871	74.360						
9	1.090	1.787	76.147						
10	1.057	1.733	77.880						
11	.910	1.491	79.372						
12	.775	1.270	80.642						
13	.768	1.260	81.902						
14	.709	1.162	83.064						
15	.660	1.081	84.145						
16	.574	.941	85.086						
17	.552	.905	85.991						
18	.536	.878	86.870						
19	.522	.856	87.726						
20	.500	.819	88.546						
21	.453	.743	89.288						
22	.428	.702	89.990						
23	.396	.649	90.639						
24	.384	.630	91.269						
25	.375	.614	91.883						
26	.350	.574	92.457						
27	.337	.553	93.010						
28	.317	.519	93.529						
29	.311	.510	94.039						
30	.291	.477	94.516						
31	.287	.470	94.985						

(Contd...)

31	.287	.470	94.985						
32	.272	.447	95.432						
33	.250	.410	95.842						
34	.241	.394	96.236						
35	.215	.352	96.588						
36	.207	.340	96.928						
37	.192	.315	97.242						
38	.184	.302	97.545						
39	.179	.293	97.838						
40	.164	.268	98.106						
41	.143	.234	98.341						
42	.124	.203	98.544						
43	.116	.191	98.734						
44	.107	.176	98.910						
45	.098	.161	99.071						
46	.092	.150	99.221						
47	.074	.121	99.342						
48	.072	.118	99.460						
49	.060	.098	99.559						
50	.051	.083	99.642						
51	.043	.071	99.713						
52	.042	.069	99.781						
53	.037	.061	99.843						
54	.027	.045	99.888						
55	.027	.043	99.931						
56	.015	.024	99.955						
57	.011	.017	99.973						
58	.009	.015	99.987						
59	.004	.006	99.994						
60	.003	.005	99.998						
61	.001	.002	100.000						

Extraction Method: Principal Axis Factoring.

Rotated Factor Matrixa						
	Factor					
	1	*2*	*3*	*4*	*5*	*6*
A5	.883					
A15	.845					
A9	.843					
A11	.841					
A6	.835					
A13	.831					
A14	.822					
A10	.816					
A12	.814					
A8	.813					
A7	.797					
A2	.781					
A4	.772					
A3	.770					
A1	.742					
R6		.797				
R10		.794				
R5		.765				
R3		.763				
R2		.760				
R11		.757				
R9		.751				
R7		.745				
R8		.715				
R4		.695				
R12		.690				
R1		.625				
R13		.624				
SN9			.865			
SN2			.861			
SN6			.856			
SN5			.842			
SN8			.838			
SN7			.809			
SN1			.798			
SN10			.797			
SN4			.779			
SN3			.777			
B1				.809		
B11				.784		
B4				.781		

(Contd...)

B6				.779		
B3				.774		
B12				.771		
B9				.758		
B10				.750		
B7				.744		
B8				.731		
B2				.715		
IB3					.804	
IB1					.801	
IB6					.751	
IB4					.748	
IB5					.654	
IB2					.620	
FL1						.758
FL2						.750
FL6						.699
FL5						.687
FL3						.665
FL8						.664

Extraction Method: Principal Axis Factoring.

Rotation Method: Varimax with Kaiser Normalization.a

a. Rotation converged in 6 iterations.

Appendix - C

Output Tables of Zero-order Constructs

Attitude

Regression Weights: (Group number 1 - Default model)

			Estimate	*S.E.*	*C.R.*	*P*	*Label*
A1	<---	Attitude	1.000				
A3	<---	Attitude	1.001	.047	21.218	***	
A4	<---	Attitude	1.013	.048	21.334	***	
A2	<---	Attitude	1.008	.047	21.448	***	
A7	<---	Attitude	1.132	.050	22.782	***	
A12	<---	Attitude	1.203	.049	24.437	***	
A8	<---	Attitude	1.199	.051	23.650	***	
A14	<---	Attitude	1.247	.051	24.682	***	
A10	<---	Attitude	1.103	.048	23.177	***	
A13	<---	Attitude	1.199	.048	24.855	***	
A6	<---	Attitude	1.136	.047	23.939	***	
A11	<---	Attitude	1.193	.047	25.115	***	
A15	<---	Attitude	1.244	.049	25.354	***	
A9	<---	Attitude	1.148	.047	24.585	***	
A5	<---	Attitude	1.169	.046	25.510	***	

Standardized Regression Weights: (Group number 1 - Default model)

			Estimate
A1	<---	Attitude	.743
A3	<---	Attitude	.779
A4	<---	Attitude	.783
A2	<---	Attitude	.786
A7	<---	Attitude	.829
A12	<---	Attitude	.881
A8	<---	Attitude	.856
A14	<---	Attitude	.888
A10	<---	Attitude	.842
A13	<---	Attitude	.894
A6	<---	Attitude	.865
A11	<---	Attitude	.902
A15	<---	Attitude	.909
A9	<---	Attitude	.885
A5	<---	Attitude	.914

Squared Multiple Correlations: (Group number 1 - Default model)

	Estimate
A5	.835
A9	.784
A15	.826
A11	.813
A6	.749
A13	.799
A10	.708
A14	.789
A8	.734
A12	.776
A7	.687
A2	.618
A4	.612
A3	.607
A1	.552

Model Fit Summary

CMIN

Model	NPAR	CMIN	DF	P	CMIN/DF
Default model	72	158.630	48	.000	3.305
Saturated model	120	.000	0		
Independence model	15	14340.484	105	.000	136.576

RMR, GFI

Model	RMR	GFI	AGFI	PGFI
Default model	.029	.968	.922	.404
Saturated model	.000	1.000		
Independence model	.688	.194	.060	.167

Baseline Comparisons

Model	NFI Delta1	RFI rho1	IFI Delta2	TLI rho2	CFI
Default model	.989	.977	.992	.983	.992
Saturated model	1.000		1.000		1.000
Independence model	.000	.000	.000	.000	.000

Parsimony-Adjusted Measures

Model	PRATIO	PNFI	PCFI
Default model	.487	.482	.483
Saturated model	.000	.000	.000
Independence model	1.000	.000	.000

NCP

Model	NCP	LO 90	HI 90
Default model	121.593	86.300	164.443
Saturated model	.000	.000	.000
Independence model	14359.042	13967.454	14756.916

FMIN

Model	FMIN	F0	LO 90	HI 90
Default model	.237	.181	.128	.244
Saturated model	.000	.000	.000	.000
Independence model	21.452	21.336	20.754	21.927

RMSEA

Model	RMSEA	LO 90	HI 90	PCLOSE
Default model	.056	.058	.080	.062
Independence model	.523	.516	.530	.000

AIC

Model	AIC	BCC	BIC	CAIC
Default model	109.381	110.610	276.370	313.370
Saturated model	110.000	111.828	358.228	413.228
Independence model	10507.358	10507.690	10552.490	10562.490

ECVI

Model	ECVI	LO 90	HI 90	MECVI
Default model	.163	.143	.194	.164
Saturated model	.163	.163	.163	.166
Independence model	15.613	15.117	16.117	15.613

HOELTER

Model	HOELTER .05	HOELTER .01
Default model	550	663
Independence model	4	5

Minimization: .006
Miscellaneous: .412
Bootstrap: .000
Total: .418

Beliefs

Regression Weights: (Group number 1 - Default model)

Regression Weights: (Group number 1 - Default model)

			Estimate	S.E.	C.R.	P	Label
B8	<---	Beliefs	1.171	.061	19.288	***	
B7	<---	Beliefs	1.251	.063	19.748	***	
B10	<---	Beliefs	1.224	.061	19.956	***	
B9	<---	Beliefs	1.222	.059	20.790	***	
B12	<---	Beliefs	1.224	.059	20.673	***	
B3	<---	Beliefs	1.180	.056	20.899	***	
B6	<---	Beliefs	1.251	.058	21.413	***	
B4	<---	Beliefs	1.206	.057	21.016	***	
B11	<---	Beliefs	1.242	.061	20.413	***	
B1	<---	Beliefs	1.268	.057	22.366	***	
B2	<---	Beliefs	1.000				

Standardized Regression Weights: (Group number 1 - Default model)

			Estimate
B8	<---	Beliefs	.741
B7	<---	Beliefs	.757
B10	<---	Beliefs	.765
B9	<---	Beliefs	.795
B12	<---	Beliefs	.790
B3	<---	Beliefs	.799
B6	<---	Beliefs	.817
B4	<---	Beliefs	.803
B11	<---	Beliefs	.781
B1	<---	Beliefs	.851
B2	<---	Beliefs	.730

Squared Multiple Correlations: (Group number 1 - Default model)

	Estimate
B2	.532
B1	.724
B11	.610
B4	.644
B6	.667
B3	.638
B12	.625
B9	.631
B10	.585
B7	.573
B8	.549

Model Fit Summary

CMIN

Model	NPAR	CMIN	DF	P	CMIN/DF
Default model	33	92.744	33	.000	2.810
Saturated model	66	.000	0		
Independence model	11	5478.743	55	.000	99.614

RMR, GFI

Model	RMR	GFI	AGFI	PGFI
Default model	.010	.975	.951	.488
Saturated model	.000	1.000		
Independence model	.298	.208	.049	.173

Baseline Comparisons

Model	NFI Delta1	RFI rho1	IFI Delta2	TLI rho2	CFI
Default model	.983	.972	.989	.982	.989
Saturated model	1.000		1.000		1.000
Independence model	.000	.000	.000	.000	.000

Parsimony-Adjusted Measures

Model	PRATIO	PNFI	PCFI
Default model	.600	.590	.593
Saturated model	.000	.000	.000
Independence model	1.000	.000	.000

NCP

Model	NCP	LO 90	HI 90
Default model	59.744	34.760	92.377
Saturated model	.000	.000	.000
Independence model	5423.743	5184.015	5669.767

FMIN

Model	FMIN	F0	LO 90	HI 90
Default model	.138	.089	.052	.137
Saturated model	.000	.000	.000	.000
Independence model	8.141	8.059	7.703	8.425

RMSEA

Model	RMSEA	LO 90	HI 90	PCLOSE
Default model	.052	.040	.064	.382
Independence model	.383	.374	.391	.000

AIC

Model	AIC	BCC	BIC	CAIC
Default model	158.744	159.942	307.681	340.681
Saturated model	132.000	134.396	429.873	495.873
Independence model	5500.743	5501.142	5550.388	5561.388

ECVI

Model	ECVI	LO 90	HI 90	MECVI
Default model	.236	.199	.284	.238
Saturated model	.196	.196	.196	.200
Independence model	8.173	7.817	8.539	8.174

HOELTER

Model	HOELTER .05	HOELTER .01
Default model	344	398
Independence model	10	11

Minimization: .002
Miscellaneous: .236
Bootstrap: .000

Investment Behavior

Regression Weights: (Group number 1 - Default model)
Regression Weights: (Group number 1 - Default model)

			Estimate	S.E.	C.R.	P	Label
IB5	<---	InvestmentBehavior	.869	.059	14.614	***	
IB4	<---	InvestmentBehavior	.876	.061	14.363	***	
IB6	<---	InvestmentBehavior	.887	.060	14.675	***	
IB1	<---	InvestmentBehavior	1.400	.069	20.408	***	
IB3	<---	InvestmentBehavior	1.441	.071	20.433	***	
IB2	<---	InvestmentBehavior	1.000				

Standardized Regression Weights: (Group number 1 - Default model)

			Estimate
IB5	<---	InvestmentBehavior	.625
IB4	<---	InvestmentBehavior	.612
IB6	<---	InvestmentBehavior	.628
IB1	<---	InvestmentBehavior	.975
IB3	<---	InvestmentBehavior	.978
IB2	<---	InvestmentBehavior	.630

Squared Multiple Correlations: (Group number 1 - Default model)

	Estimate
IB2	.397
IB3	.956
IB1	.950
IB6	.394
IB4	.375
IB5	.391

Model Fit Summary
CMIN

Model	NPAR	CMIN	DF	P	CMIN/DF
Default model	19	6.671	2	.036	3.336
Saturated model	21	.000	0		
Independence model	6	4008.472	15	.000	267.231

RMR, GFI

Model	RMR	GFI	AGFI	PGFI
Default model	.003	.997	.966	.095
Saturated model	.000	1.000		
Independence model	.620	.326	.057	.233

Baseline Comparisons

Model	NFI Delta1	RFI rho1	IFI Delta2	TLI rho2	CFI
Default model	.998	.988	.999	.991	.999
Saturated model	1.000		1.000		1.000
Independence model	.000	.000	.000	.000	.000

Parsimony-Adjusted Measures

Model	PRATIO	PNFI	PCFI
Default model	.133	.133	.133
Saturated model	.000	.000	.000
Independence model	1.000	.000	.000

NCP

Model	NCP	LO 90	HI 90
Default model	4.671	.234	16.582
Saturated model	.000	.000	.000
Independence model	3993.472	3788.938	4205.267

FMIN

Model	FMIN	F0	LO 90	HI 90
Default model	.010	.007	.000	.025
Saturated model	.000	.000	.000	.000
Independence model	5.956	5.934	5.630	6.249

RMSEA

Model	RMSEA	LO 90	HI 90	PCLOSE
Default model	.059	.013	.111	.305
Independence model	.629	.613	.645	.000

AIC

Model	AIC	BCC	BIC	CAIC
Default model	44.671	45.070	130.422	149.422
Saturated model	42.000	42.441	136.778	157.778
Independence model	4020.472	4020.599	4047.552	4053.552

ECVI

Model	ECVI	LO 90	HI 90	MECVI
Default model	.066	.060	.084	.067
Saturated model	.062	.062	.062	.063
Independence model	5.974	5.670	6.289	5.974

HOELTER

Model	HOELTER .05	HOELTER .01
Default model	605	930
Independence model	5	6

Minimization: .001
Miscellaneous: .162
Bootstrap: .000
Total: .163

Financial Literacy

Regression Weights: (Group number 1 - Default model)
Regression Weights: (Group number 1 - Default model)

			Estimate	S.E.	C.R.	P	Label
FL3	<---	FinancialLiteracy	.997	.004	240.706	***	
FL5	<---	FinancialLiteracy	1.388	.105	13.242	***	
FL6	<---	FinancialLiteracy	1.392	.104	13.346	***	
FL2	<---	FinancialLiteracy	1.753	.098	17.808	***	
FL1	<---	FinancialLiteracy	1.782	.102	17.465	***	
FL8	<---	FinancialLiteracy	1.000				

Standardized Regression Weights: (Group number 1 - Default model)

			Estimate
FL3	<---	FinancialLiteracy	.597
FL5	<---	FinancialLiteracy	.620
FL6	<---	FinancialLiteracy	.626
FL2	<---	FinancialLiteracy	.972
FL1	<---	FinancialLiteracy	.981
FL8	<---	FinancialLiteracy	.595

Squared Multiple Correlations: (Group number 1 - Default model)

	Estimate
FL8	.334
FL1	.976
FL2	.937
FL6	.370
FL5	.363
FL3	.334

Model Fit Summary

CMIN

Model	NPAR	CMIN	DF	P	CMIN/DF
Default model	15	27.056	6	.000	4.509
Saturated model	21	.000	0		
Independence model	6	7972.744	15	.000	531.516

RMR, GFI

Model	RMR	GFI	AGFI	PGFI
Default model	.049	.987	.954	.282
Saturated model	.000	1.000		
Independence model	.552	.321	.049	.229

Baseline Comparisons

Model	NFI Delta1	RFI rho1	IFI Delta2	TLI rho2	CFI
Default model	.997	.992	.997	.993	.997
Saturated model	1.000		1.000		1.000
Independence model	.000	.000	.000	.000	.000

Parsimony-Adjusted Measures

Model	PRATIO	PNFI	PCFI
Default model	.400	.399	.399
Saturated model	.000	.000	.000
Independence model	1.000	.000	.000

NCP

Model	NCP	LO 90	HI 90
Default model	21.056	8.528	41.113
Saturated model	.000	.000	.000
Independence model	7957.744	7667.292	8254.474

FMIN

Model	FMIN	F0	LO 90	HI 90
Default model	.040	.031	.013	.061
Saturated model	.000	.000	.000	.000
Independence model	11.847	11.824	11.393	12.265

RMSEA

Model	RMSEA	LO 90	HI 90	PCLOSE
Default model	.052	.046	.101	.079
Independence model	.888	.872	.904	.000

AIC

Model	AIC	BCC	BIC	CAIC
Default model	57.056	57.372	124.755	139.755
Saturated model	42.000	42.441	136.778	157.778
Independence model	7984.744	7984.870	8011.823	8017.823

ECVI

Model	ECVI	LO 90	HI 90	MECVI
Default model	.085	.066	.115	.085
Saturated model	.062	.062	.062	.063
Independence model	11.864	11.433	12.305	11.865

HOELTER

Model	HOELTER .05	HOELTER .01
Default model	314	419
Independence model	3	3

Minimization: .002
Miscellaneous: .239
Bootstrap: .000
Total: .241

Appendix D

Results of the Measurement Model

			Estimate	S.E.	C.R.	P	Label
A5	<---	Attitude	1.000				
A15	<---	Attitude	1.062	.027	39.108	***	
A9	<---	Attitude	.991	.026	37.475	***	
A11	<---	Attitude	1.026	.026	39.073	***	
A6	<---	Attitude	.970	.024	40.184	***	
A13	<---	Attitude	1.026	.027	37.552	***	
A14	<---	Attitude	1.060	.029	36.735	***	
A10	<---	Attitude	.949	.029	32.767	***	
A12	<---	Attitude	1.026	.028	36.139	***	
A8	<---	Attitude	1.024	.031	33.520	***	
A7	<---	Attitude	.962	.031	30.811	***	
A2	<---	Attitude	.847	.031	27.105	***	
A4	<---	Attitude	.851	.032	26.834	***	
A3	<---	Attitude	.842	.032	26.668	***	
A1	<---	Attitude	.837	.034	24.269	***	
R6	<---	RiskAppetite	1.000				
R10	<---	RiskAppetite	1.009	.006	160.883	***	
R5	<---	RiskAppetite	.776	.030	26.190	***	
R3	<---	RiskAppetite	.635	.031	20.431	***	
R2	<---	RiskAppetite	.565	.030	18.963	***	
R11	<---	RiskAppetite	.567	.030	18.834	***	
R9	<---	RiskAppetite	.655	.029	22.217	***	
R7	<---	RiskAppetite	.614	.027	23.109	***	
R8	<---	RiskAppetite	.563	.031	18.191	***	
R4	<---	RiskAppetite	.513	.029	17.549	***	
R12	<---	RiskAppetite	.505	.029	17.434	***	
R1	<---	RiskAppetite	.474	.032	14.801	***	
R13	<---	RiskAppetite	.476	.033	14.574	***	
SN9	<---	SubjectiveNorms	1.000				
SN2	<---	SubjectiveNorms	.993	.006	164.752	***	
SN6	<---	SubjectiveNorms	1.073	.030	35.186	***	
SN5	<---	SubjectiveNorms	1.067	.031	34.133	***	
SN8	<---	SubjectiveNorms	1.084	.032	34.140	***	
SN7	<---	SubjectiveNorms	1.070	.034	31.746	***	
SN1	<---	SubjectiveNorms	.969	.032	30.331	***	
SN10	<---	SubjectiveNorms	.994	.034	29.260	***	
SN4	<---	SubjectiveNorms	1.011	.033	30.325	***	
SN3	<---	SubjectiveNorms	.996	.036	27.820	***	
B1	<---	Beliefs	1.000				
B11	<---	Beliefs	.975	.039	24.796	***	
B4	<---	Beliefs	.949	.037	25.972	***	
B6	<---	Beliefs	.986	.037	26.826	***	
B3	<---	Beliefs	.929	.036	25.818	***	
B12	<---	Beliefs	.963	.038	25.343	***	
B9	<---	Beliefs	.963	.038	25.637	***	
B10	<---	Beliefs	.963	.040	24.057	***	
B7	<---	Beliefs	.984	.042	23.683	***	
B8	<---	Beliefs	.921	.040	22.888	***	
B2	<---	Beliefs	.786	.035	22.375	***	

(Contd...)

IB3	<---	InvestmentBehavior	1.000			
IB1	<---	InvestmentBehavior	.969	.014	70.039	***
IB6	<---	InvestmentBehavior	.602	.031	19.746	***
IB4	<---	InvestmentBehavior	.595	.031	18.953	***
IB5	<---	InvestmentBehavior	.597	.030	19.945	***
IB2	<---	InvestmentBehavior	.691	.034	20.395	***
FL1	<---	FinancialLiteracy	1.000			
FL2	<---	FinancialLiteracy	.988	.015	66.776	***
FL6	<---	FinancialLiteracy	.787	.040	19.556	***
FL5	<---	FinancialLiteracy	.784	.041	19.254	***
FL3	<---	FinancialLiteracy	.565	.031	18.098	***
FL8	<---	FinancialLiteracy	.566	.031	18.096	***

Standardized Regression Weights: (Group number 1 - Default model)

			Estimate
A5	<---	Attitude	.912
A15	<---	Attitude	.905
A9	<---	Attitude	.892
A11	<---	Attitude	.905
A6	<---	Attitude	.862
A13	<---	Attitude	.892
A14	<---	Attitude	.885
A10	<---	Attitude	.845
A12	<---	Attitude	.880
A8	<---	Attitude	.853
A7	<---	Attitude	.822
A2	<---	Attitude	.771
A4	<---	Attitude	.767
A3	<---	Attitude	.764
A1	<---	Attitude	.725
R6	<---	RiskAppetite	.994
R10	<---	RiskAppetite	.995
R5	<---	RiskAppetite	.714
R3	<---	RiskAppetite	.621
R2	<---	RiskAppetite	.592
R11	<---	RiskAppetite	.594
R9	<---	RiskAppetite	.653
R7	<---	RiskAppetite	.668
R8	<---	RiskAppetite	.576
R4	<---	RiskAppetite	.562
R12	<---	RiskAppetite	.560
R1	<---	RiskAppetite	.497
R13	<---	RiskAppetite	.491
SN9	<---	SubjectiveNorms	.881
SN2	<---	SubjectiveNorms	.882
SN6	<---	SubjectiveNorms	.902
SN5	<---	SubjectiveNorms	.893
SN8	<---	SubjectiveNorms	.893
SN7	<---	SubjectiveNorms	.863
SN1	<---	SubjectiveNorms	.844

(*Contd...*)

SN10	<---	SubjectiveNorms	.829
SN4	<---	SubjectiveNorms	.844
SN3	<---	SubjectiveNorms	.807
B1	<---	Beliefs	.852
B11	<---	Beliefs	.779
B4	<---	Beliefs	.802
B6	<---	Beliefs	.818
B3	<---	Beliefs	.799
B12	<---	Beliefs	.790
B9	<---	Beliefs	.796
B10	<---	Beliefs	.764
B7	<---	Beliefs	.757
B8	<---	Beliefs	.740
B2	<---	Beliefs	.729
IB3	<---	InvestmentBehavior	.980
IB1	<---	InvestmentBehavior	.974
IB6	<---	InvestmentBehavior	.616
IB4	<---	InvestmentBehavior	.600
IB5	<---	InvestmentBehavior	.620
IB2	<---	InvestmentBehavior	.629
FL1	<---	FinancialLiteracy	.986
FL2	<---	FinancialLiteracy	.970
FL6	<---	FinancialLiteracy	.612
FL5	<---	FinancialLiteracy	.605
FL3	<---	FinancialLiteracy	.581
FL8	<---	FinancialLiteracy	.581

Correlations: (Group number 1 - Default model)

			Estimate
Attitude	<-->	RiskAppetite	.265
Attitude	<-->	SubjectiveNorms	.447
Attitude	<-->	Beliefs	.271
Attitude	<-->	InvestmentBehavior	.288
Attitude	<-->	FinancialLiteracy	.299
RiskAppetite	<-->	SubjectiveNorms	.182
RiskAppetite	<-->	Beliefs	.241
RiskAppetite	<-->	InvestmentBehavior	.124
RiskAppetite	<-->	FinancialLiteracy	.453
SubjectiveNorms	<-->	Beliefs	.200
SubjectiveNorms	<-->	InvestmentBehavior	.460
SubjectiveNorms	<-->	FinancialLiteracy	.209
Beliefs	<-->	InvestmentBehavior	.175
Beliefs	<-->	FinancialLiteracy	.294
InvestmentBehavior	<-->	FinancialLiteracy	.077
e60	<-->	e61	.997
e58	<-->	e59	.952
e36	<-->	e38	.908
e29	<-->	e30	.959
e27	<-->	e28	.953

(*Contd...*)

e25	<-->	e26	.971
e20	<-->	e21	.982
e52	<-->	e53	.847
e19	<-->	e22	.908
e12	<-->	e15	.842
e13	<-->	e14	.741
e10	<-->	e11	.479
e19	<-->	e25	-.054
e16	<-->	e21	-.129
e23	<-->	e24	.480
e57	<-->	e61	-.028
e21	<-->	e28	.018
e1	<-->	e5	.276
e2	<-->	e7	.384
e6	<-->	e9	.345
e7	<-->	e9	.337
e19	<-->	e20	-.019
e29	<-->	e31	.003
e30	<-->	e31	-.093

Model fit summary

CMIN

Model	NPAR	CMIN	DF	P	CMIN/DF
Default model	128	1537.069	775	.000	1.983
Saturated model	903	.000	0		
Independence model	42	9986.223	861	.000	11.598

RMR, GFI

Model	RMR	GFI	AGFI	PGFI
Default model	.054	.961	.938	.939
Saturated model	.000	1.000		
Independence model	.393	.264	.228	.252

Baseline Comparisons

Model	NFI Delta1	RFI rho1	IFI Delta2	TLI rho2	CFI
Default model	.946	.829	.917	.907	.916
Saturated model	1.000		1.000		1.000
Independence model	.000	.000	.000	.000	.000

Parsimony-Adjusted Measures

Model	PRATIO	PNFI	PCFI
Default model	.900	.762	.825
Saturated model	.000	.000	.000
Independence model	1.000	.000	.000

NCP

Model	NCP	LO 90	HI 90
Default model	762.069	654.379	877.522
Saturated model	.000	.000	.000
Independence model	9125.223	8806.887	9450.029

FMIN

Model	FMIN	F0	LO 90	HI 90
Default model	3.446	1.709	1.467	1.968
Saturated model	.000	.000	.000	.000
Independence model	22.391	20.460	19.746	21.188

RMSEA

Model	RMSEA	LO 90	HI 90	PCLOSE
Default model	.047	.044	.050	.927
Independence model	.154	.151	.157	.000

AIC

Model	AIC	BCC	BIC	CAIC
Default model	1793.069	1820.384	2318.197	2446.197
Saturated model	1806.000	1998.700	5510.610	6413.610
Independence model	10070.223	10079.185	10242.530	10284.530

ECVI

Model	ECVI	LO 90	HI 90	MECVI
Default model	4.020	3.779	4.279	4.082
Saturated model	4.049	4.049	4.049	4.481
Independence model	22.579	21.865	23.307	22.599

HOELTER

Model	HOELTER .05	HOELTER .01
Default model	244	253
Independence model	42	43

Appendix F

Initial SEM MODEL Output

Regression Weights: (Group number 1 - Default model)

Regression Weights: (Group number 1 - Default model)

			Estimate	S.E.	C.R.	P	Label
Attitude	<---	FinancialLiteracy	.111	.030	3.675	***	par_43
Attitude	<---	RiskAppetite	.073	.023	3.125	.002	par_44
Attitude	<---	SubjectiveNorms	.246	.025	9.801	***	par_45
Attitude	<---	Beliefs	.157	.043	3.625	***	par_46
InvestmentBehavior	<---	Attitude	.454	.055	8.302	***	par_47
A11	<---	Attitude	1.010	.026	39.131	***	par_1
A6	<---	Attitude	.977	.027	36.521	***	par_2
A13	<---	Attitude	1.018	.027	38.378	***	par_3
A14	<---	Attitude	1.043	.028	37.143	***	par_4
A10	<---	Attitude	.944	.028	33.506	***	par_5
A12	<---	Attitude	1.014	.028	36.186	***	par_6
A8	<---	Attitude	1.028	.029	35.231	***	par_7
A7	<---	Attitude	.970	.030	32.509	***	par_8
A4	<---	Attitude	.856	.031	27.893	***	par_9
A3	<---	Attitude	.844	.031	27.494	***	par_10
A1	<---	Attitude	.839	.034	25.004	***	par_11
R6	<---	RiskAppetite	1.000				
R10	<---	RiskAppetite	1.011	.008	131.884	***	par_12
R5	<---	RiskAppetite	.776	.030	26.082	***	par_13
SN9	<---	SubjectiveNorms	1.000				

(Contd...)

SN2	<---	SubjectiveNorms	.991	.006	170.117	***	par_14
SN6	<---	SubjectiveNorms	.842	.025	34.286	***	par_15
SN5	<---	SubjectiveNorms	.822	.026	31.695	***	par_16
SN8	<---	SubjectiveNorms	.883	.024	36.850	***	par_17
SN7	<---	SubjectiveNorms	.847	.027	31.213	***	par_18
SN1	<---	SubjectiveNorms	.781	.025	30.870	***	par_19
SN10	<---	SubjectiveNorms	.784	.028	28.142	***	par_20
SN4	<---	SubjectiveNorms	.803	.027	29.815	***	par_21
SN3	<---	SubjectiveNorms	.783	.030	26.422	***	par_22
B1	<---	Beliefs	1.000				
B11	<---	Beliefs	.976	.039	24.796	***	par_23
B4	<---	Beliefs	.949	.037	25.957	***	par_24
B6	<---	Beliefs	.986	.037	26.807	***	par_25
B3	<---	Beliefs	.930	.036	25.803	***	par_26
B12	<---	Beliefs	.963	.038	25.330	***	par_27
B9	<---	Beliefs	.963	.038	25.620	***	par_28
B10	<---	Beliefs	.964	.040	24.053	***	par_29
B7	<---	Beliefs	.984	.042	23.672	***	par_30
B8	<---	Beliefs	.922	.040	22.897	***	par_31
B2	<---	Beliefs	.787	.035	22.374	***	par_32
IB3	<---	InvestmentBehavior	1.000				
IB5	<---	InvestmentBehavior	.798	.048	16.586	***	par_33
IB2	<---	InvestmentBehavior	.973	.057	17.213	***	par_34
FL1	<---	FinancialLiteracy	1.000				
FL2	<---	FinancialLiteracy	.981	.023	43.292	***	par_35
A2	<---	Attitude	.847	.027	30.907	***	par_48
A9	<---	Attitude	.979	.026	37.901	***	par_52
A15	<---	Attitude	1.051	.026	39.791	***	par_53
A5	<---	Attitude	1.000				

Standardized Regression Weights: (Group number 1 - Default model)

			Estimate
Attitude	<---	FinancialLiteracy	.145
Attitude	<---	RiskAppetite	.120
Attitude	<---	SubjectiveNorms	.347
Attitude	<---	Beliefs	.136
InvestmentBehavior	<---	Attitude	.351
A11	<---	Attitude	.898
A6	<---	Attitude	.875
A13	<---	Attitude	.891
A14	<---	Attitude	.881
A10	<---	Attitude	.846
A12	<---	Attitude	.872
A8	<---	Attitude	.863
A7	<---	Attitude	.835
A4	<---	Attitude	.777
A3	<---	Attitude	.771
A1	<---	Attitude	.733

(*Contd...*)

R6	<---	RiskAppetite	.993
R10	<---	RiskAppetite	.996
R5	<---	RiskAppetite	.713
SN9	<---	SubjectiveNorms	.995
SN2	<---	SubjectiveNorms	.994
SN6	<---	SubjectiveNorms	.801
SN5	<---	SubjectiveNorms	.777
SN8	<---	SubjectiveNorms	.821
SN7	<---	SubjectiveNorms	.772
SN1	<---	SubjectiveNorms	.769
SN10	<---	SubjectiveNorms	.738
SN4	<---	SubjectiveNorms	.758
SN3	<---	SubjectiveNorms	.716
B1	<---	Beliefs	.852
B11	<---	Beliefs	.780
B4	<---	Beliefs	.802
B6	<---	Beliefs	.818
B3	<---	Beliefs	.799
B12	<---	Beliefs	.790
B9	<---	Beliefs	.796
B10	<---	Beliefs	.764
B7	<---	Beliefs	.757
B8	<---	Beliefs	.740
B2	<---	Beliefs	.729
IB3	<---	InvestmentBehavior	.833
IB5	<---	InvestmentBehavior	.704
IB2	<---	InvestmentBehavior	.753
FL1	<---	FinancialLiteracy	.989
FL2	<---	FinancialLiteracy	.967
A2	<---	Attitude	.816
A9	<---	Attitude	.887
A15	<---	Attitude	.903
A5	<---	Attitude	.919

Covariances: (Group number 1 - Default model)

			Estimate	S.E.	C.R.	P	Label
RiskAppetite	<-->	FinancialLiteracy	.470	.045	10.481	***	par_38
SubjectiveNorms	<-->	FinancialLiteracy	.148	.035	4.179	***	par_39
Beliefs	<-->	FinancialLiteracy	.159	.023	6.913	***	par_40
RiskAppetite	<-->	SubjectiveNorms	.157	.044	3.541	***	par_41
SubjectiveNorms	<-->	Beliefs	.115	.024	4.803	***	par_42
RiskAppetite	<-->	Beliefs	.166	.029	5.825	***	par_54
e36	<-->	e38	.493	.028	17.611	***	par_36
e2	<-->	e7	.050	.006	8.795	***	par_37
e12	<-->	e14	.067	.006	11.144	***	par_49
e12	<-->	e15	.171	.011	15.642	***	par_50
e7	<-->	e9	.062	.007	9.533	***	par_51

Squared Multiple Correlations: (Group number 1 - Default model)

	Estimate
Attitude	.255
InvestmentBehavior	.123
FL2	.935
FL1	.978
IB2	.567
IB5	.496
IB3	.694
B2	.531
B8	.548
B7	.572
B10	.584
B9	.633
B12	.624
B3	.639
B6	.669
B4	.643
B11	.608
B1	.726
SN3	.513
SN4	.574
SN10	.545
SN1	.591
SN7	.596
SN8	.675
SN5	.604
SN6	.641
SN2	.989
SN9	.990
R5	.508
R10	.991
R6	.987
A1	.537
A3	.595
A4	.604
A2	.666
A7	.697
A8	.745
A12	.761
A10	.716
A14	.776
A13	.795
A6	.766
A11	.806
A9	.788
A15	.815
A5	.844

Model Fit Summary

CMIN

Model	NPAR	CMIN	DF	P	CMIN/DF
Default model	112	2130.580	629	.000	3.387
Saturated model	741	.000	0		
Independence model	38	16445.738	703	.000	23.394

RMR, GFI

Model	RMR	GFI	AGFI	PGFI
Default model	.075	.981	.960	.748
Saturated model	.000	1.000		
Independence model	.413	.274	.235	.260

Baseline Comparisons

Model	NFI Delta1	RFI rho1	IFI Delta2	TLI rho2	CFI
Default model	.870	.855	.905	.893	.905
Saturated model	1.000		1.000		1.000
Independence model	.000	.000	.000	.000	.000

Parsimony-Adjusted Measures

Model	PRATIO	PNFI	PCFI
Default model	.895	.779	.809
Saturated model	.000	.000	.000
Independence model	1.000	.000	.000

NCP

Model	NCP	LO 90	HI 90
Default model	1501.580	1365.122	1645.590
Saturated model	.000	.000	.000
Independence model	15742.738	15328.588	16163.259

FMIN

Model	FMIN	F0	LO 90	HI 90
Default model	2.611	1.840	1.673	2.017
Saturated model	.000	.000	.000	.000
Independence model	20.154	19.293	18.785	19.808

RMSEA

Model	RMSEA	LO 90	HI 90	PCLOSE
Default model	.054	.052	.057	.634
Independence model	.166	.163	.168	.000

AIC

Model	AIC	BCC	BIC	CAIC
Default model	2354.580	2365.823	2881.611	2993.611
Saturated model	1482.000	1556.386	4968.879	5709.879
Independence model	16521.738	16525.552	16700.552	16738.552

ECVI

Model	ECVI	LO 90	HI 90	MECVI
Default model	2.886	2.718	3.062	2.899
Saturated model	1.816	1.816	1.816	1.907
Independence model	20.247	19.740	20.763	20.252

HOELTER

Model	HOELTER .05	HOELTER .01
Default model	264	274
Independence model	38	40

Execution time summary

Minimization: .093
Miscellaneous: .906
Bootstrap: .000
Total: .999

Appendix E

Final Interaction Model

Regression Weights: (All - Default model)

			Estimate	S.E.	C.R.	P	Label
ZAttitude	<---	ZBeliefs	.078	.038	2.062	.039	par_1
ZAttitude	<---	RA_x_B	-.101	.029	-3.518	***	par_2
ZAttitude	<---	ZRiskAppetite	.111	.037	3.014	.003	par_3
ZAttitude	<---	ZFinancialLiteracy	.130	.038	3.424	***	par_25
ZAttitude	<---	ZSubjectiveNorms	.361	.034	10.669	***	par_26

Standardized Regression Weights: (All - Default model)

			Estimate
ZAttitude	<---	ZBeliefs	.078
ZAttitude	<---	RA_x_B	-.131
ZAttitude	<---	ZRiskAppetite	.111
ZAttitude	<---	ZFinancialLiteracy	.130
ZAttitude	<---	ZSubjectiveNorms	.361

Squared Multiple Correlations: (All - Default model)

	Estimate
ZAttitude	.297

Model Fit Summary

CMIN

Model	NPAR	CMIN	DF	P	CMIN/DF
Default model	112	1501.423	629	.000	2.387
Saturated model	741	.000	0		
Independence model	38	16445.738	703	.000	23.394

RMR, GFI

Model	RMR	GFI	AGFI	PGFI
Default model	.075	.981	.960	.748
Saturated model	.000	1.000		
Independence model	.413	.274	.235	.260

Baseline Comparisons

Model	NFI Delta1	RFI rho1	IFI Delta2	TLI rho2	CFI
Default model	.970	.855	.905	.883	.995
Saturated model	1.000		1.000		1.000
Independence model	.000	.000	.000	.000	.000

Parsimony-Adjusted Measures

Model	PRATIO	PNFI	PCFI
Default model	.895	.779	.809
Saturated model	.000	.000	.000
Independence model	1.000	.000	.000

NCP

Model	NCP	LO 90	HI 90
Default model	1501.580	1365.122	1645.590
Saturated model	.000	.000	.000
Independence model	15742.738	15328.588	16163.259

FMIN

Model	FMIN	F0	LO 90	HI 90
Default model	2.611	1.840	1.673	2.017
Saturated model	.000	.000	.000	.000
Independence model	20.154	19.293	18.785	19.808

RMSEA

Model	RMSEA	LO 90	HI 90	PCLOSE
Default model	.064	.052	.057	.634
Independence model	.166	.163	.168	.000

AIC

Model	AIC	BCC	BIC	CAIC
Default model	2354.580	2365.823	2881.611	2993.611
Saturated model	1482.000	1556.386	4968.879	5709.879
Independence model	16521.738	16525.552	16700.552	16738.552

ECVI

Model	ECVI	LO 90	HI 90	MECVI
Default model	2.886	2.718	3.062	2.899
Saturated model	1.816	1.816	1.816	1.907
Independence model	20.247	19.740	20.763	20.252

HOELTER

Model	HOELTER .05	HOELTER .01
Default model	264	274
Independence model	38	40

Execution time summary

Minimization:	.093
Miscellaneous:	.906
Bootstrap:	.000
Total:	.999

Appendix F

SEM MODEL MEDIATION Output

Direct Effects Model

Regression Weights: (Group no 1 - Default model)

			Estimate	S.E.	C.R.	P	Label
InvestmentBehavior	<---	FinancialLiteracy	.081	.046	-1.759	.079	
InvestmentBehavior	<---	RiskAppetite	.050	.035	1.439	.150	
InvestmentBehavior	<---	Beliefs	.163	.065	2.532	.011	
InvestmentBehavior	<---	SubjectiveNorms	.538	.041	13.206	***	

Standardized Regression Weights: (Group no 1 - Default model)

			Estimate
InvestmentBehavior	<---	FinancialLiteracy	.069
InvestmentBehavior	<---	RiskAppetite	.055
InvestmentBehavior	<---	Beliefs	.091
InvestmentBehavior	<---	SubjectiveNorms	.462

Covariances: (Group no 1 - Default model)

			Estimate	S.E.	C.R.	P	Label
Beliefs	<-->	SubjectiveNorms	.113	.021	5.422	***	
SubjectiveNorms	<-->	RiskAppetite	.188	.041	4.645	***	
SubjectiveNorms	<-->	FinancialLiteracy	.170	.032	5.384	***	
Beliefs	<-->	RiskAppetite	.169	.027	6.325	***	
Beliefs	<-->	FinancialLiteracy	.163	.021	7.733	***	
RiskAppetite	<-->	FinancialLiteracy	.481	.044	10.999	***	

Correlations: (Group no 1 - Default model)

			Estimate
Beliefs	<-->	SubjectiveNorms	.214
SubjectiveNorms	<-->	RiskAppetite	.182
SubjectiveNorms	<-->	FinancialLiteracy	.212
Beliefs	<-->	RiskAppetite	.251
Beliefs	<-->	FinancialLiteracy	.312
RiskAppetite	<-->	FinancialLiteracy	.468

Total Effects (Group no 1 - Default model)

	FinancialLiteracy	RiskAppetite	SubjectiveNorms	Beliefs
InvestmentBehavior	.081	.050	.538	.163

Standardized Total Effects (Group no 1 - Default model)

	FinancialLiteracy	RiskAppetite	SubjectiveNorms	Beliefs
InvestmentBehavior	.069	.055	.462	.091

Direct Effects (Group no 1 - Default model)

	FinancialLiteracy	RiskAppetite	SubjectiveNorms	Beliefs
InvestmentBehavior	.081	.050	.538	.163

Standardized Direct Effects (Group no 1 - Default model)

	FinancialLiteracy	RiskAppetite	SubjectiveNorms	Beliefs
InvestmentBehavior	.069	.055	.462	.091

Indirect Effects (Group no 1 - Default model)

	FinancialLiteracy	RiskAppetite	SubjectiveNorms	Beliefs
InvestmentBehavior	.000	.000	.000	.000

Standardized Indirect Effects (Group no 1 - Default model)

	FinancialLiteracy	RiskAppetite	SubjectiveNorms	Beliefs
InvestmentBehavior	.000	.000	.000	.000

Model Fit Summary

CMIN

Model	NPAR	CMIN	DF	P	CMIN/DF
Default model	108	1442.412	927	.000	1.556
Saturated model	1035	.000	0		
Independence model	45	42679.479	990	.000	43.111

RMR, GFI

Model	RMR	GFI	AGFI	PGFI
Default model	.055	.952	.911	.584
Saturated model	.000	1.000		
Independence model	.342	.163	.125	.156

Baseline Comparisons

Model	NFI Delta1	RFI rho1	IFI Delta2	TLI rho2	CFI
Default model	.971	.955	.988	.973	.988
Saturated model	1.000		1.000		1.000
Independence model	.000	.000	.000	.000	.000

Parsimony-Adjusted Measures

Model	PRATIO	PNFI	PCFI
Default model	.936	.922	.937
Saturated model	.000	.000	.000
Independence model	1.000	.000	.000

NCP

Model	NCP	LO 90	HI 90
Default model	8858.833	8544.458	9179.697
Saturated model	.000	.000	.000
Independence model	41689.479	41016.978	42368.306

FMIN

Model	FMIN	F0	LO 90	HI 90
Default model	14.541	13.163	12.696	13.640
Saturated model	.000	.000	.000	.000
Independence model	63.417	61.946	60.946	62.954

RMSEA

Model	RMSEA	LO 90	HI 90	PCLOSE
Default model	.119	.117	.121	.124
Independence model	.250	.248	.252	.000

AIC

Model	AIC	BCC	BIC	CAIC
Default model	10001.833	10017.680	10489.262	10597.262
Saturated model	2070.000	2221.866	6741.193	7776.193
Independence model	42769.479	42776.082	42972.574	43017.574

ECVI

Model	ECVI	LO 90	HI 90	MECVI
Default model	14.862	14.394	15.338	14.885
Saturated model	3.076	3.076	3.076	3.301
Independence model	63.550	62.551	64.559	63.560

HOELTER

Model	HOELTER .05	HOELTER .01
Default model	69	71
Independence model	17	18

Minimization:	.159
Miscellaneous:	4.007
Bootstrap:	.000
Total:	4.166

SEM MEDIATION results

Regression Weights: (Group no 1 - Default model)

Regression Weights: (Group no 1 - Default model)

			Estimate	S.E.	C.R.	P	Label
Attitude	<---	FinancialLiteracy	.110	.029	3.744	***	
Attitude	<---	RiskAppetite	.064	.022	2.874	.004	
Attitude	<---	Beliefs	.157	.041	3.822	***	
Attitude	<---	SubjectiveNorms	.288	.026	11.120	***	
InvestmentBehavior	<---	Attitude	.128	.060	2.115	.034	
InvestmentBehavior	<---	FinancialLiteracy	.095	.046	-2.049	.041	
InvestmentBehavior	<---	RiskAppetite	.042	.035	1.202	.229	
InvestmentBehavior	<---	Beliefs	.143	.065	2.205	.027	
InvestmentBehavior	<---	SubjectiveNorms	.501	.044	11.345	***	

Standardized Regression Weights: (Group no 1 - Default model)

			Estimate
Attitude	<---	FinancialLiteracy	.143
Attitude	<---	RiskAppetite	.107
Attitude	<---	Beliefs	.134
Attitude	<---	SubjectiveNorms	.377
InvestmentBehavior	<---	Attitude	.084
InvestmentBehavior	<---	FinancialLiteracy	.081
InvestmentBehavior	<---	RiskAppetite	.046
InvestmentBehavior	<---	Beliefs	.080
InvestmentBehavior	<---	SubjectiveNorms	.430

Covariances: (Group no 1 - Default model)

			Estimate	S.E.	C.R.	P	Label
Beliefs	<-->	Subjective Norms	.113	.021	5.422	***	
Risk Appetite	<-->	Subjective Norms	.188	.041	4.645	***	
Financial Literacy	<-->	Subjective Norms	.170	.032	5.384	***	
Risk Appetite	<-->	Beliefs	.169	.027	6.325	***	
Financial Literacy	<-->	Beliefs	.163	.021	7.733	***	
Financial Literacy	<-->	Risk Appetite	.481	.044	10.999	***	

Correlations: (Group no 1 - Default model)

			Estimate
Beliefs	<-->	Subjective Norms	.214
RiskAppetite	<-->	Subjective Norms	.182
Financial Literacy	<-->	Subjective Norms	.212
Risk Appetite	<-->	Beliefs	.251
Financial Literacy	<-->	Beliefs	.312
Financial Literacy	<-->	Risk Appetite	.468

Squared Multiple Correlations: (Group no 1 - Default model)

	Estimate
Attitude	.284
Investment Behavior	.243

Bootstrap Results

Standardized Indirect Effects (Group no 1 - Default model)

	SubjectiveNorms	Beliefs	RiskAppetite	FinancialLiteracy	Attitude
Attitude	.000	.000	.000	.000	.000
Investment Behavior	.032	.011	.009	.012	.000

Standardized Indirect Effects - Standard Errors (Group no 1 - Default model)

	SubjectiveNorms	Beliefs	RiskAppetite	FinancialLiteracy	Attitude
Attitude	.000	.000	.000	.000	.000
Investment Behavior	.018	.007	.006	.008	.000

Standardized Indirect Effects - Lower Bounds (BC) (Group no 1 - Default model)

	SubjectiveNorms	Beliefs	RiskAppetite	FinancialLiteracy	Attitude
Attitude	.000	.000	.000	.000	.000
Investment Behavior	.003	.001	.001	.003	.000

Standardized Indirect Effects - Upper Bounds (BC) (Group no 1 - Default model)

	SubjectiveNorms	Beliefs	RiskAppetite	FinancialLiteracy	Attitude
Attitude	.000	.000	.000	.000	.000
Investment Behavior	.062	.026	.022	.030	.000

Standardized Indirect Effects - Two Tailed Significance (BC) (Group no 1 - Default model)

	SubjectiveNorms	Beliefs	RiskAppetite	FinancialLiteracy	Attitude
Attitude	...	...	...	...	...
Investment Behavior	.061	.042	.037	.029	...

Std Direct Effects

Standardized Direct Effects (Group no 1 - Default model)

	SubjectiveNorms	Beliefs	RiskAppetite	FinancialLiteracy	Attitude
Attitude	.377	.134	.107	.143	.000
InvestmentBehavior	.430	.080	.046	-.081	.084

Standardized Direct Effects - Standard Errors (Group no 1 - Default model)

	SubjectiveNorms	Beliefs	RiskAppetite	FinancialLiteracy	Attitude
Attitude	.045	.042	.043	.050	.000
InvestmentBehavior	.048	.037	.046	.047	.046

Standardized Direct Effects - Lower Bounds (BC) (Group no 1 - Default model)

	SubjectiveNorms	Beliefs	RiskAppetite	FinancialLiteracy	Attitude
Attitude	.289	.052	.024	.042	.000
InvestmentBehavior	.327	.009	-.043	-.181	-.008

Standardized Direct Effects - Upper Bounds (BC) (Group no 1 - Default model)

	SubjectiveNorms	Beliefs	RiskAppetite	FinancialLiteracy	Attitude
Attitude	.465	.218	.196	.240	.000
InvestmentBehavior	.517	.158	.135	.012	.172

Standardized Direct Effects - Two Tailed Significance (BC) (Group no 1 - Default model)

	SubjectiveNorms	Beliefs	RiskAppetite	FinancialLiteracy	Attitude
Attitude	.002	.002	.009	.008	...
InvestmentBehavior	.003	.031	.280	.080	.064

Index

O

P

Q

R